MARY'S TITLES

Biblical reflections on the titles of
Mary in the Litany of Loreto

ELIZABETH G. BRYSON

WESTBOW
PRESS®
A DIVISION OF THOMAS NELSON
& ZONDERVAN

WestBow Press books may be ordered through booksellers or by contacting:

WestBow Press
A Division of Thomas Nelson & Zondervan
1663 Liberty Drive
Bloomington, IN 47403
www.westbowpress.com
844-714-3454

Scripture quotations taken from The Holy Bible, New International Version® NIV® Copyright © 1973 1978 1984 2011 by Biblica, Inc. TM. Used by permission. All rights reserved worldwide.

ISBN: 978-1-6642-6004-7 (sc)
ISBN: 978-1-6642-6003-0 (e)

Print information available on the last page.

WestBow Press rev. date: 03/11/2022

ACKNOWLEDGEMENTS

My husband Fr Neil Bryson for his support and encouragement in the many hours that I have spent researching and writing this book. I appreciate discussing some of my reflections with him and thank him for his proof-reading and sub-editing.

Fr Peter Anthony whose Article, *What is the Ark?* In the December 2010 [1]*Walsingham Review* inspired me to write Talks about some of the titles of Mary in the Litany, which have now grown and developed into this book.

The late **Doris Gilbart-Smith** who introduced me to the joy of Biblical 'word studies' and gave me [2]Young's *Analytical Concordance to the Holy Bible* at Christmas 1976, which I have referred to when writing many of the chapters. She gave me this verse: 'Study to shew thyself approved unto God, a workman that needeth not to be ashamed, rightly dividing the word of truth' *(Timothy 2:15 AV)*. I hope to have achieved that by the Biblical references and interpretations that I have presented.

My parents **June Doran** and the late **Rev Sidney Doran** with thanks for their prayers, support and their encouragement for me to read the Bible from a young age.

---

[1] Walsingham Review, December 2010, 'Do you know what the Ark is?' Fr Peter Anthony, p. 10

[2] Analytical Concordance to the Holy Bible, Robert Young, United Society for Christian Literature, Lutterworth Press London, 1973

Revd. Lesley Ludlow and **Dr Jacki Thomas** with appreciation for their encouragement and prayers about the writing of this book.

Fr Kevin Smith, the Administrator at the Shrine of Our Lady of Walsingham, with thanks for his interest and encouragement about the writing of this book.

The Walsingham Group at the Parish Church of St Michael and All Angels Maidstone, who have listened with interest and appreciated my Talks on some of the titles of Mary.

Pilgrims to Walsingham from All Saints', Boyne Hill Maidenhead, who listened to the first five Talks and encouraged me to continue with this research.

All the Bible verses, quoted in this book are from the [3] *New International Version* of the Bible or from the *British Hodder's NIV* on the [4] *Glo Computer Bible*, unless otherwise stated.

I have referenced other books, booklets and internet articles at the bottom of each page. I include five photographs that I have taken: they are in Chapters 6, 10, 11, 14 and 21. Prior Francis at Aylesford Friary has given permission to use the images in Chapters 10 and 11. The other three images in Chapters 14, 20 and 22 are free to modify, share and use commercially; retrieved from the Internet showing the date of retrieval.

I have listed all the books and booklets in the Bibliography.

The colour photograph on the front cover is a statue of Our Lady of Walsingham © Graham Howard.

---

[3] *Holy Bible,* New International Version, Zondervan, International Bible Society, 1984

[4] *British Hodder's NIV Glo Computer Bible,* Glo Premium ISBN 978-0-9826978-8-7, Immersion Digital, 2010

CONTENTS

CHAPTER 1

INTRODUCTION

When I first took part in the First Visit in the Holy House at Walsingham in Norfolk, England, and we recited the *Litany of Our Lady*; I wondered 'why and how do we address Mary with these titles?' That was the beginning of a long journey of Bible study, research, reading and reflection that has led to this book. In each Chapter I study and reflect on relevant Bible texts, consider and research into how Mary can be given this title and finally for each title suggest 'What does this mean for us?' I hope and pray that this book will be helpful to other curious and questioning people and to those who would like to look with fresh eyes at some of the Catholic teaching they received as children.

When you have the First Visit to the Holy House at Walsingham with *The Litany of Our Lady* in the ⁵Walsingham Manual; 'Our Lady of Walsingham' is listed at the end. I hope and pray that, when you ask Mary to pray for you, using the 51 titles listed there; as a result of reading this book you will have a greater understanding about the Biblical background

---

⁵ The Walsingham Pilgrim Manual 2016, p.12-14

and the reasons why Mary is addressed with these titles. Just as Mary always points us to Jesus, so I hope and pray that this book will draw you closer to Jesus.

This Litany of the Blessed Virgin Mary [6]'dates from between 1150 and 1200, and it was probably of Persian origin, originally approved in 1587 by Pope Sixtus V. It is known as the *Litany of Loreto* from the famous Italian Shrine where its use is attested for the year 1558, but its existence far antedates this year.' The list of 50 titles that praise Mary [7]'owes much to prayers of the Greek Church, in particular to the Akathist Hymn. The alternation of admiring contemplation and confident supplication makes the Litany a prayer at once simple and complete.'

Margaret Barker wrote: [8] 'some of the titles for Mary were known by 431 AD, when Cyril of Alexandria delivered his elaborate homily during the Council of Ephesus. There are earlier examples of her titles, evidence of an established and consistent pattern, much of which draws on Old Testament imagery... What do the images of Mary in the *Litany of Loreto* suggest? Surely, that there is an important element of the earliest Christian teaching about Mary that has been neglected and almost lost.' In this book I explore the deep biblical meaning of these titles and discover their symbolic meaning and relevance in our lives, so we grow closer to God. Mary points us to Jesus, saying 'do whatever he tells you' *(John 2:5)*. My prayer is that you grow into a closer relationship with Jesus; increase in Biblical knowledge as well as developing in your understanding and appreciation of his Mother Mary, through focusing on titles that she has been given.

Michael Rear tells us about the Holy House at Loreto: [9]'On the Adriatic coast of Italy, in a region known as the Marches, there is a town called Loreto, above which stands a fine Basilica built in the fifteenth

---

[6] Dictionary of Mary 'Behold your Mother', Catholic Book Publishing Co. New Jersey 1997, 1985, p.241

[7] Ibid.

[8] The Images of Mary in the Litany of Loreto, Margaret Barker, Usus Antiquior, Vol 1, No. 2, July 2010, p. 110, p. 131

[9] Walsingham Pilgrims and Pilgrimage: Michael Rear, Gracewing, 2019, p. 39 - 41

century, containing, it is said, the House of Mary, which once stood in Nazareth... The story is that in 1291 the House of Mary was miraculously rescued from Nazareth and transported by angels... It became a revered place of pilgrimage, for if faith could move mountains how much easier to move a mere house? The medieval mind saw no difficulty in this, even if modern minds are, perhaps, more sceptical... Giuseppi Lappoponi, personal physician to Pope Leo XIII and Pope St Pius X discovered in the Vatican archives documents stating that during the Moslem invasion of the Holy Land in the thirteenth century a noble Byzantine family, surnamed Angeli, descended from the Emperors of Constantinople, had saved the 'materials' of Our Lady's House in Nazareth and transported them to Loreto.... Examination of the building shows that three sides of it, up to a height of three yards, are built of stone not found in the Marches region of Italy, but of a type quarried in Palestine... This is very significant because it suggests that the three stone walls abutted the cave in Nazareth.' So, this suggests that the 'angels' who moved the Holy House from Nazareth to Loreto were in fact the family with the surname of 'Angeli'.

Fr Peter Anthony recently visited Loreto on Pilgrimage and he was amazed to see how the Holy House at Loreto reminded him of the Holy House at Walsingham. He writes: [10]'we can be pretty sure that the bricks which form the core of the present Holy House of Loreto come from the building that had been venerated since the earliest of times as the House of Mary in Nazareth.' This is the House that [11]'In 1061 according to tradition' the Virgin Mary showed in a vision to Lady Richeldis de Faverche at Walsingham asking her 'to build a replica of Mary's house in Nazareth, the house where Gabriel appeared to Mary'.

Fr Peter Anthony writes: [12]'The great titles of Our Lady in the Litany of Loreto all speak of Mary in terms of rich imagery from the Old Testament scriptures: Ivory Tower; Mystic Rose; Ark of the Covenant;

[10] Notes of a pilgrimage to Loreto, Subiaco and Rome: Fr Peter Anthony, The Walsingham Review, Candlemas 2020, Issue 165, p. 6–7
[11] The Shrine of Our Lady of Walsingham booklet, Jarrold Publishing and Guardians of the Shrine of Walsingham 2002, p.2
[12] Anthony, op. cit., p.7

Gate of Heaven. We see in these Marian titles of Loreto the fulfilment of God's ancient promises to his people Israel. To claim these titles for Our Lady is not Ultramontane whimsy, nor some sort of ill-thought-through saccharine piety. Rather, it is to deeply root our claims about Christ and his Mother in the assertions of scripture and the loving purposes of God revealed to his pilgrim people in ancient times.'

All of the titles given to Our Lady have meaning and significance for the Church because Mary is seen as a 'type' of the Church. [13]St Ambrose 340-397, said 'Mary is explicitly said to be the type figure of the Church, which in effect means that she is the Church's pattern or model.... The Church, like the Virgin, is bride of Christ, each is mother of Christians and bearer of Christ to the world.' McBrien[14] tells us about typology that a 'Type' is: 'A person in whom the qualities of a greater or later reality are somehow 'typified' or anticipated e.g., Mary as a 'type' of the Church.' [15]Scott Hahn writes: 'The study of typology shows us that the Church can learn from the example of Mary's life.'

Esther can be seen as a 'type figure' of Mary. [16]'Esther is a type of Mary who won God's love by the splendour of her goodness, drew Him into her heart, and saved her people from the devil by the Redeemer whom she bore, while she became Queen of the World in the process.' Esther interceded for her people *(Esther 4:15-16)*. We can ask Mary to pray for us and for those in need. It is interesting that [17]'in 1563 the *Hail Mary* was introduced into the Divine Office.' We can ask Mary to pray for us: [18]*Hail Mary, full of grace, the Lord is with thee. Blessed art thou amongst women,*

---

[13] MARY the Complete Resource edited by Sarah Jane Boss, Oxford University Press 2007, p. 149

[14] Catholicism: Richard P. McBrien, HarperCollins, 1994, p. 1253

[15] 'Hail, Holy Queen': Scott Hahn, Darton, Longman and Todd Ltd, London 2010, p. 24

[16] Dictionary of Mary 'Behold your Mother', Catholic Book Publishing Co. New Jersey 1997, 1985, p. 306

[17] Dictionary of Mary 'Behold your Mother', Catholic Book Publishing Co. New Jersey 1997, 1985, p. 547

[18] Walsingham Pilgrim Manual 2016, p. 53

and blessed is the fruit of thy womb, Jesus. Holy Mary, Mother of God, pray for us sinners now and at the hour of our death. Amen.

Max Thurian explains that Mary is a 'type' of the Church as [19]'her function was to be a 'type' of the Church, the Mother to the faithful. And the various episodes in the Gospels in which Mary is involved will reveal to us the function of the Church under this symbol. Meditation on the vocation and life of Mary is therefore at one and the same time a meditation also on the vocation and life of the Church; and, as a consequence, we shall come to understand better our own Christian vocation and life in relation to the Church which is 'mother of the faithful.'' The questions at the end of each Chapter of this Book are to encourage us to grow in faith and serve the Lord in the ways He is calling us.

Through our reflections on the titles of Mary in the *Litany of Loreto*, we will reflect and learn from them to grow into a closer relationship with Jesus and discover ways to serve the Lord and His people. In each Chapter we will consider and explore:

What does the Bible tell us about each title?
How can Mary be described as that title?
What does this mean for us?

We will reflect on the spoken words of Mary in this book. [20]'In addition to revealing her personality and her role, Mary's words hold special meaning for us. As the servant of God, she is the model for all Christians... Meditation on her words and on her life will inevitably open up ways in which we too can grow in our servanthood.' There are seven recorded words [21] of Mary described as 'childlike wonder' *(Luke 1:34)*; obedient servant *(Luke 1:38)*; Scriptural knowledge *(Luke 1:38)*; joyful praise *(Luke 1:46-55)*; gentle authority *(Luke 2:48)*; tender charity *(John 2:3)*; and deep faith *(John 2:5)*.

---

[19] Mary Mother of the Lord Figure of the Church: Max Thurian, The Faith Press, Tufton Street London, 1963, p. 12

[20] Dictionary of Mary 'Behold your Mother', op. cit., p. 498

[21] Ibid. p. 498-501

Rev Thomas Flynn appreciated the titles of Mary in the *Litany of Loreto* as: [22] 'Like a diamond, which reveals its many facets when struck by light, so is the collection of Marian titles known as the *Litany of Loreto*.... Each one of the titles of Our Blessed Mother preserved in this venerable collection seems, on first sight, to offer a single vantage point from which to view her. However, on closer inspection, we find that they are multifaceted titles, revealing more and more of Mary's glory and prerogatives as we shine more 'light' upon them.'

[23]'The Society of Mary, whilst being one of the Catholic Societies of the Church of England, has members in churches and countries all over the world. The objects of the Society are:

- to love and honour Mary;
- to spread devotion to her in reparation for past neglect and misunderstanding and in the cause of Christian Unity;
- to take Mary as a model in purity, personal relationships, and family life.'

These objectives are what I am hoping to achieve in this book. In the reflections about why Mary is given each title she is loved and honoured. As misunderstandings are explained here, this would lead to increased devotion to Mary. The third section of many Chapters asking '**What does this mean for us?**' often uses Mary as a good example for us to follow in purity, personal relationships and family life.

Here is a list of the 50 titles in the [24]*Litany of Loreto*, showing their number, with the title from the [25]Walsingham Manual in brackets, where that differs. I add the title *Our Lady of Walsingham* at the end, as I focus on that in the concluding Chapter 30.

---

[22] http://www.catholictradition.org/Mary/house-gold.htm, Rev Thomas Flynn, *The Litany of Loreto*, 1954 July 1st 2017

[23] https://societyofmary.weebly.com/ 14th March 2021

[24] Dictionary of Mary 'Behold your Mother', Catholic Book Publishing Co. New Jersey 1997, 1985, p.241

[25] The Walsingham Pilgrim Manual 2016, p.12-14

1. Holy Mary, *pray for us.*
2. Holy Mother of God, *pray for us.*
3. Holy Virgin of Virgins, [*etc.*]
4. Mother of Christ,
5. Mother of divine grace,
6. Mother most pure,
7. Mother most chaste,
8. Mother inviolate,
9. Mother undefiled (Mother unstained),
10. Mother most amiable (Mother most lovable),
11. Mother most admirable (Mother most wonderful),
12. Mother of good Counsel,
13. Mother of our Creator (Mother of the Creator),
14. Mother of our Saviour (Mother of the Saviour),
15. Virgin most prudent,
16. Virgin most venerable (Virgin most worshipful),
17. Virgin most renowned,
18. Virgin most powerful (Virgin most mighty),
19. Virgin most merciful (Virgin most clement),
20. Virgin most faithful,
21. Mirror of justice (Mirror of righteousness),
22. Seat of wisdom,
23. Cause of our joy (Cause of gladness),
24. Spiritual vessel (Vessel of the Spirit),
25. Vessel of honour,
26. Singular vessel of devotion (Vessel of devotion wondrous),
27. Mystical rose (Mystic Rose),
28. Tower of David,
29. Tower of ivory,
30. House of gold,
31. Ark of the covenant,
32. Gate of heaven,
33. Morning star,
34. Health of the sick,
35. Refuge of sinners,

36. Comforter of the afflicted (Consoler of the afflicted),
37. Help of Christians,
38. Queen of Angels,
39. Queen of Patriarchs,
40. Queen of Prophets,
41. Queen of Apostles,
42. Queen of Martyrs,
43. Queen of Confessors,
44. Queen of Virgins,
45. Queen of all Saints,
46. Queen conceived without original sin (Queen conceived without stain),
47. Queen assumed into heaven (Queen taken up to heaven),
48. Queen of the most holy Rosary,
49. Queen of families,
50. Queen of peace,
51. (Our Lady of Walsingham).

[26] 'Controversy around Mary links to controversy about authority in the Church. At the Reformation a section of Christendom prided itself in testing doctrine and devotion against the plain sense of scripture. St Paul, who has no mention of Mary in his writings, is a key influence. Roman Catholic doctrine, formulated from scripture and tradition by the consensus of bishops headed by the Pope, is seen by Protestants as weak in its biblical basis. The doctrines of Mary's conception without sin, perpetual virginity and bodily assumption are rejected in consequence by many although none are contradicted by scripture. The 2005 Anglican-RC statement on Mary says, 'we agree that doctrines and devotions which are contrary to Scripture cannot be said to be revealed by God nor to be the teaching of the Church'. This agreement captures the spirit of the Second Vatican Council (1962-5) whose Constitution on the Church states: 'This Synod earnestly exhorts theologians and preachers of the divine word that

---

[26] This is from a post by John Twistleton on *The Society*'s Facebook group. References to the Anglican-RC statement and to Vatican II, 15th May 2021

in treating of the unique dignity of the Mother of God, they carefully and equally avoid the falsity of exaggeration on the one hand, and the excess of narrow-mindedness on the other... Pursuing the study of the sacred scripture, the holy Fathers, the doctors and liturgies of the church, and under the guidance of the church's teaching authority, let them rightly explain the offices [roles] and privileges of the Blessed Virgin which are always related to Christ, the source of all truth, sanctity and piety'.

In this Book about the Titles of Mary in the Litany of Loreto I explain the roles and privileges of the Blessed Virgin Mary which are always related to Christ. I include hymns, prayers and pictures, to help our understanding of these titles. Mary's role is recognised in [27]'art, liturgy, and popular devotion'.

The hymn [28]*Take my life and let it be consecrated, Lord, to thee*; expresses my feelings of love and commitment to the Lord. The third verse *Take my intellect, and use every power as thou shalt choose*; has been inspirational in the writing of this book.

I hope and pray that all those who read this book will grow into a closer relationship with Jesus; that they increase in Biblical knowledge while developing understanding and appreciation of his Mother Mary, through focusing on her given titles.

---

[27] *The Images of Mary in the Litany of Loreto*, Margaret Barker, Usus Antiquior, Vol 1, No. 2, July 2010, p. 111

[28] *Celebration Hymnal for Everyone*, McCrimmon Publishing Company Ltd, 1994, hymn 677, Frances R. Havergal 1836-1879

CHAPTER 2

HOLY MARY

'**Holy Mary**' is the first title of Mary in the Litany of Our Lady, the [29]*Litany of Loreto.*

'**Mary**' is the English name for the name that is Μαριά in New Testament Greek, from the Hebrew: מְרִי meaning 'bitter', [30] which is significant because Mary's life had many times of sorrow and affliction. Ruth's mother-in-law Naomi said "Don't call me Naomi," she told them. "Call me Mara, because the Almighty has made my life very bitter" *(Ruth 1:20).* [31]'In the ancient Near East, a person's name was often descriptive. Naomi's choice of name and her explanation for it provide the most poignant disclosure of her sense of desolation—even her God is against her.' God later brought many blessings into Naomi's life. Mary experienced

---

[29] Dictionary of Mary 'Behold your Mother', Catholic Book Publishing Co. New Jersey 1997, 1985, p.241

[30] Analytical Concordance to the Holy Bible, Robert Young, United Society for Christian Literature, Lutterworth Press London, 1973, p.647

[31] Glo Computer Commentary for Ruth 1:20

many trials and bitter affliction, but God was certainly for her and gave her many blessings.

What does the Bible tell us about 'holy'?

God is Holy. This means [32]"God is absolutely pure." We read in Isaiah 'Holy, holy, holy is the LORD Almighty' *(Isaiah 6:3)*. This is the Hebrew word [33] *qâdôsh* קָדוֹשׁ meaning 'set apart'. [34]"God is called the Holy One of Israel about thirty times in Isaiah, and is so called also in Jeremiah and Ezekiel.' In the New Testament, God the Son is spoken of and recognised as the 'Holy One.' The demon-possessed man said "I know who you are - the Holy One of God!" *(Mark 1:24)*. Peter called Jesus 'the Holy One' after the healing of the lame man: 'You disowned the Holy and Righteous One' *(Acts 3:14a)*. The Holy Spirit, the Third Person of the Trinity who filled the disciples on the day of Pentecost *(Acts 2:5)* is the **Holy** Spirit. Paul prays for the Corinthians, may 'the fellowship of the Holy Spirit be with you all' *(II Corinthians 13:14)*. So, God is Holy.

God wants to have a holy people who are set apart, pure and consecrated to Him. God makes us holy *(Leviticus 21:8)*. The story of the Old Testament is God's reaching out in love to His people, wanting them to walk in His ways and receive His blessings *(Leviticus 20:24)*. The Ten Commandments and other laws were given so the people know how to live to please God *(Exodus 20-23)*. The sacrificial system *(Leviticus 1-7)* was for the people to recognise and confess their sins, so they could be a holy people following God's ways.

The New Testament Greek word for '**holy**' is [35]*hagios* (ἁγιος) and is translated 'separate from common condition and use, dedicated', when used to describe things and of people 'holy' and 'saints'. This is the root word meaning 'sanctification, sanctify, holiness' and as a verb it means

---

[32] What the Bible Teaches': R.A. Torrey, Nisbet & Co., Ltd, London, early 20th century p.37

[33] Young, op. cit., p.487

[34] What the Bible Teaches': R.A. Torrey, Nisbet & Co., Ltd, London, early 20th century p.36

[35] Analytical Greek Lexicon, Samuel Bagster & Sons Ltd, London, 1973, p.3

'to separate, consecrate, sanctify, regard or reverence as holy'. This word is [36]'used of believers. When people believe in Jesus and choose to follow Him they are 'set apart to God' and 'God's work of grace in making each believer holy begins.' [37]'All members of the Church of God already are sanctified in Christ Jesus.'

The letter to the Hebrews tells us about Jesus' death on the cross that 'by one sacrifice he has made perfect for ever those who are being made holy' *(Hebrews 10:14).* God is making us holy. [38]'Sanctification is the process of setting apart or state of being set apart for God.' God wants us to **be holy** by being different from the world. We read in Romans 'Do not conform any longer to the pattern of this world, but be transformed by the renewing of your mind. Then you will be able to test and approve what God's will is – his good, pleasing and perfect will' *(Romans 12:2).* We should follow the teachings of Jesus and 'do to others as you would have them do to you' *(Luke 6:31).*

The Beatitudes in St Luke's Gospel are followed by challenging teaching from Jesus about our attitude and behaviour to those who have harmed us: Jesus said 'Love your enemies, do good to those who hate you' *(Luke 6:27).* Jesus [39]'commands that we love everyone – even our enemies' and tells us to pray for them *(Luke 6:28).* [40]'The Beatitudes, and trying to live them out, is one of the best ways of loving God with all your heart and understanding the Christian vision for the world.' [41] They 'describe what it means to live as a child of the kingdom of God' rather than following the ways of the world.

Sanctification is God's changing us and **making us holy**. The Holy Spirit convicts us of sin, *(John 16:8)* we repent and try to live lives that are

---

[36] *An Expository Dictionary of Biblical Words*: W.E. Vine, Thomas Nelson Publishers, 1985 p.544

[37] *What the Bible Teaches*: R.A. Torrey Nisbet & Co, p.347

[38] *What the Bible Teaches*: R.A. Torrey Nisbet & Co p.340

[39] Glo Computer Commentary for this verse

[40] *Pilgrim Course for the Christian Journey The Beatitudes* Church House Publishing 2015 p.9

[41] *Ibid.,* p. 11

pleasing to the Lord: 'for it is God who works in you to will and to act according to his good purpose.' *(Philippians 2:13)* We need to confess our sins and receive absolution because 'the blood of Jesus, purifies us from all sin' *(I John 1:7)*. As a caterpillar changes into a butterfly: 'we, who with unveiled faces all reflect the Lord's glory, are being transformed into his likeness with ever-increasing glory, which comes from the Lord, who is the Spirit' *(II Corinthians 3:18)*.

To grow in holiness, **the fruit of the Holy Spirit** should be growing in our lives: 'the fruit of the Spirit is love, joy, peace, patience, kindness, goodness, faithfulness, gentleness and self-control' *(Galatians 5:22-23)*. These qualities and virtues should be increasing in the lives of those who know, love and follow Jesus.

Many hymns proclaim the holiness and majesty of God, for example:

> [42] *Holy, holy, holy! Lord God Almighty,*
> *Early in the morning our song shall rise to Thee;*
> *Holy, holy, holy, merciful and mighty!*
> *God in three Persons, blessed Trinity!*

The Bible tells us that **God is holy** and He calls all His followers to **be holy.**

'How can Mary be described as 'Holy Mary'?

Mary was chosen to be the Mother of Jesus. The Gospel of Luke begins its account of Mary's life with the Annunciation, when the angel Gabriel appeared to her and announced her divine selection to be the mother of Jesus *(Luke 1:26-28)*. God chose Mary because she was the perfect young woman prepared by God to be the Mother of His Son. The Church celebrates the Annunciation on 25th March. [43]'The feast marks

---

[42] The New English Hymnal, Canterbury Press, Norwich, 1987, p. 156, hymn 146, v. 1, Reginald Heber 1783-1826

[43] *Exciting Holiness* Collects and Readings for the Festivals and Lesser Festivals, Canterbury Press, 2012, p. 702

the conception of Christ in the womb of Mary' and on this day 'his virgin mother still has a unique place of honour.' We refer to Mary as 'The Blessed Virgin Mary'. Mary wanted her life to be holy, dedicated and set apart.

Mary is 'Holy Mary' because she said 'yes' to God. At the Annunciation, on hearing the amazing plan that God had for her life, Mary answered, "I am the Lord's servant... May it be to me as you have said" *(Luke 1:38)*. Mary was letting God fulfil His perfect plan and purposes in her life; dedicating herself to God's will. Mary is '**Holy Mary**' because she remained a Virgin, as we explore in Chapter 5. Christians believe that she conceived her son while a virgin by the Holy Spirit. The miraculous birth took place when she was already betrothed to Joseph *(Matthew 1:22-25)*.

Mary is called '**Holy Mary**' by some Christians, because they believe she herself was conceived without sin. This belief is called the Immaculate Conception, which we explore in Chapter 26.

Mary is '**Holy Mary**' because **the fruit of the Holy Spirit** is seen clearly in her life. In the places in the Bible where we meet Mary, we can see these qualities of 'love, joy, peace, patience, kindness, goodness, faithfulness, gentleness and self-control' *(Galatians 5:22-23)*. After the visit of the Shepherds *(Luke 2: 8-20)* Mary felt love, joy and peace while she 'treasured up all these things and pondered them in her heart'. At the Wedding at Cana *(John 2:1-11)* we see her love, joy, kindness, goodness and gentleness in helping the family by asking Jesus to help them. When following Jesus on his teaching journeys *(Luke 8:19-21)* Mary showed love, patience, faithfulness and self-control. Standing by the Cross of Jesus, *(John 19:25-27)* Mary displayed love and faithfulness. Thus, the fruit of the Holy Spirit is clearly seen in the life of Holy Mary.

What does this mean for us?

All believers are called to be '**holy**' and by God's grace the work of sanctification, becoming more holy, continues in our lives. Jesus said: 'Do to others as you would have them do to you' *(Luke 6:31)*. We need to confess our sins and receive absolution *(I John 1:7)*. The Holy Spirit helps, convicts and challenges so that we are changed to be more like Jesus, just as a caterpillar changes into a butterfly *(II Corinthians 3:18)*. How is the Lord changing you?

God calls us to **live holy lives** and to share the love of Jesus with others. St Paul commended the Ephesian Christians on 'their love' *(Ephesians 1:15)* and we know Jesus' new commandment: 'Love one another' *(John 13:34)*. We are called to live as saints by loving acts of care and kindness that make the world a better place. How can you **live a holy life** by giving care and help to people to show the love and kindness of Jesus?

Like Holy Mary, we should say **Yes** to whatever God is calling us to do, trusting that the Lord has a perfect plan for our lives as 'we know that in all things God works for the good of those who love him, who have been called according to his purpose' *(Romans 8:28)*. Is the Lord calling you to new ways to serve and share the love of Jesus?

To grow in holiness, **the fruit of the Holy Spirit** *(Galatians 5:22-23)* should be growing in our lives. These qualities and virtues should be increasing in the lives of those who know, love and follow Jesus. Which of these qualities need to grow in your life?

[44]Holy Mary, *pray for us.*

---

[44] The Walsingham Pilgrim Manual 2016, p.12

CHAPTER 3

HOLY MOTHER OF GOD AND MORE 'MOTHER' TITLES

'Holy Mother of God' is the second title in the [45]*Litany of Loreto.*

What does the Bible tell us about 'Holy Mother of God'?

In the previous chapter we explored the word **'holy'**. The Bible tells us that **God is holy** and He calls all His followers to **be holy**.

In the Bible the word **Mother** is [46] *'êm* אֵם in Hebrew, which means 'ancestress'. In the New Testament the Greek word for 'mother' is [47] *mētēr*,

---

[45] Dictionary of Mary 'Behold your Mother', Catholic Book Publishing Co. New Jersey 1997, 1985, p.241

[46] Analytical Concordance to the Holy Bible, Robert Young, United Society for Christian Literature, Lutterworth Press London, 1973, p.672

[47] Ibid., p.483

μήτηρ meaning [48]'mother' and 'parent' with the same root word as 'womb', because to be a mother means a baby has grown in the womb. The word *mētēr* is often used to refer to Mary, the mother of Jesus. 'His mother Mary was pledged to be married to Joseph, but before they came together, she was found to be with child through the Holy Spirit' *(Matthew 1:18)*.

The Bible tells us that Mary is the Mother of Jesus. The Angel Gabriel told Mary 'The Holy Spirit will come upon you, and the power of the Most High will overshadow you. So the holy one to be born will be called the Son of God' *(Luke 1:35)*. In Bethlehem 'she gave birth to her firstborn, a son' *(Luke 2:7)*. The Wise Men 'saw the child with his **mother** Mary' *(Matthew 2:11)*.

Mary is referred to as the **mother** of Jesus in many places in the Bible. In the Temple in Jerusalem when Jesus was forty days old, at his Presentation, 'Simeon blessed them and said to Mary, his **mother**, "This child is destined to cause the falling and rising of many in Israel, ... And a sword will pierce your own soul too" *(Luke 2:34-35)*. After the visit to Jerusalem when Jesus was twelve years old, 'his **mother** treasured all these things in her heart' *(Luke 2:51)*. At the Wedding at Cana 'Jesus' **mother** was there' *(John 2:1-11)* and 'his mother said to the servants, 'Do whatever he tells you' *(v.5)*. Mary followed Jesus on some of his journeys *(Luke 8: 19-21)*. 'Near the cross of Jesus stood his **mother**' *(John 19:25)*; when Mary suffered great anguish seeing the suffering of her beloved Son, maybe remembering Simeon's words 'a sword will pierce your own soul too'. How wonderful that on the Day of Pentecost 'Mary the **mother** of Jesus' *(Acts 1:14)* was in the room praying with the disciples waiting for God to send the Holy Spirit.

The Bible tells us that Jesus is God. 'In the beginning was the Word, and the Word was with God, and the Word was God... The **Word became flesh** and made his dwelling among us...' *(John 1:1,14)*. An angel reassured Joseph that Mary's expected baby was 'from the Holy Spirit' and will be called **Immanuel**, meaning '**God with us**' *(Matthew 1:18-25)*. At Jesus's Baptism, God the Father spoke from heaven saying: "This is **my Son**, whom I love, with him I am well pleased" *(Matthew 3:17)*. The

---

[48] Analytical Greek Lexicon, Samuel Bagster & Sons Ltd, London, 1973, p.269

demon-possessed man in the synagogue in Capernaum recognised that Jesus is God, saying: "I know who you are – **the Holy One of God**" *(Mark 1:24)*. At Caesarea Philippi Simon Peter said to Jesus "You are **the Christ, the Son of the living God**" *(Matthew 16:13)*. At the Transfiguration Jesus was revealed as God's Son: "This is my **Son**" *(Matthew 17:1-8)*. When Thomas saw Jesus a week after the Resurrection, 'Thomas said to him "**My Lord and my God**"' *(John 20:28)*. John wrote about the signs he recorded: 'These are written that you may believe that **Jesus is the Christ, the Son of God**, and that by believing you may have life in his name' *(John 19:30-31)*. On the Day of Pentecost Peter told the crowd: "God has made this Jesus, whom you crucified, both **Lord and Christ**" *(Acts 2:36b)*.

The phrase **'Holy Mother of God'** is not in the Bible. [49]Jacques Bur explains: 'The expression 'mother of God' is not found in the Bible. However, we read there that Jesus is the Son of God and that the Virgin Mary is the mother of Jesus…. Mary is truly mother of Jesus, the true Son of God.'

Then how can Mary be described as 'Holy Mother of God'?

The doctrine called **Theotokos** helps us to understand how Mary can be described as **'Holy Mother of God'**. [50]Bur writes: 'From the third century onwards, the title *Theotokos* was given to Mary. It means 'mother of God' or, more accurately, 'the one who gave birth to God'. Its use spread during the fourth century. [51]St Gregory of Nazianzus, for example, wrote about 382: 'Anyone who does not recognise Mary as the mother of God is separated from the divinity…. If Jesus is one and the same divine being, the Son, having two distinct natures, divine and human, then Mary, in giving human life to the person of the Son of God, gave birth to God himself, in the person of his Son.' There were debates and discussions about this doctrine and it was opposed by Nestorius because he was alarmed and

---

[49] How to understand the Virgin Mary: Jacques Bur, SCM Press Ltd, Translation 1994 John Bowden and Margaret Lydamore, P.1

[50] Ibid.

[51] Theological letters of St Gregory of Nazianzus 101.4

did not want to [52]'deny the humanity of Christ.' His teaching is called 'Nestorianism' and it is recognised as heresy. [53]'This teaching, condemned by the Council of Ephesus that posited two separate persons in Jesus Christ, the one human and the other divine.' This was argued against by Cyril of Alexandria who taught the belief in the doctrine of *Theotokos* as [54]'the Word was Son of God by nature, but He was also naturally Mary's son too, since the humanity conceived in Mary's womb was exclusively and inalienably His'.

Cyril also wrote: [55]'If anyone does not confess that the Emmanuel is truly God and that for this reason the Holy Virgin is **mother of God** (since she bore in the flesh the Word of God made flesh), let him be anathema.' At this time [56]'a failure to agree that Mary was the 'mother of God' became seen as tantamount to a refusal to accept the divinity of Christ.' The Council of Ephesus in 412 agreed [57]'we confess the holy Virgin as *Theotokos* because the divine Word became flesh and was made man and from the very conception united to Himself the Temple taken from her.' This important Council agreed that Mary is indeed the **Holy Mother of God**. So [58]'the term *Theotokos* was adopted by the Council of Ephesus' in 412 and later it 'was reinforced by the definition of the Council of Chalcedon in 451 and by the second Council of Constantinople in 553.' *Theotokos* is defined by McBrien as: [59]'Literally "the bearer of God." The title given to Mary at the Council of Ephesus (431) to establish that Mary is truly the "**Mother of God**" and not only the mother of the human Jesus.' *Theotokos* is defined as: [60]'Literally, "the bearer of God." A Greek term

[52] Christian Theology: Alister E. McGrath, Fifth Edition, Wiley-Blackwell, 2011, p. 280

[53] Catholicism: Richard P. McBrien, HarperCollins, 1994, p. 1246

[54] Early Christian Doctrines Fifth Edition, J.N.D.Kelly, Continuum, 2011, P. 322

[55] How to understand the Virgin Mary: Jacques Bur, SCM Press Ltd, Translation 1994 John Bowden and Margaret Lydamore, P.2

[56] McGrath, op. cit., p. 280

[57] Early Christian Doctrines Fifth Edition, J.N.D.Kelly, Continuum, 2011, P. 329

[58] Bur, op. cit., p.2

[59] McBrien, op. cit., p. 1252

[60] Christian Theology: Alister E. McGrath, Fifth Edition, Wiley-Blackwell, 2011, p. 470

used to refer to Mary, the mother of Jesus Christ, with the intention of reinforcing the central insight of the doctrine of the incarnation – that is, that Jesus Christ is none other than God. The term was extensively used by writers of the Eastern Church, especially around the time of the Nestorian controversy, to articulate both the divinity of Christ and the reality of the incarnation.' Michael Rear elucidates: [61]'Theotokos means that Jesus is born both truly God and truly human. The Word was made flesh in the womb of the Blessed Virgin Mary.'

An understanding of the **hypostatic union** helps us to understand the incarnation, that is how 'The Word became flesh' *(John 1:14)* in Mary's womb. The hypostatic union is: [62]'The permanent union of divine and human natures in the one divine person of the Word in Jesus Christ.' This is the belief of all Christians. Jacques Bur explains: [63]'In affirming that Mary is the mother of God, one is necessarily affirming that there are two real natures in Jesus Christ, divine and human, substantially united in a single divine being. This union of persons is called the 'hypostatic union', that is to say, the union of two natures in a single person.' So Christians believe in the dual-nature of Christ; that Jesus is one person in two natures. From the Jews 'is traced the human ancestry of Christ, who is God over all, for ever praised!' *(Romans 9:5)*.

The **Incarnation** is: [64]'A term used to refer to the assumption of human nature by God, in the person of Jesus Christ.' At Christmas carol services the wonderful Bible reading from John 1:1-14 is announced as, 'St John unfolds the great mystery of the Incarnation'. 'The Word became flesh and made his dwelling among us. We have seen his glory...' *(John 1:14)*. St Paul writes about God 'regarding his Son, who as to his human nature was a descendant of David, and who through the Spirit of holiness was declared with power to be the Son of God, by his resurrection from the

[61] Walsingham Pilgrims and Pilgrimage: Michael Rear, Gracewing, 2019, p. 84

[62] Catholicism: Richard P. McBrien, HarperCollins, 1994, p. 1241

[63] How to understand the Virgin Mary: Jacques Bur, SCM Press Ltd, Translation 1994 John Bowden and Margaret Lydamore, P.2

[64] Christian Theology: Alister E. McGrath, Fifth Edition, Wiley-Blackwell, 2011, p. 468

dead: Jesus Christ our Lord' *(Romans 1:3-4)*. A lovely Christmas hymn[65] teaches us about the Incarnation; how Jesus left heaven to come to earth: *Thou didst leave Thy throne and Thy kingly crown, when Thou camest to earth for me; ... But of lowly birth didst Thou come to earth, and in great humility.*

It is essential that we have an understanding of the **Trinity** in order to appreciate the title, **Mary Mother of God**. The doctrine of the Trinity is defined in Article 1 of the Church of England's 39 Articles as: [66]'There is one living and true God ... And in unity of this Godhead there be three Persons, of one substance, power and eternity; the Father, the Son and Holy Ghost'. Jesus' great commission told the disciples to baptize new believers 'in the name of the Father and of the Son and of the Holy Spirit' *(Matthew 28:19)*. Paul's words *(II Corinthians 13:14)* support the Trinitarian belief in the one Being of God as eternally three Persons: 'May the grace of the Lord Jesus Christ, and the love of God, and the fellowship of the Holy Spirit be with you all'. Gumbel writes: [67]'The concept of the Trinity permeates the pages of the New Testament and (there are) hints of this doctrine even in the Old Testament'. The Creeds were written to clarify beliefs and to be statements of faith to oppose heresy, thus protecting the Church from wrong teaching. In 325 the Council of Nicaea discussed the doctrine of the Trinity, including the Arian question of [68]'how Christ the Son of God was himself God' and they debated the Christology issue of how Christ was man and God. This led to the Nicene Creed's being agreed by the Bishops to be [69]'universally binding' at the Council of Constantinople in 381.

Jesus is God, the second Person of the Holy Trinity. Mary is the mother of Jesus who is God. She is not the mother of God the Father or of the Holy Spirit. It is paramount that we understand this, because then

---

[65] Hymns Ancient & Modern Revised, William Clowes & Sons, pre 1964, p. 287, hymn number 363, Emily Elliott 1836-1897

[66] A Guide to the Church of England: M. Davie, Mowbray, London, 2008, p.88

[67] Searching Issues: Nicky Gumbel, Kingsway, Eastbourne, 2004, p. 103

[68] The History of Christianity: A Lion Handbook: T. Dowley, Lion Publishing, Berkhamstead, 1977, p. 156

[69] Ibid., p. 169

we can come to recognise and address Mary with some of her other titles in [70]*The Litany of Loreto*: the 4th, **Mother of Christ**; the 5th, **Mother of divine grace**; the 13th, **Mother of our Creator;** and the 14th title, **Mother of our Saviour.**

The New Testament Greek word for **Christ** is '*Christos*' which means anointed. [71]Young explains this word is: 'The official appellation of the long-promised and long-expected Saviour, denoting his kingly authority and mediatorial position as 'Servant of the Lord'. Jesus was his common name among men during his lifetime and he is generally so called in the Gospels, while Christ or Jesus Christ is generally used in the Epistles.' The Jewish people had been waiting for centuries for God to send the Messiah, the anointed One who would save His people. **Mary is the mother of Jesus who is the Christ**, so we can call Mary **Mother of Christ**.

Mother of divine grace is the 5th title in [72]The Litany of Loreto. 'Grace is the New Testament Greek word '*charis*' which means 'gracious'. Jesus shows us the love and grace of God, so he has 'divine grace'. John tells us that at the Incarnation, when Jesus was conceived in Mary's womb, 'The Word became flesh and made his dwelling among us. We have seen his glory, the glory of the One and Only, who came from the Father, full of **grace** and truth' *(John 1:14)*. Jesus was 'full of grace' and as a child 'the **grace** of God was upon him' *(Luke 2:40)*. 'From the fullness of his grace we have all received one blessing after another.... **grace** and truth came through Jesus Christ' *(John 1:16-17)*. Mary is the mother of Jesus who is divine grace, so we can call Mary **Mother of divine grace**. Jacques Bur explains: [73]'Mary is 'mother of grace' because she has made us be born to the life of grace by engendering the one who is the author of this life. But she is also 'mother of grace' for a second reason: being the first to welcome

[70] The Walsingham Pilgrim Manual 2016, p.13

[71] Analytical Concordance to the Holy Bible, Robert Young, United Society for Christian Literature, Lutterworth Press London, 1973, p.165

[72] The Walsingham Pilgrim Manual 2016, p.13

[73] How to understand the Virgin Mary: Jacques Bur, SCM Press Ltd, Translation 1994 John Bowden and Margaret Lydamore, p. 106

Christ, the source of all blessings, by her faith, she continues to be the one who opens us up to all grace.'

Is Jesus the **Creator**? God created the world, as we read in Genesis. God is three Persons: the Father, the Son and the Holy Spirit. God created the world. 'In the beginning God created the heavens and the earth' *(Genesis 1:1)*. Jesus is the Word and 'In the beginning was the Word, and the Word was with God, and the Word was God.... Through him all things were made; without him nothing was made that has been made' *(John 1:1-3)*. Jesus Christ 'is the image of the invisible God, the firstborn over all creation. For by him all things were created: things in heaven and on earth' *(Colossians 1:15-16)*. **Jesus is the Creator**, so Mary can be addressed as **Mother of our Creator** because she is the Mother of Jesus who along with God the Father and the Holy Spirit created the world.

The name 'Jesus' means[74] **Saviour**. The angel told Joseph that Mary 'will give birth to a son, and you are to give him the name Jesus, because he will **save** his people from their sins' *(Matthew 1:21)*. Jesus lived to show God's love and then died on the Cross to 'save us' from our sins. Jesus did no wrong, He was without sin; so only Jesus could be our **Saviour** and take upon Himself the sins of the world and be that one perfect sacrifice for sin. Christ 'gave himself up for us as a fragrant offering and sacrifice to God' *(Ephesians 5:2)*. Jesus is our wonderful **Saviour** because He was both our ransom and our Redeemer as we were 'bought at a price' *(I Corinthians 6:20)*: we were redeemed 'with the precious blood of Christ' *(I Peter 1:19)*. Jesus' death on the cross is the ransom that has set us free as 'he has died as a ransom to set (us) free from the sins committed' *(Hebrews 9:12; John 3:16)*. Christ came 'to do away with sin by the sacrifice of himself' *(Hebrews 9:26)*. God forgives us because 'the blood of Jesus, his Son, purifies us from all sin' *(I John 1:7)*.

Brother Ramon explains: [75]'**Salvation** in its fullness, means a whole body, a clear mind and a pure heart.' The New Testament Greek word

---

[74] Analytical Concordance to the Holy Bible, Robert Young, United Society for Christian Literature, Lutterworth Press London, 1973, p.541

[75] When they crucified my Lord', Brother Ramon, The Bible Reading Fellowship, Abingdon, 1999, p. 53

for 'salvation' is *sōtēria*, σωτηρία which means [76]'soundness and safety.' Jesus demonstrated the coming of his kingdom with many miracles of healing *(Matthew 4:23)*. Through Jesus' death on the Cross we can receive forgiveness and healing. 'Surely he took up our infirmities and carried our sorrows... But he was pierced for our transgressions, he was crushed for our iniquities; the punishment that brought us peace was upon him, and by his wounds we are healed' *(Isaiah 53:4-5)*. Our **Saviour** gives physical and emotional healing as well as forgiveness of sins. Mary is the mother of Jesus Christ who is our **Saviour**, through his death on the Cross, so we can call Mary **Mother of our Saviour**. We sing about Jesus' being our **Saviour** in the lovely hymn [77]*There is a green hill far away*, where we reflect on the amazing love of Jesus in dying on the Cross to save us.

We now focus on six more 'Mother' titles for Our Lady, with their number in the Litany.[78]They are adjectives describing her: 6th **Mother most pure**; 7th **Mother most chaste**; 8th **Mother inviolate**; 9th **Mother unstained**; 10th **Mother most loveable;** and 11th **Mother most wonderful**.

Mary is the Mother most **pure, chaste, inviolate** and **unstained** because she remained a virgin. No other mother is a virgin. Chapter 5 explores the '**Virgin**' titles of Mary in more detail. Mary is the Mother most **pure, chaste, inviolate** and **unstained** because she was conceived without sin. I explore the theology of the Immaculate Conception in Chapter 26 **Queen conceived without original sin.**

The title **Mother most loveable** can be understood when realising that Mary's motherly love extends to all Christians who turn to her. Mothers love their own children but Mary's love reaches out to everyone. Thus, the title **Mother most wonderful** seems appropriate for Mary as she is full of wonderful, special, admirable motherly care and concern for all who ask

---

[76] Analytical Concordance to the Holy Bible, Robert Young, United Society for Christian Literature, Lutterworth Press London, 1973, p.833

[77] Hymns Ancient & Modern Revised, William Clowes & Sons, pre 1964, p. 177, hymn number 214, Mrs C. F. Alexander 1818-1895

[78] The Walsingham Pilgrim Manual 2016, p.12-13

for her help. We remember this in the *Prayer to Our Lady of Walsingham* at the [79]Last Visit to the Holy House:

*O Mary, recall the solemn moment when Jesus, your divine Son, dying on the cross, confided us to your maternal care. You are **our Mother**, we desire ever to remain your devout children. Let us therefore feel the effects of your powerful intercession with Jesus Christ.... Pray, O **holy Mother of God** for the conversion of England, restoration of the sick, consolation for the afflicted, repentance of sinners, peace to the departed.*

There are hymns and other prayers that refer to Mary as **Mother of God**. We sing [80] *I'll sing a hymn to Mary, **The Mother of my God**.* [81]*How sweet thou art, my Mother* contains the phrases: ***Thou Mother of Our Lord divine*** and *How **pure** thou art, **my Mother*** and ***spotless Mother**,* meaning **pure, chaste, inviolate** and **unstained**. We sing [82]*For Mary, **Mother of our Lord**, God's holy name be praised.* In [83]*Hear thy children, gentlest Mother*, we describe Mary as *sweet Mother* and ***dearest Mother**,* showing she is **Mother most loveable** and **Mother most wonderful**. We sing: [84] *In splendour arrayed, in vesture of gold, the **Mother of God** In glory behold!* The last verse has the phrase *A **Mother all-pure**;* reminds us of Our Lady's titles **Mother most pure, Mother most chaste, Mother inviolate** and **Mother unstained**.

There are many pictures, paintings and statues that show Mary the Mother of Jesus. The Statue of Our Lady of Walsingham, on the front cover, shows Mary **Holy Mother of God** is holding Jesus out to us.

What does this mean for us?

We should be living **holy** lives. To grow in holiness, **the fruit of the Holy Spirit** should be growing in our lives *(Galatians 5:22-23)*. These qualities

---

[79] Walsingham Pilgrim Manual, 2016, p. 75

[80] Ibid., p. 108, hymn number 20 v.1, John Wyse 1825-1898

[81] Ibid., p. 107, hymn number 19, Anon traditional

[82] Ibid., p. 97, hymn number 8, J.R. Peacey 1896-1971

[83] Ibid., p. 103-4, hymn number 15, Francis Stanfield 1835-1914

[84] Ibid., p. 109 -10, hymn number 21, St John Henry Newman 1801- 1890

and virtues should be increasing in the lives of those who know, love and follow Jesus so we are 'transformed into his likeness' *(II Corinthians 3:18).* Which of these qualities do you need more? To grow in **holiness,** we need to confess our sins and receive absolution *(I John 1:7).* God wants us to **be holy** by being different from the world *(Romans 12:2).* We should follow the teachings of Jesus and 'do to others as you would have them do to you' *(Luke 6:31).*

Jesus is our **Saviour:** we need to confess sins and receive forgiveness. Christ came 'to do away with sin by the sacrifice of himself' *(Hebrews 9:26).* Are there sins you need to repent of, confess and receive forgiveness for? Jesus our **Saviour** died for our healing too. Pray for the sick and ask others to pray for you if you need healing.

Let us receive the **grace** of Our Lord Jesus Christ *(Romans 13:14)* and realise that Jesus sympathises with our weakness because He has been tempted in every way, yet was without sin. Let us approach the throne of grace with confidence, so we may receive grace and mercy in our times of need *(Hebrews 4: 14-15).*

Let us give thanks for the beauty of **Creation.** God's love is shown to us in creation. Let us appreciate, enjoy and care for the beautiful world that God created. The Church of England's 5th Mark of Mission is: [85]'To strive to safeguard the integrity of creation, and sustain and renew the life of the earth'. We are increasingly aware of how the way we live impacts on the world around us and how we need to change. How can you care for the world?

After reflecting on this theme of **Mother,** how wonderful that Jesus said we must be born again *(John 3:3).* We can know Jesus is 'born in us' and with us by asking Him to come into our hearts.

[86]*O holy Child of Bethlehem, descend to us, we pray; cast out our sin and enter in, be born in us today... Oh, come to us, abide with us, Our Lord*

---

[85] https://www.anglicancommunion.org/mission/marks-of-mission.aspx 25th October 2019

[86] Celebration Hymnal for Everyone, McCrimmons, Great Wavering, Essex, hymn number 540, v. 5, Phillips Brooks 1835-1893

Emmanuel! [87] *O come to my heart, Lord Jesus, there is room in my heart for Thee.*

Our response to Jesus' amazing love should be to love Him more. [88] *O dearly, dearly has He loved, and we must love Him, too, and trust in His redeeming blood, and try His works to do.*

What are the 'works' that God is calling you to do at this time?

[89] Holy Mother of God, *pray for us.*

---

[87] Hymns Ancient & Modern Revised, William Clowes & Sons, pre-1964, p. 287, hymn number 363, Emily Elliott 1836-1897

[88] Ibid., p. 177, hymn number 214, Mrs C.F. Alexander 1818-1895

[89] The Walsingham Pilgrim Manual 2016, p.12

CHAPTER 4

MOTHER OF GOOD COUNSEL

Mother of good counsel is the 12th title in the[90] *Litany of Loreto.*

What does the Bible tell us about good counsel?

The Bible tells us much about '**good counsel**', which means[91] 'to advice, counsel and to consult'. David experienced the Lord's guiding, protecting, helping, directing him and giving him **good counsel**. He writes that God says: 'I will instruct you and teach you in the way you should go; I will **counsel** you and watch over you. Do not be like the horse or like the mule, which have no understanding, which must be controlled by bit and bridle' *(Psalm 32:8-9).* We should be open and ready to listen to the **good counsel** that the Lord will give us in many ways. Good counsel is wise advice.

---

[90] Dictionary of Mary 'Behold your Mother', Catholic Book Publishing Co. New Jersey 1997, 1985, p.241

[91] 'An Expository Dictionary of Biblical Words: W.E. Vine p. 49

God guides and gives us **good counsel** through verses and passages in the Bible as God's word written in the Bible can be like a torch showing us the right path to take in the darkness. 'Your word is a lamp to my feet' *(Psalm 119:105)*.

Verses from Proverbs encourage us to pray and seek God's direction and help in all we do. 'Trust in the LORD with all your heart; and lean not on your own understanding; in all your ways acknowledge him, and he will make your paths straight' *(Proverbs 3:4-5)*. Praying, reading the Bible and reflecting are important ways that God guides and gives us **good counsel**.

God can use other people to guide us through wise advice and **good counsel**: 'Make plans by seeking advice' *(Proverbs 20:18)*. Jehoshaphat wanted to 'First seek the **counsel** of the LORD', *(I Kings 22:5)* before leading his men into the battle at Ramoth Gilead. Many Prophets were then called to give advice. Micaiah, 'a prophet of the Lord' *(I Kings 22:7)* spoke the truth.

Moses appreciated God's guidance through the words of his father-in-law. Jethro gave '**good counsel**' to Moses: "Listen now to my voice; I will give you **counsel**, and God will be with you" *(Exodus 18:19)*. This **good counsel** was for Moses to appoint elders to assist him in the work of teaching God's laws, guiding and directing the people. This was wise and **good counsel** for Moses to hear, otherwise Jethro warned Moses that he would wear himself out because "the work is too heavy for you; you cannot handle it alone" *(Exodus 18: 17)*. Moses could not continue or he would become exhausted.

Isaiah prophesised that the Messiah will be called '**Wonderful Counsellor**' *(Isaiah 9:6)*. Jesus is called the '**Wonderful Counsellor**' who gives **good counsel**. The Hebrew word for '**counsel**', which is *yâsad* יָסַד meaning [92]'to have a firm foundation laid'. If we follow the **good counsel** that Jesus gives us, then our lives will have a firm foundation. Jesus said: "Everyone who hears these words of Mine, and puts them into practice is like a wise man who built his house on the rock" *(Matthew 7:24)*. Jesus tells us not only to listen, but also to <u>do</u> what He tells us, so that we will

---

[92] Analytical Concordance to the Holy Bible, Robert Young, United Society for Christian Literature, Lutterworth Press London, 1973, p. 205

then 'stand firm' in the storms of life. We need to pray, trust and follow Jesus, so we grow to know the Lord more in the reality of our daily lives.

Jesus tells us that the Holy Spirit is '**The Counsellor**'. He told the disciples: 'When the **Counsellor** comes, whom I will send to you from the Father, the Spirit of truth who goes out from the Father, he will testify about me' *(John 14:26)*. The Holy Spirit 'will guide you into all truth' *(John 16:13)*. Jesus said the **Counsellor** will 'teach you all things and will remind you of everything I have said to you' *(John 14:26)*. This is the New Testament Greek word *paraklētos* παράκλητος meaning [93]'one called or sent for to assist another, an advocate, one who pleads the cause of another, one present to render beneficial service.' The Holy Spirit gives us **good counsel**, coming alongside to give us advice, comfort and help. God says: 'I will put my laws in their minds and write them on their hearts' *(Hebrews 8:10)*. The Holy Spirit will direct and guide us through giving us peace about what is right *(Colossians 3:15)*. The Holy Spirit is **The Counsellor** and gives us **good counsel**, which is wise advice.

How can Mary be described as 'Mother of 'good counsel'?

Mary can be described as '**Mother of good counsel**' because the Holy Spirit, the **Counsellor** overshadowed and filled her. The Angel told Mary: 'The Holy Spirit will come upon you, and the power of the Most High will overshadow you. So, the holy one to be born will be called the Son of God' *(Luke 1:35)*. The Holy Spirit, the Counsellor, overshadowed Mary enabling her to become the Mother of Jesus, God's Son. Mary, **Mother of good counsel** gave love, protection, nurture, teaching and **good counsel** to the baby and young child Jesus as He grew in the home at Nazareth *(Luke 2:40)*.

At Walsingham we think much about the home at Nazareth, where the Angel came to Mary and where the young child Jesus grew, played, laughed and learned in the care of His Mother and Joseph. When He was a teenager, 'Jesus grew in wisdom and stature and in favour with God and men' *(Luke 2:52)*. Mary continued to be a '**Mother of good counsel**' to

---

[93] Analytical Greek Lexicon, Samuel Bagster & Sons Ltd, London, 1973, p. 303

her Son through all those years in the home at Nazareth until He began His Ministry at about the age of 30 years old. Mary can be described as '**Mother** of good counsel': she understands family situations, being a mother at the home in Nazareth.

We can imagine that Mary was a wonderful friend and neighbour, being one of those people always ready to listen and give **good counsel** in her home or by the well in Nazareth, listening to friends and neighbours pour out their troubles and giving **good counsel** helping those troubled people in their difficult situations. The Holy Spirit, the Counsellor, overshadowed, filled and remained with Mary, so she could help others.

Mary can be described as '**Mother of good counsel**' because Jesus gave His Mother to the Church. While He hung on the Cross *(John 19:26-27)*, Jesus gave John to His Mother, saying 'Here is your son' and He gave His Mother to John, saying 'Here is your mother'. 'From that time on this disciple took her into his home'. Mary was with John and the other disciples after Jesus' ascension where 'they all joined together constantly in prayer' *(Acts 1:14)*. Jesus not only gave Mary into John's care, He said she was his <u>Mother</u>! Mary became the Mother of the Church. Scott Hahn thinks that it is amazing that Jesus gave his Mother to the Church. He writes: [94]'for Jesus to have given His mother to us – that's something great beyond imagining!' Mary is given to the Church and we can learn from her motherly **good counsel**.

The woman in Revelation chapter 12 is seen to be Mary *(Revelation 12:1-2)*. Later in that chapter we are told about the woman's other children: 'Then the dragon was enraged at the woman and went off to make war against the rest of her offspring – those who obey God's commandments and hold to the testimony of Jesus' *(Revelation 12: 17)*. The reference to 'the rest of her children' contextually refers to the whole body of Christians. This is further Biblical evidence that Mary is the Mother of the Church and that she can give motherly **good counsel** to all Christians.

---

[94] Hail, Holy Queen, Scott Hahn Darton. Longman + Todd London 2001, reprinted 2010 p.136

Pope Pius X [95]wrote: 'For is not Mary the Mother of Christ? Then she is our Mother also. …In heaven Mary prays for us.' Hahn develops this idea by referring to writings of Saint Augustine, [96] explaining: 'Mary, then, is a mother to the family of God. She is a model for that family, and she actively participates in the children's 'birth and <u>education</u>". Mary, the **Mother of good counsel** educates by teaching us through her words, prayers, attitudes and actions. John,[97] Bishop of Plymouth, suggests that we 'join her in the pages of the Scriptures, linger and pray as you read of God's call to her and of her life-long response…. Let her teach you.' So we can learn by reflecting on the example of Mary's life. Mary can be recognised **Mother of good counsel** because she is also given the title **Seat of Wisdom**, which I investigate in Chapter 7.

Mary can be described as **'Mother of good counsel'** because as a good Mother she gives wise advice and we can learn from the words that Mary spoke that are recorded in the Bible. Mary said to the Angel, 'Let it be with me according to your word' *(Luke 1:38)*. Mary's cooperation in saying Yes to God means that Jesus, the **'Wonderful Counsellor'** was born. Mary accepted that God knew what was best for her life, she did not doubt or argue with God, but she only wanted God's word and plans to be fulfilled in her life. That is a real place of peace to reach, when we are wondering about what we should be doing. We can find deep peace when we say Yes to God and, 'Let it be with me according to Your word', concerning decisions. At the wedding at Cana, Mary said to the servants 'Do whatever He tells you' *(John 2:5)*. This is **'good counsel'** for us all to follow – to listen to Jesus speaking to us through our prayers, Bible reading and other people and 'do whatever He tells you.'

Mary can be described as **'Mother of good counsel'** because she gave Him her heart and we are encouraged to follow her example and "[98]with

---

[95] Hail, Holy Queen, Scott Hahn Darton. Longman + Todd London 2001, reprinted 2010 p. 122- 123 quoting the 2nd Vatican Council

[96] Ibid., p 142 quoting Lumen Gentium 53 by Saint Augustine

[97] Booklet for 'Glastonbury Pilgrimage' 2013 p.1 'A welcome from the Bishop of Plymouth'

[98] Title page of The Walsingham 'Pastoral and Liturgical Guidebook for leaders 2013

Mary give Him your heart.' We can pray: [99]*O come to my heart Lord Jesus, there is room in my heart for Thee.*

Mary can be described as **'Mother of good counsel'** because she understands sorrow and grief. Simeon had prophesied to Mary that "a sword will pierce your own soul too" *(Luke 2:35)*. When Mary stood at the cross, watching the agony, pain and suffering of her beloved Son, then indeed she experienced great sorrow and it felt like a sword was piercing her soul. Brother Ramon[100] says 'at this moment Mary is called **'Mother of sorrows'** as she entered into that maternal grief in which she can only stand and watch and wait.' Brother Ramon imagines Mary standing at the foot of the cross; [101]'she can only hope, only reach out in faith, only weep in the tender loyalty that roots her to this very spot.' He also writes that [102]'the foot of the cross is not only the place of forgiveness and salvation, but the place of waiting, reflection and contemplation.' In times of sorrow and grief Mary is a **'Mother of good counsel'** because we can follow her example of 'tender loyalty', 'waiting, reflection' and prayer; knowing that Mary understands sorrow and grief.

What does this mean for us?

Mary the Mother of Jesus is seen as a 'type' of the Church. So as Our Lady is given the title **'Mother of good counsel'** this has significance and challenge for every member of the Church. Let us follow the example of the life of Mary, the **Mother of good counsel.** So 'with Mary give Him our hearts,' praying with the words of a hymn[103] *O come to my heart, Lord Jesus; there is room in my heart for thee.*

---

[99] The New English Hymnal, The Canterbury Press, Norwich, 1987, p. 461, hymn 465 chorus

[100] When they Crucified my Lord: Brother Ramon, BRF, 1999, p 164

[101] Ibid.

[102] 'The Way of Love': Brother Ramon, BRF, 1994, p.213

[103] The New English Hymnal, The Canterbury Press, Norwich, 1987, p. 461, hymn 465 chorus, Emily Elliott 1836-1897

Are you wondering about an important decision? Ask the Lord to guide you and say Yes to God, and 'let it be with me according to Your word' (*Luke 1:38*). 'Let the peace of Christ rule in your hearts', because the Lord will give you peace about the right choice that He is calling you to make (*Colossians 3:15*).

We need to give **good counsel** to people who come to us for advice. Like Mary, we need to be filled with the Holy Spirit, pray and <u>listen</u> to the Lord, so we know what is the right advice and **good counsel** to give to those who ask for our help. We need to grow into a closer relationship with God, so we can help those who turn to us for help.

[104]John, the Bishop of Plymouth, encourages us to read and reflect on Bible passages about Mary so that you 'let her teach you.' We will discover that Mary, is the **Mother of good counsel**. Let us follow this **good counsel** by Bible reading and reflection, being open for God to counsel us through our Bible reading and the advice of people.

Jethro's advice to Moses (*Exodus 18: 17*) has been used to help many over-worked people in the Church to realise that they need to delegate some of the tasks that need to be done, by involving more people in leading as part of a team. This passage of Scripture has been helpful for many people who are almost 'wearing themselves out.' It is great when many people are actively involved in the Church, rather than just a few people. Do you need to ask more people to help you so you are not over-worked? Do you recognise some ways that you could help in the Church so other people do not try to do too much and become worn out?

We can ask Mary to pray for those we are concerned about. We can know that Mary understands with motherly love, and that she will pray for them.

[105]*Mother of good counsel, pray for us.*

---

[104] Booklet for 'Glastonbury Pilgrimage' 2013 p.1 'A welcome from the Bishop of Plymouth'

[105] The Walsingham Pilgrim Manual 2016, p.13

CHAPTER 5

MARY'S TITLES CONCERNING HER VIRGINITY

'Holy Virgin of Virgins' is the third title of Mary in the [106]*Litany of Loreto*. We will also explore the other '**Virgin**' titles of Mary.

What does the Bible tell us about 'Virgins'?

The Hebrew word for [107]'virgin' is *bethûlâh,* הָלֹוּתְב which is first used in the Bible to describe Rebecca *(Genesis 24:16)*. Later *bethûlâh* is used in Esther when King Xerxes's personal attendants said 'Let a search be made for beautiful young virgins for the king' *(Esther 2:2)*. Esther 'won his favour

[106] Dictionary of Mary 'Behold your Mother', Catholic Book Publishing Co. New Jersey 1997, 1985, p.241

[107] Analytical Concordance to the Holy Bible, Robert Young, United Society for Christian Literature, Lutterworth Press London, 1973, p. 1026

and approval more than any of the other virgins' *(Esther 2:17)*. Esther was the beautiful virgin who was chosen to be the queen.

Another Hebrew word for 'virgin' is *'almâh* עַלְמָה, which is a virgin who is engaged. *'Almâh* is used in Isaiah's prophecy 'the LORD himself will give you a sign. The virgin will give birth to a son, and will call him Immanuel' *(Isaiah 7:14)*. This was fulfilled when the Virgin Mary who was engaged to Joseph, gave birth to Jesus. The angel of the Lord revealed this amazing news to Joseph: '"Do not be afraid to take Mary home as your wife, because what is conceived in her is from the Holy Spirit. She will give birth to a son, and you are to give him the name Jesus, because he will save his people from their sins." All this took place to fulfil what the Lord had said through the prophet: "The virgin will be with child and will give birth to a son, and they will call him Immanuel – which means 'God with us'" *(Matthew 1:20-23)*. Joseph 'took Mary home as his wife. But he had no union with her' *(Matthew 1:24)*. Mary was an *'almâh*, a virgin who is engaged and so she perfectly fulfils Isaiah's prophecy that an *'almâh* will give birth to a son' *(Isaiah 7:14)*.

In the Old Testament we read the phrase 'Virgin Daughter of Zion', in Lamentations. The Lord says: 'What can I say for you? With what can I compare you, O Daughter of Jerusalem? To what can I liken you, that I may comfort you, O **Virgin Daughter of Zion**? Your wound is as deep as the sea. Who can heal you?' *(Lamentations 2:13)* Fr Nicholas Turner[108] suggests that this phrase conveys hope for the people. In Exile in Babylon they are a wounded and defeated people; and yet God sees them as a 'Virgin'. The Lord will cleanse and forgive the past sins of the people; giving them hope and restoration. The Annunciation echoes this prophecy *(Luke 1:26-38)* as the Virgin Mary will give birth to Jesus, through whom we receive cleansing, forgiveness and hope.

The New Testament Greek word for virgin is παρθένος *(parthénos)*, which means [109]'a virgin, maid and chaste'. This is the word used when the angel Gabriel was sent 'to a virgin pledged to be married to a man named

---

[108] Talk at Walsingham Bible Week, Our Lady in the Old Testament, Tuesday 24th October 2017

[109] Analytical Greek Lexicon, Samuel Bagster & Sons Ltd, London, 1973, p.309

Joseph' *(Luke 1:27)*. After Gabriel told her that she has 'found favour with God' *(v 30)* and been chosen to be the mother of Jesus, we read, 'How will this be,' Mary asked the angel, 'since I am a virgin?' *(Luke 1:24)*. The angel says: 'The Holy Spirit will come upon you, and the power of the Most High will overshadow you. So the holy one to be born will be called the Son of God' *(Luke 1:35)*. Mary said, 'May it be to me as you have said' *(Luke 1:38)*.

We recall this in the Nicene Creed,[110] proclaiming our belief in: 'one Lord, Jesus Christ, the only Son of the Father' who: 'For us and our salvation he came down from heaven, was incarnate from the Holy Spirit and the Virgin Mary and was made man.'

How can Mary be described as 'Holy Virgin of Virgins' and the other Virgin titles in the Litany[111]: the 15th 'Virgin most prudent'; the 16th 'Virgin most venerable'; the 17th 'Virgin most renowned'; the 18th title is 'Virgin most powerful'; the 19th title 'Virgin most merciful'; the 20th 'Virgin most faithful'; and the 44th title in the *Litany of Loreto* which is 'Queen of Virgins'?

The [112]Advent Antiphon for the Magnificat on December 23rd is 'O *Virgo Virginum*'. This describes Mary as the **'Holy Virgin of Virgins'**: 'O Virgin of virgins, how shall this be? For neither before thee was any like thee, nor shall there be after. Daughters of Jerusalem, why marvel ye at me? The thing which ye behold is a divine mystery.' The 'divine mystery' was Mary, who remained a Virgin and became the mother of Jesus, God's Son. This Antiphon is said before the Magnificat on 23rd December and also sometimes read at Advent Carol Services. These words were [113]'in the old Sarum rite'.

---

[110] Common Worship Services and Prayers for the Church of England, Church House Publishing, 2000, P. 173

[111] The Walsingham Pilgrim Manual 2016, p.13-14

[112] The English Hymnal with tunes, Oxford University Press, London, W 1, 1967, P. 885

[113] *Exciting Holiness* Collects and Readings for the Festivals and Lesser Festivals, Canterbury Press, 2012 p. 563

[114]Blessed Albertus Magnus tells us why Mary is given the title 'Virgin of Virgins' as he said: 'For good reason is Mary called the Virgin of virgins; for she without the counsel or example of others, was the first who offered her virginity to God.' Saint Ambrose honoured Mary as the **Holy Virgin of Virgins** by saying: 'Mary was such, that her life alone was a model for all. Let the virginity and life of Mary be to you as a faithful image, in which the form of virtue shines brilliantly. Then learn how to live, what to correct, what to avoid, and what to retain.' He sees Mary as a wonderful example of virtue.

Mary is **Holy Virgin of Virgins**. We explored '**holy**' in Chapter 2. Mary was set apart and dedicated to God, being the **Holy Virgin of Virgins**. Mary is considered to be the **Holy Virgin of Virgins** by some because they think she had chosen to live as a virgin. Her response to the Angel, "I know not a man" *(Luke 1:34 AV)*, suggests her chaste attitude toward her chosen life with perfect cooperation with God's love *(Luke 1:38)*.

We often refer to Mary as [115]'The Blessed Virgin Mary' which reminds us that she is the **Holy Virgin of Virgins**. We can recognise Mary as the **Holy Virgin of Virgins** when we reflect that she was conceived without sin. I explore the teaching about the Immaculate Conception in Chapter 26. Mary is the Virgin Mother who remained a Virgin, and so we address Mary **Holy Virgin of Virgins**. We see Mary's purity in the image of a Statue of Our Lady of Walsingham on the front cover. Laurenceau explains about the perpetual virginity of Mary: [116]'In calling Mary 'ever virgin', Tradition is saying that after conceiving Jesus in virginity Mary always remained a virgin, abstaining from all conjugal relations. This also implies that the birth of Jesus left intact the virginity of His Mother'; giving Mary the title **Virgin of Virgins**.

---

[114] http://www.maryqueenofallsaints.com/MarysTitles/03VirginOfVirgins/03HolyVirginOfVirgins.htm 25th November 2016

[115] *Exciting Holiness* Collects and Readings for the Festivals and Lesser Festivals, Canterbury Press, 2012 p 702

[116] Dictionary of Mary 'Behold Your Mother', Catholic Book Publishing Co., New Jersey, 1985, p. 485

Hymns from the first millennium of the Eastern and Western Churches praise Mary as the **Virgin of Virgins**. [117]Gregory of Nyssa wrote of Mary: *Blessed are you among women! For you have been placed above all virgins, for you have been found worthy to give shelter to the Lord.* The fact that Mary was chosen to be the mother of Jesus places her above other virgins. The [118]Akathistos Hymn proclaims: *You are the protector of virgins, O Virgin Mother of God.* Theodore of Ancyra[119] wrote in praise of Mary: *Hail, you who give honour to virginity.* Augustine marvelled that the Virgin Mary became the mother of Jesus. He reflected on the incarnation[120]: *The One who created you will be born in you. Whence came to you such a great goodness? You are virgin, you are holy...When he was conceived, you were a virgin; a virgin still, when he was born.*

There are other titles of Mary in the [121]Litany of Loreto that begin 'Virgin most......' They are superlative adjectives describing qualities of Mary. They are Virgin most **prudent**, most **venerable**, most **renowned**, most **powerful**, most **merciful** and most **faithful**.

Prudent means sensible, wise and careful. Just like the 'wife of noble character' described in Proverbs chapter 31, Mary 'speaks with wisdom, and faithful instruction is on her tongue' *(Proverbs 31:26)*. At the wedding at Cana, Mary gave the wise and sensible advice to the servants, "Do whatever He tells you" *(John 2:5)*. This is good advice for everyone to follow, so we can recognise that Mary is **Virgin most prudent**.

Venerable means respected, honoured, admired. Mary is indeed respected, honoured and admired by Catholic Christians today and by Christians through all the history of Christianity. The [122]Litany of Our Lady in the Walsingham Manual has '**Virgin most worshipful**' as the 16th

---

[117] In Praise of Mary, Hymns from the first millennium of the Eastern and Western Churches, St Paul Publications, Slough, 1981, p. 26, Gregory of Nyssa

[118] Ibid., p. 39, Anonymous Hymn 5th- 6th century

[119] Ibid., p. 48, Theodore of Ancyra

[120] Ibid., p. 50, Augustine

[121] Dictionary of Mary 'Behold your Mother', Catholic Book Publishing Co. New Jersey 1997, 1985, p.241

[122] The Walsingham Pilgrim Manual 2016, p.13

title for Mary. Saint Augustine taught that Mary [123]'is not to be offered the worship that is owed to God alone, but her unique status as Mother of God means that she is marked out above other holy men and women. *Latreia* is the worship and adoration due only to God. *Hyperdoulia* for Mary is a type of devotion that is somewhat greater than that due to the other saints.' So, Mary is called '**venerable**'. **Renowned** means famous, well known, celebrated. Mary must be the most famous, well known and celebrated Virgin who has ever lived and so indeed deserves this title.

Powerful means influential and great. Mary is attributed with great power and influence, because Catholics ask her to pray for them and thank her for the answers to those prayers. The [124]Litany of Our Lady in the Walsingham Manual has '**Virgin most mighty**' for this 18th title of Our Lady. Mary is entitled **Health of the Sick**, **Comforter of the Afflicted** and **Help of Christians**. These are mighty, powerful titles of great influence as Christians are trusting Mary to pray for them. **Virgin most powerful** is a true title for Mary who is the most powerful Virgin interceding to Jesus for the needy.

Merciful means compassionate, kind, generous, sympathetic and forgiving. We see kindness and generosity in Mary's helping the family at the wedding at Cana *(John 2:1-11)*. Mary wanted others to be close to Jesus and was compassionate and sympathetic to their needs rather than pushing herself forward. She did not take offence when Jesus was busy. Jesus said 'My mother and brothers are those who hear God's word and put it into practice' *(Luke 8:21)*. Hilda Graf reflects on this passage and writes of Mary that: [125]'She didn't take advantage of being his mother to push her way through the crowd.' The [126]Litany of Our Lady in the Walsingham Manual has '**Virgin most clement**' for this 19th title of Our Lady, which

---

[123] MARY the Complete Resource edited by Sarah Jane Boss, Oxford University Press 2007, p. 156

[124] The Walsingham Pilgrim Manual 2016, p.13

[125] 'Mary A History of Doctrine and Devotion': Hilda Graef, Christian Classics Westminster, 1987, The Liturgical Press Collegeville Minnesota p. 83

[126] The Walsingham Pilgrim Manual 2016, p.13

means mild, gentle, lenient and merciful. We pray in the *Salve Regina*: [127]'O **clement**, O loving, O sweet Virgin Mary' showing we can address Our Lady as the **Virgin most merciful**.

Faithful means true, loyal and constant. Mary showed wonderful true loyalty and constant devotion to Jesus by always being there for Him. Mary followed Jesus in His ministry *(Luke 8: 20)*. Mary accompanied Jesus on the way to the Cross, as we remember at the fourth Station of the Cross when 'Jesus Meets His Afflicted Mother'. Mary did not leave Jesus to walk to the Cross alone. She walked with him and was loyal when most of the disciples had left him. Mary must have given great comfort to Jesus in being there for him with her constant motherly love and care. Mary continued to be **faithful**, loyal and constant as she stood by the Cross when Jesus suffered and died. 'Near the cross of Jesus stood his mother' *(John 19: 25)*. Most of Jesus' disciples left Him but Mary was there at the Cross with John, her sister and two friends *(John 19: 25-27)*. Mary is indeed **Virgin most faithful**. Office Hymns in the ancient [128]Walsingham Breviary show Mary's deep love, sorrow and faithfulness when she stood by the Cross:

> *Now of Mary's sevenfold sorrow*
> *Let my tongue the mystery sing;*
> *She the **ever-Virgin Mother***
> *Of the world's eternal King,*
> *Standing by her Son, the Victim*
> *On the cross of suffering…*
> *Whose pure heart the sharp sword pierced*
> *In the Passion of her Son.*
> [129]*Who is there that can truly tell the agonies that then befell*
> *The **Virgin Mother** as her eye gazed on her Son about to die?*

---

[127] Ibid. p. 15

[128] Walsingham Pilgrims and Pilgrimage: Michael Rear, Gracewing, 2019, p. 341-342, translated by Fr W.H. Sandell

[129] Ibid. p. 342, translated by Mgr. Bruce Harbert

We now move onto the eighth title in the Litany of Loreto about Mary's Virginity. This is the 44th title **'Queen of Virgins'**. In Chapter 20 **'Queen assumed into heaven'** I explore how and why we address Mary with the title **'Queen'**. I include **'Queen of Virgins'** now as it is the last **'Virgin'** title in the [130]Litany of Loreto. If we accept that Mary is Queen in Heaven; then we can recognise that she is Queen over all the people who are in Heaven, which includes virgins. Sarah Jane Boss recognises [131] **'The Virgin's Queenship'** as [132]'throughout the early and high Middle Ages, the Virgin's queenship was a central aspect of her cult.' Mary's purity, holiness and humility show she is the most special of Virgins and so she is called the **'Queen of Virgins'**. Mary is **Queen of Virgins** because she is **Queen conceived without original sin** explored in Chapter 26.

Some **hymns** remind us about the virginity of the **Virgin Mary**. We sing:

> [133]*Holy Virgin, by God's decree,*
> *You were called eternally;*
> *That he could give his Son to our race.*
> *Mary, we praise you, hail full of grace.*

At Christmas in our carols we remember that Mary was the **Virgin** Mother of Jesus. In *Once in royal David's city*[134] we sing:

> *And through all his wondrous childhood*
> *He would honour and obey,*
> *Love and watch the **lowly maiden***
> *In whose gentle arms he lay.*

---

[130] Dictionary of Mary 'Behold your Mother', Catholic Book Publishing Co. New Jersey 1997, 1985, p.241

[131] MARY the Complete Resource edited by Sarah Jane Boss, Oxford University Press 2007, p. 156

[132] Ibid., p. 156

[133] The Walsingham Pilgrim Manual 2016 p. 106 Hymn 18 v. 1, Jean-Paul Lécot 1947-

[134] The English Hymnal Service Book, London, Oxford University Press, A.R. Mowbray & Co., Ltd. 1969, p. 254, Hymn 200, Mrs C. F. Alexander 1818-1895

In the bleak mid-winter has the moving words:
[135]*But only His mother in her **maiden** bliss, worshipped the Beloved with a kiss.*

Mary is addressed as Queen in many **Hymns**. Here [136]she is addressed as Virgin as well:

> **Hail, Queen of the heavens,** *hail Mistress of earth;*
> *Hail,* **Virgin most pure** *of immaculate birth...*
> *Hail, Mother most pure, hail,* **Virgin renowned**
> **Hail, Queen with the stars as a diadem crowned;**
> *Above all the angels in glory untold,*
> **Set next to the King in a vesture of gold.**

What does this mean for us?

Mary is seen as a 'type' of the Church. [137]The study of typology shows us that the Church can learn from the example of Mary's life. When God calls us to serve Him and His people our response should be to say Yes, just like the Virgin Mary; and to say to the Lord, 'May it be to me as You have said' *(Luke 1:38)*. We can learn from the example of Mary's life to live pleasing the Lord. We should '*imitate*' Mary, as we sing in the hymn [138]*I'll sing a hymn to Mary,* when we sing that Mary is 'The **Virgin of all Virgins**'.

Is God calling you showing you ways that He would like you to serve now? We can trust that the Lord has a perfect plan for our lives, since 'in all things God works for the good of those who love him, who have been called according to his purpose' *(Romans 8:28)*.

---

[135] Ibid., p. 144, Hymn 107, Christina Rossetti 1830-1894

[136] Universalis App, Universalis publishing, 1996-2019, Birthday of BM, Vespers, Office Hymn, Edward Caswall 1814-1878

[137] 'Hail, Holy Queen': Scott Hahn, Darton, Longman and Todd Ltd, London 2010, p. 24

[138] The Walsingham Pilgrim Manual 2016 p. 108, Hymn 20, v. 1, Edward Caswall 1814-1878

Let us follow the Blessed Virgin Mary's example and be **prudent**, wise sensible and careful. Let us become more **merciful**, compassionate, kind, generous, sympathetic, clement, forgiving and **faithful** being true, loyal and constant.

[139]Holy Virgin of virgins, *pray for us.*

---

[139] Ibid., p.12

CHAPTER 6

MIRROR OF JUSTICE AND MIRROR OF RIGHTEOUSNESS

Mirror of justice is the 21st title of Mary in the [140]*Litany of Loreto*. In the [141]Walsingham Manual this 21st title is called **Mirror of righteousness** in the suggested Litany for the First Visit to the Holy House.

What does the Bible tell us about Mirror of justice and **Mirror of righteousness?**

The phrases **Mirror of justice** and **Mirror of righteousness** are not in the Bible, so we shall first explore the Biblical references to 'mirror' and then discover what the Bible tells us about 'justice' and 'righteousness'.

---

[140] Dictionary of Mary 'Behold your Mother', Catholic Book Publishing Co. New Jersey 1997, 1985, p.241

[141] The Walsingham Pilgrim Manual 2016, p.13

Mirrors reflect what is there. Moses' face shone and reflected God's glory when he had been with the Lord *(Exodus 34:29-35)*. Moses' radiant face was **reflecting** the glory of the Lord, like a mirror. Our faces can shine too when we have been close to the Lord in worship. When Moses was arranging the construction of the altar of burnt offerings in the Tabernacle, 'They made the bronze basin and its bronze stand from the **mirrors** of the women who served at the entrance to the Tent of Meeting' *(Exodus 38:8)*. The women gave up and sacrificed their mirrors so they could be used to make utensils for the Altar of Burnt Offering in the worship of God and helping people to know God's forgiveness. Mirrors can be seen as encouraging vanity, *(Isaiah 3:23)* as Isaiah says the 'haughty' women *(Isaiah 3:16)* will have their **mirrors** and finery taken away.

The word 'mirror' helps us to think about the wonders of heaven. 'Now we see but a poor reflection as in a **mirror**; then we shall see face to face. Now I know in part; then I shall know fully, even as I am fully known' *(I Corinthians 13:12)*. The New Testament Greek word here for 'mirror' is[142] ἔσοπτρον *(esoptron)*, meaning 'a mirror, spectrum'. We see only 'a poor reflection' now, but in heaven we will see God's amazing glory.

St Paul later reminds the Corinthians about how Moses' face shone when he had been in the presence of the Lord. 'We are not like Moses, who would put a veil over his face to keep the Israelites from gazing at it while the radiance was fading away' *(II Corinthians 3:18)*. We should look to Jesus and be changed to be more like Him. The word 'changed' here is the word '[143]μεταμορφόω *(metamorphoō)* from which we have the word 'metamorphosis', describing what happens in the cocoon when a caterpillar changes into a butterfly. The Lord wants to change us just as fundamentally as we look to Him and **reflect** his love in our lives *(II Corinthians 3:18)*.

The word 'reflect' is the New Testament Greek word κατοπτρίζομαι *(katoptridzomenai)* meaning [144]'mirror, to have a clear image presented, to

---

[142] The Analytical Greek Lexicon, London: Samuel Bagster and Sons Ltd, 1973, p. 168

[143] The Interlinear Greek-English New Testament, London: Samuel Bagster and Sons Ltd, 1958

[144] The Analytical Greek Lexicon, London: Samuel Bagster and Sons Ltd, 1973, p. 226

reflect'. How amazing that the likeness of Jesus will be seen in us as we spend time with Him and seek to change to be more like Him. The fruit of the Holy Spirit needs to grow in our lives for this to happen *(Galatians 5: 22-23)*.

This word κατοπτριξομενοι is used by James. 'Do not merely listen to the word, and so deceive yourselves. Do what it says. A nyone who listens to the word but does not do what it says is like a man who looks at his face in a **mirror** and, after looking at himself, goes away and immediately forgets what he looks like *(James 1:22-25)*. We should be careful to be <u>doers</u> by hearing and doing what the Lord shows us to be right.

The same root Hebrew word is used for '**justice**' and '**righteousness**', צָדֵק. This is [145]*tsaddiq* meaning right, righteous and just; and *tsadaq* meaning to be justified or to become right. Abraham's faith showed his righteousness. 'Abram believed the Lord, and he credited it to him as **righteousness**' *(Genesis 15:6)*. Moses told the people, 'If we are careful to obey all this law before the LORD our God, as he has commanded us, that will be are righteousness' *(Deuteronomy 6:25)*. The Jews had to keep all the laws to be righteous. So we pray for help: 'Lead me, O LORD, in your righteousness' *(Psalm 5:8)*. David trusts that 'I – in righteousness I shall see your face' *(Psalm 17:15)*. He writes 'I will proclaim your **righteousness**, yours alone' *(Psalm 71:16)*. 'Wicked men are overthrown and are no more, but the house of the righteous stands firm' *(Proverbs 12:7)*, because the Lord protects the righteous who seek to obey and follow His ways. Isaiah prophesies about the Messiah that 'with righteousness he will judge the needy, with justice he will give decisions for the poor of the earth ... **Righteousness** shall be his belt' *(Isaiah 11:4-5)*. Zephaniah says: 'Seek the Lord... Seek righteousness, seek humility' *(Zephaniah 2:3)*. We see here the connection between justice and righteousness, which is doing what is right.

---

[145] Analytical Concordance to the Holy Bible, Robert Young, United Society for Christian Literature, Lutterworth Press London, 1973, p. 559 and p. 819

The New Testament Greek word [146] δικαιοσυνή (dikaiosune) means rightness and justice. It means [147]'the character or quality of being right or just.' We read this word often in Romans when St Paul is explaining about salvation. The good news is that through Jesus' death on the Cross we can be made righteous and be justified before God. 'This **righteousness** from God comes through <u>faith</u> in Jesus Christ to all who believe. There is no difference, for all have sinned and fall short of the glory of God, and are **justified** freely by his grace through the redemption that came by Christ Jesus' (Romans 3: 21-24). How wonderful that 'since we have been **justified** through <u>faith</u>, we have peace with God through our Lord Jesus Christ' (Romans 5:1)! Through believing and accepting that Jesus died on the Cross, we can be forgiven and restored into a **right** relationship with God. On the Cross Jesus took the punishment for our sins so now it is "just if I'd never sinned"! Justification is [148]'the event by which God, acting in Jesus Christ, makes us holy (just)'. How wonderful that 'Christ is the end of the law so that there may be righteousness for everyone who believes' (Romans 10:4)!

We are made righteous through <u>faith</u> and not by our own attempts to keep God's laws. Jesus is 'our righteousness, holiness and redemption' (I Corinthians 1:30). We need to 'put on the full armour of God' including 'the breastplate of **righteousness**' (Ephesians 6:10-18). Paul tells Timothy to 'pursue righteousness' (I Timothy 6:11). James encourages us to be peacemakers 'who sow in peace (and) raise a harvest of righteousness' (James 3:18). Vine explains: [149]'with righteousness, or 'justification': Paul is occupied with a right relationship with God, James with right conduct.' We are restored to a right relationship with God through Jesus' death on the Cross; and then we need 'to do good works, which God prepared in advance for us to do' (Ephesians 2:10).

---

[146] Ibid., p. 819

[147] An Expository Dictionary of Biblical Words: W.E. Vine, Thomas Nelson, Inc, 1984, p. 535

[148] Catholicism: Richard P. McBrien, HarperCollins, 1994, p. 1243

[149] Vine, op. cit., p. 340

How can Mary be described as **Mirror of justice** and **Mirror of righteousness?**

Professor Michael Ogunu writes about **Mirror of Justice** [150] 'As explained in a book entitled *Our Lady in Catholic Life*, in biblical language justice is the perfect observance of God's commandments. Mary was perfectly responsive to the will of God; thus, she is the reflection (mirror) of God's own holiness.' Mary is a mirror of all that is right and 'righteous' because she obeyed all God's commandments.

Mary was close to Jesus and reflected Him. Margaret Barker writes that Mary [151]'is a reflection of eternal light, a spotless mirror of the working of God, an image of his goodness' as she is 'the flawless mirror of the active power of God and the image of his goodness' *(Wisdom 7:26).*

[152] 'Cardinal Newman writes: 'Here first we must consider what is meant by *justice*, for the word as used by the Church has not that sense which it bears in ordinary English. By "justice" is not meant the virtue of fairness, equity, uprightness in our dealings; but it is a word denoting all virtues at once, a perfect, virtuous state of soul—righteousness, or moral perfection; so that it answers very nearly to what is meant by *sanctity*. Therefore when Our Lady is called the "Mirror of Justice," it is meant to say that she is the Mirror of sanctity, holiness, goodness... Mary is the *"Speculum Justitiæ,"* the Mirror of Justice.'... A mirror is a surface which reflects, as still water, polished steel, or a looking-glass. What did Mary reflect? She reflected our Lord—but *He* is infinite *Sanctity*. She then, as far as a creature could, reflected His Divine sanctity, and therefore she is the *Mirror* of Sanctity, or, as the Litany says, of *Justice*. Do we ask how she came to reflect His Sanctity?—it was by living with Him. We see every day how like people get to each other who live with those they love...

---

[150] http://christendom-awake.org/pages/litany-of-loreto/litany+ogunu+article+1.htm, Our Lady in Catholic Life, Lawrence G. Lovasik, The MacMillan Company, 29th June 2017

[151] The Images of Mary in the Litany of Loreto, Margaret Barker, Usus Antiquior, Vol 1, No. 2, July 2010, p. 113

[152] http://www.cardinaljohnhenrynewman.com/mary-mirror-of-justice-cardinal-newman/ 10th July 2017

Now, consider that Mary loved her Divine Son with an unutterable love; and consider too she had Him all to herself for thirty years. Do we not see that, as she was full of grace *before* she conceived Him in her womb, she must have had a vast incomprehensible sanctity when she had lived close to God for thirty years?... The very house in which the Holy Family lived became a sanctuary of holiness, and is worthy of veneration by the faithful... It was in this holy dwelling that Mary grew to be the "Mirror of Justice," from Her constant reflection on the virtues of Jesus.' Mary reflects the love, holiness, justice and righteousness of Jesus, after living with Him for thirty years; just as a mirror reflects what is in front of it.

What does this mean for us?

How wonderful that, 'since we have been **justified** through <u>faith</u>, we have peace with God through our Lord Jesus Christ' *(Romans 5:1)*! Through believing and accepting that Jesus died on the Cross so we can be forgiven, we can receive forgiveness and be restored into a **right** relationship with God. Have you come into this relationship with God through Jesus? Jesus says to you: 'Here I am! I stand at the door and knock. If anyone hears my voice and opens the door, I will come in and eat with him, and he with me' *(Revelation 3:20)*. Have you 'opened the door' and asked Jesus to come into your life? Here is a prayer to pray so we can have the assurance that we have been **justified** and made **righteous** by Jesus:

[153]*Lord Jesus Christ, I am sorry for the things I have done wrong in my life.... Please forgive me. I now turn from everything that I know is wrong. Thank you that you died on the cross for me so that I could be forgiven and set free. Thank you that you offer me forgiveness and the gift of your Spirit. I now receive that gift. Please come into my life by your Holy Spirit to be with me forever. Thank you, Lord Jesus. Amen*

James tells us: 'Do not merely listen to the word, and so deceive yourselves. Do what it says' *(James 1: 22-25)*. What have you read or heard recently that you now need to do? 'And we, who with unveiled faces all

---

[153] Why Jesus? Nicky Gumbel, Kingsway Publications Ltd, 2013, p.18

reflect the Lord's glory, are being transformed into his likeness with ever-increasing glory' *(II Corinthians 3:18)*. We should increasingly reflect the likeness, glory and love of Jesus. How is the Lord changing you now? What fruit of the Holy Spirit needs to grow in your life *(Galatians 5:22-23)*?

I love walking by rivers and have enjoyed walking the Thames Path and the Medway Valley Path, when I have time to think, pray and reflect. I am often inspired by reflections. Just as the river is being a 'mirror' here, reflecting perfectly the trees, bushes and the sky, so I want my life to be a more perfect reflection of the love and light of Jesus. Do you long for your life to be a mirror reflecting the 'love, joy, peace, patience, kindness, goodness, faithfulness, gentleness and self-control' *(Galatians 5:22-23)* of Jesus? Does your life reflect the love of Jesus like Mary's life? Paul tells Timothy to 'pursue righteousness' *(I Timothy 6:11)*. James encourages us to be peacemakers as: 'Peacemakers who sow in peace raise a harvest of righteousness' *(James 3:18)*. John instructs us that 'he who does what is right is righteous' *(I John 3:7)*. How can you be a peacemaker and do what is right?

We are restored to a right relationship with God through Jesus' death on the Cross; and then we need 'to do good works, which God prepared in advance for us to do' *(Ephesians 2:10)*. What 'good works' is the Lord leading you to do at this time?

May we all grow closer to Jesus so that our lives increasingly reflect His love, light, joy and peace to those we meet. May our lives become a 'mirror' of the love of Jesus to those around us. **Amen.**

[154] Mirror of Righteousness, *pray for us.*

---

[154] The Walsingham Pilgrim Manual 2016, p.12

CHAPTER 7

SEAT OF WISDOM

Seat of wisdom is the 22nd title of Mary in the Litany of Our Lady, the [155]*Litany of Loreto.*

What does the Bible tell us about Seat of wisdom?

The Bible does not mention the phrase 'seat of wisdom'; however, there are many references to 'wisdom'. The Hebrew word most frequently used in the Bible is חָכְמָה[156], *chokmah* meaning wisdom and skill. The New Testament Greek word for wisdom is [157]*sophia* σοφια which means being 'wise, shrewd, clever and learned; while having knowledge and enlightenment'. Wisdom is needed to give good counsel.

[155] Dictionary of Mary 'Behold your Mother', Catholic Book Publishing Co. New Jersey 1997, 1985, p.241

[156] Analytical Concordance to the Holy Bible, Robert Young, United Society for Christian Literature, Lutterworth Press London, 1973 p. 1059-1060

[157] Analytical Greek Lexicon, Samuel Bagster & Sons Ltd, London, 1973, p.371

'Wisdom' is a theme which runs through the Bible. Seeking 'sound wisdom' is encouraged in the book of Proverbs *(Proverbs 2:7, 3:21, 8:14)*. We are encouraged to 'find wisdom' *(Proverbs 3:13)* as 'she is more precious than jewels' *(Proverbs 3:15)* and 'all her paths are peace' *(Proverbs 3:17)*. Wisdom is 'a tree of life' giving happiness. The 'wife of noble character' depicted in Proverbs 'speaks with wisdom' *(Proverbs 31:26)*. Isaiah prophesied that the Messiah will have 'the Spirit of wisdom and understanding' *(Isaiah 11:2)*.

Joseph was recognised by Pharaoh as being a man of wisdom, because he correctly interpreted dreams. However, Joseph acknowledged that God was the source of his wisdom, saying 'I cannot do it, but God will give Pharaoh the answer he desires' *(Genesis 41:16)*. Joseph was then put in charge in Egypt *(Genesis 41:39)*. Joseph's wisdom was a gift from God and used to help other people.

King Solomon had great wisdom. Solomon felt the need for wisdom when he became king *(I Kings 3:9)* and God said 'I will give you a wise and discerning heart' *(I Kings 3:12)*. God was pleased that Solomon recognised his need for wisdom, in order to be a good King who made right decisions. 'God gave Solomon wisdom and very great insight and a breadth of understanding as measureless as the sand on the seashore' *(I Kings 4:29)*. Solomon's wisdom became famous after his wise judgement in the dispute between the two prostitutes about their babies *(I Kings 3:16-28)*. Visitors came to Jerusalem to hear his wisdom. The Queen of Sheba *(I Kings 10:1-12)* was very impressed with King Solomon's wisdom. Solomon's throne was: 'a great throne inlaid with ivory and overlaid with fine gold. The throne had six steps, and its back had a rounded top. On both sides of the seat were armrests, with a lion standing beside each of them. Twelve lions stood on the six steps, one at either end of each step. Nothing like it had ever been made for any other kingdom' *(I Kings 10:18-20)*. King Solomon sat there to speak words of wisdom.

Daniel praises God that 'wisdom and power are his. He gives wisdom to the wise and knowledge to the discerning. He reveals deep and hidden things' *(Daniel 2:20-21)*. God gave Daniel the wisdom to interpret dreams, so that people could learn from them. Just like Joseph, Daniel acknowledged that God was his source of wisdom.

Jesus as a young child 'was filled with wisdom, and the grace of God was upon him' *(Luke 2: 40)*. After the visit to Jerusalem when Jesus was twelve years old, 'Jesus grew in wisdom and stature, and in favour with God and men' *(Luke 2:52)*. Later Jesus told the parable of the wise and foolish builders, *(Matthew 7:24-29)* showing that to be wise we need to hear the words of Jesus and put them into practice.

James tells us much about wisdom. He writes 'if any of you lacks wisdom, he should ask God, who gives generously', *(James 1:5)* explaining that there are two types of wisdom: earthly and heavenly wisdom. We should grow in heavenly wisdom that 'is first of all pure; then peace-loving, considerate, submissive, full of mercy and good fruit, impartial and sincere' *(James 3:17)*. Paul tells us to 'walk in wisdom' and 'be wise in the way you act towards outsiders, make the most of every opportunity.' *(Colossians 4:5)* This encourages us to be open to the Lord showing us what to say and how to speak with grace, love and wisdom. Paul recognised that 'wisdom' is a person, Jesus is wisdom. **Christ** is **'the wisdom of God'** *(I Corinthians 1:24)*. 'Christ has become for us wisdom from God' *(I Corinthians 1:30)*.

Jesus Himself is wisdom. Origen explains about this: [158]'First we must know this that in Christ there is one nature, his deity, because he is the only-begotten Son of the Father, and another human nature, which in very recent times he took upon him to fulfil the divine purpose…. He is called "wisdom," as Solomon said…. He is also called "firstborn," as the apostle Paul says: "who is the firstborn of all creation" *(Colossians 1:15)*. The firstborn is not, however, by nature a different being from wisdom but is one and the same. Finally, the apostle Paul says, "Christ the power of God and the wisdom of God" *(I Corinthians 1:24)*.' It is important to establish that **Christ is 'the wisdom of God'**.

God has revealed His secret wisdom to us by the Holy Spirit *(Ephesians 2:7,10)*. 'God's secret wisdom' 'has been hidden' *(I Corinthians 2:7)*. This mystery is 'Christ in you, the hope of glory' *(Colossians 1:27)*. 'God has revealed it to us by his Spirit' *(I Corinthians 2:10)*. This is an amazing revelation, to realise that 'Christ may dwell in your hearts through faith' *(Ephesians 3:17)*. How wonderful that we know God because Jesus comes to live in our hearts, giving us wisdom and understanding by the Holy Spirit. Jesus told the

---

[158] Believer's Bible Commentary, Early Church Writings, online version, 23rd January 2018

disciples 'if anyone loves me, he will obey my teaching. My father will love him and we will come to him and make our home with him' *(John 14:23).* Paul prays that God will give: 'the Spirit of wisdom and revelation, so that you may know him better' *(Ephesians 1:17).* Wisdom is one of the gifts of the Holy Spirit for the Church *(I Corinthians 12: 9).* We grow in wisdom as we come to know Jesus more by growing into a closer relationship with Jesus. [159]*'O come to my heart, Lord Jesus; there is room in my heart for thee.'*

How can Mary be described as "Seat of wisdom"?

A 'seat' is a place where you can sit. When holding a baby or a young child on your lap, then you are being a 'seat', because he is sitting on you. Christ is 'the wisdom of God', so Jesus is wisdom. When she sat holding baby Jesus, Mary was being his 'seat' and therefore she was being the **seat of wisdom.** This title is recognising that in her motherly role Mary was a seat for Christ who is 'the wisdom of God' *(1 Corinthians 1:24).* When carrying Jesus in her womb, that was where the growing baby 'sat' when Mary was being the **Seat of Wisdom.** [160]'The Virgin is not just enthroned: she is herself a throne. For Christ is enthroned on her lap.'

The statue of **Our Lady of Walsingham**, as on the front cover, shows Mary sitting and holding Jesus out to us. She is pointing at her Son inviting us to meet with him. [161]'The modern statue of Our Lady of Walsingham is based upon the record of the 13th century statue, which is preserved for us in the Mediaeval seal of Walsingham Priory... known as *Sedes Sapientiae,* the Seat of Wisdom'. Michael Rear explains that [162]'The image of Our Lady of Walsingham, and similar statues, also show Mary seated on a throne, a Seat of Wisdom. She is crowned Virgin-Mother. But not only

[159] The New English Hymnal, The Canterbury Press, Norwich, 1987, p. 461, hymn 465 chorus, Emily Elliott 1836-1897

[160] MARY the Complete Resource: edited by Sarah Jane Boss, Oxford University Press 2007, p 166

[161] The Virgin Mary as Seat of Wisdom by Pamela Tudor-Craig, Lady Wedgewood p 1 of *The 1986 Assumptiontide Lecture*

[162] Walsingham Pilgrims and Pilgrimage: Michael Rear, Gracewing, 2019, p. 83

is Mary enthroned; Christ is enthroned on her knee: she herself becomes the Seat of Wisdom'. Mary is being a seat for Christ who is the Wisdom of God *(I Corinthians 1:24)*. The throne also links to Mary's title **'Queen'**, which I explore in Chapter 20 **Queen Assumed into Heaven.**

[163]'Mary has the title because the Son of God Who is called in Sacred Scripture the Word and Wisdom of God, once dwelt in her, and then after His birth from her was carried in her arms and seated on her lap in His first years. Hence in Cardinal Newman's words since she was 'the human throne of Him Who reigns in Heaven, she is called the **Seat of Wisdom.'** The Theology of Mary as Seat of Wisdom explains that Mary is understood as both the Mother of God and the cathedra or seat of Jesus who is 'Logos incarnate.' Jesus is described in John's Gospel as 'the Word became flesh' *(John 1:14)'*.

In a painting, the Lucca Madonna by Jan van Eyck, Mary is sitting on an ornate throne with lions carved on the arm and back of the throne, like King Solomon's throne *(I Kings 10:18-20, II Chronicles 9:17–19)*. Mary is breast-feeding the baby Jesus while sitting on that ornate throne; depicting the concept of Mary as **'seat of wisdom'** while reminding us that she is the mother of Jesus by breast-feeding her precious baby. In paintings and statues of Mary, seat of wisdom, Mary is holding baby Jesus on her lap so she is being a 'seat' for Jesus who is God's wisdom. Hence 'Seat of wisdom' is glorifying Jesus, who is sitting on the lap of His Mother, while also honouring Mary.

The theology of Mary's being 'Seat of Wisdom' is explained by Catherine Combier-Donovan: '[164]As a mother Mary supports her son in her lap, yet as the Mother of God she serves as a throne for the incarnation of Divine Wisdom, whom she is holding and presenting to the world.' She tells us that Mary, '[165]the all-holy ever-virgin Mother of God, is the masterwork of the mission of the Son and the Spirit in the fullness of time. For the first time in the plan of salvation and because his Spirit had

---

[163] Dictionary of Mary 'Behold your Mother', Catholic Book Publishing Co, New Jersey 1997, 1985 page 300

[164] Mary throne of Wisdom: Catherine Combier-Donovan

[165] Ibid.

prepared her, the Father found a dwelling place where his Son and his Spirit could dwell among men.'

Margaret Barker writes: '[166]In the title the Seat of Wisdom, the Litany of Loreto sums up an ancient way of describing the Mother of the Lord... that she was the throne of the King.' Mary was being a throne or seat for Jesus.

Pamela Tudor-Craig tells us that Mary was associated with wisdom [167]'in the Middle Ages' 'the glorious poetry of the Wisdom literature in the Old Testament was taken to apply to her.' In Proverbs we read: 'Does not wisdom call out? Does not understanding raise her voice? For wisdom is more precious than rubies, and nothing you desire can compare with her' *(Proverbs 8:1, 11)*.

Margaret Barker supports this view as she writes: [168]'The Lady was Wisdom. The 'seat of Wisdom' was not the seat on which Wisdom sat, but was Wisdom herself. The throne in the holy of holies 'was' the Lady, and the one enthroned there was her son'. She wrote: [169]'I shall show that Wisdom was a fundamental figure in the ancient faith of Jerusalem, that the Church claimed Wisdom titles for Mary from the very beginning, and that by the time the Litany of Loreto was composed, the meaning of some of these titles was fading.... Mary as Wisdom is not so explicit as in the much older Akathistos Hymn of the Orthodox Church, where she is addressed as 'The One who surpasses the knowledge of the wise'. Margaret explains why there is this alternative view of Mary herself being 'Wisdom'. She writes:[170] 'The problem is gender. Wisdom is feminine, and her other titles imply a female figure. Despite this, the Church has emphasised that Jesus was the incarnation of Wisdom, on the basis of I Corinthians 1:24:

---

[166] The Images of Mary in the Litany of Loreto, Margaret Barker, Usus Antiquior, Vol 1, No. 2, July 2010, p. 119

[167] 'The Virgin Mary as Seat of Wisdom' by Pamela Tudor-Craig, Lady Wedgewood p.2 of The 1986 Assumptiontide Lecture

[168] The Images of Mary in the Litany of Loreto, Margaret Barker, Usus Antiquior, Vol 1, No. 2, July 2010, p. 114

[169] Ibid., p. 112

[170] Ibid., p. 130

'Christ is the power of God and the wisdom of God.' Taking account of iconography and the texts of the liturgy, it seems that Mary, too, has a strong claim to the title of Wisdom. Fiene has argued that 'from the very beginning of Sophia iconography, images of the Theotokos in association with Wisdom on the one hand, tended to compete with images of Jesus Christ linked with Wisdom on the other – often yielding provocatively ambivalent compositions. Though church doctrine insisted on always interpreting any image of Wisdom as Christ or the Logos, the actual iconography often seemed to the naïve viewer to signify a female figure, the Mother of God in particular.'

This link to Our Lady's being Wisdom is implicit because the noun meaning wisdom is feminine in the Greek and Hebrew. The poetic use of the feminine pronoun has led to misunderstanding about Wisdom's being a woman. The noun here is feminine, so this is grammatical gender. Hebrew calls wisdom "she" because it is feminine in gender. So, when personified, wisdom becomes a woman. It is paramount that: [171] 'In the New Testament, Christian authors apply Old Testament texts about Wisdom to Christ.' We have seen this in I Corinthians 1:24 that **Christ is 'the wisdom of God'**. However, we can recognise that Mary had much wisdom, because she had lived with Jesus for thirty years from his birth until he began his ministry.

What does this mean for us?

Mary can be understood as '**Seat of wisdom**', because we can learn from the wisdom that we recognise in her. Wisdom seems to 'sit' in her and is shown by Mary's attitudes, words and actions. Mary was wise after living with Christ for thirty years. Mary demonstrates wisdom in the recorded events in her life; showing wisdom in saying 'yes' to God at the Annunciation *(Luke 1:26-38).* She trusted that God's plan was good, right and perfect. We need to say 'yes' to what the Lord is prompting us to do.

---

[171] MARY the Complete Resource: edited by Sarah Jane Boss, Oxford University Press 2007, p.167

Mary spent time pondering and reflecting. After the visit of the shepherds 'Mary treasured up all these things and pondered them in her heart' *(Luke 1:19)*. After the visit to Jerusalem 'his mother treasured all these things in her heart' *(Luke 2:51)*. We will grow in wisdom if we take time to reflect, ponder, think and pray.

In Jerusalem for Passover when Jesus was twelve years old, Mary showed wisdom in letting Jesus grow up. He became a man at that time in the Jewish religion and Mary had to allow Jesus to make his own decisions and choices. He chose 'to be in my Father's house' *(Luke 2:49)* that day. Mothers can learn wisdom from Mary by 'letting our children go' whilst being there to support and help them.

Mary teaches us wisdom by telling the servants at the wedding at Cana 'Do whatever he tells you' *(John 3:5)*. Mary trusted that Jesus would help the family at the wedding when they ran out of wine. In the parable of the two houses, Jesus says the wise man represents 'everyone who hears these words of mine and puts them into practice' *(Matthew 7:24)*. What is Jesus telling you to do?

Mary showed wisdom in not demanding Jesus' time, understanding that he needed to proclaim the Kingdom of God *(Matthew 4:23)*. Mary followed at a distance while allowing other people to be near her Son. Mary did not take offence when Jesus was busy. Jesus said 'My mother and brothers are those who hear God's word and put it into practice' *(Luke 8:21)*. Hilda Graf reflects on this passage and writes of Mary that: [172]'She didn't take advantage of being his mother to push her way through the crowd.' We need to learn from this wisdom and be ready to support and help people.

Mothers listen to the daily news of their children with interest, attention and speaking encouraging words of wisdom. Mary gave motherly wisdom in the home at Nazareth when Jesus was a boy and a young man. She was **Mother of Good Counsel**. Later John took Mary into his home, where Mary gave encouragement and consolation to John as he talked about the news of his day. Bishop Lindsay reflects on this when he

---

[172] Mary: A History of Doctrine and Devotion: Hilda Graef, Christian Classics, Westminster, 1987, The Liturgical Press Collegeville, Minnesota, p. 83

imagines Easter Sunday morning, after John has visited the tomb when 'he saw and believed' *(John 20: 8)* and then went home. Bishop Lindsay writes: [173]'There can surely be little doubt that the first person John told of his experience and his believing was the woman who was there at his homecoming. Mary! What a wonderful time that must have been. What joy must have filled that house!'

We should listen to other people and be ready to share their joys and give wise advice. At Walsingham we are encouraged to: [174]'Spend time with Mary in the Holy House, and be sure to spend time with her in your own home.' Mary always points us to Jesus and in the Holy House she invites us to meet Her Son. Let us follow Mary's wisdom and point people to Jesus.

Jesus wants our hearts to be '**seats of wisdom**' because **we** know that Christ dwells in our hearts through faith'; *(Ephesians 3:17)* as we know Jesus is in us and we grow to know, love and follow Jesus more; while we remember that Christ is 'the wisdom of God' *(I Corinthians 1:24)*. This is amazing! We are being invited to become 'seats of wisdom' by knowing Jesus is living in our hearts! God has revealed the hidden wisdom and mystery, which is 'Christ **in** you, the hope of glory' *(Colossians 1:27)*. 'God has revealed it to us by his Spirit.' *(I Corinthians 2:10)*. Let us grow in wisdom by coming to know Jesus more.

We should grow in heavenly wisdom *(James 3:17)*. Paul tells us to 'walk in wisdom' and 'be wise in the way you act towards outsiders, make the most of every opportunity. Let your conversation be always full of grace, so that you may know how to answer everyone' *(Colossians 4:5)*. Let us share our faith.

[175]*'O come to my heart, Lord Jesus; there is room in my heart for thee.'*

[176] Mary, Seat of Wisdom, *pray for us.*

---

[173] Walsingham Pilgrim Manual 2014 p. 2 and 3

[174] Ibid., p. 3

[175] The New English Hymnal, The Canterbury Press, Norwich, 1987, p. 461, hymn 465 chorus, Emily Elliott 1836-1897

[176] The Walsingham Pilgrim Manual 2016, p.12

CHAPTER 8

CAUSE OF JOY

Cause of joy is the 23rd title of Mary in the Litany of Our Lady, the [177]Litany of Loreto.

What does the Bible tell us about joy and gladness?

Joy and **gladness** are the Hebrew words [178] *gîyl* גִּיל, *gîylâh* גִּילָה, *mâśôś* מָשׂוֹשׂ, *rinnâh* רִנָּה, *simchâh* שִׂמְחָה, *śâśôn* שָׂשׂוֹן and *terû'âh* תְּרוּעָה, which also mean rejoicing and can mean 'mirth'. [179]The New Testament Greek word

---

[177] Dictionary of Mary 'Behold your Mother', Catholic Book Publishing Co. New Jersey 1997, 1985, p.241

[178] Analytical Concordance to the Holy Bible, Robert Young, United Society for Christian Literature, Lutterworth Press London, 1973, p. 552

[179] Ibid, p. 553

is χαρα *chara*, which means '[180]joy, gladness, rejoicing' and [181]'joy, delight'. The Bible tells us that [182]'God himself is the ground and object of the believer's joy.' God is the source of joy: 'I go to the altar of God, **to God, my joy** and my delight. *(Psalm 43:4).*

Moses told the people that God would show them their place of worship where they 'shall **rejoice** in everything you have put your hand to, because the LORD your God has blessed you' *(Deuteronomy 12:7).* The people worshipped and thanked God for their many blessings. The Psalms express worship, praise and rejoicing in God who gives joy. '**Rejoice** in the LORD and be glad, you righteous; sing, all you who are upright in heart!' *(Psalm 32:11)* 'But let all who take refuge in you be glad; let them ever sing for **joy**' *(Psalm 5:11).* We say: 'my soul will rejoice in the LORD and delight in his salvation' *(Psalm 35:9).* We feel joy when we praise the Lord. 'Shout for joy to the LORD, come before him with **joyful** songs' *(Psalm 100:1-2).* Isaiah rejoices: 'I will greatly rejoice in the LORD, my soul shall be **joyful** in my God; for He has clothed me with the garments of salvation' *(Isaiah 61:10).*

Ezra records the great joy of the people when the Temple was re-built and re-dedicated after the Exile, celebrating 'with **joy**' *(Ezra 6:16).* Later the Passover was joyful and God was the **source of their joy** as 'the Lord had filled them with joy' *(Ezra 6:22)* by changing the attitude of the Assyrian king. This shows God's providential care.

Jesus brought joy to people. Jesus was the **cause of their joy** by bringing healing to the sick *(Matthew 4:23).* Joy also came to the Samaritan woman at the well *(John 4).* Zacchaeus experienced joy when he repented and received Jesus's forgiveness *(Luke 19:1-10).* At the breakfast by the lake with a charcoal fire *(John 21:15-19)* Peter received Jesus' forgiveness. Peter denied knowing Jesus following his arrest in the Garden of Gethsemane; when Peter was in the courtyard of the High Priest, warming his hands at the other charcoal fire mentioned in the Gospel *(Luke 22:54-62).* Peter

---

[180] The Analytical Greek Lexicon, London: Samuel Bagster and Sons Ltd, 1973, p.433

[181] An Expository Dictionary of Biblical Words: W.E. Vine, Thomas Nelson, Inc, 1984, p. 335

[182] Ibid., p.336

Waddell comments: [183]'The restoration of Peter shows the effect of Jesus' **joy** in one man's life.' How wonderful that Peter became one of the main leaders in the Early Church. Jesus told the disciples to 'rejoice that your names are written in heaven' *(Luke 10:20b)*. In the parable of the talents Jesus said that on judgement day, those who have served him faithfully will be told: '...enter thou into the **joy** of thy lord' *(Matthew 25:21 AV)*. John's vision pictures great rejoicing in heaven' *(Revelation 19:7)*.

The Bible tells us to **rejoice** and be glad because of all that God has done for us. We have been reconciled to God through Jesus *(Romans 5:11)* and now grow to experience more of His presence in our lives. St Paul wrote to Timothy that God 'richly provides us with everything for our enjoyment' *(I Timothy 6:17)*. This does not mean that our lives will be free from difficulties. James writes: 'Consider it pure **joy**, my brothers, whenever you face trials of many kinds, because you know that the testing of your faith develops perseverance' *(James 1:2-4)*. Happiness depends on what <u>happens</u>, but we can feel joy even in difficult situations. [184] 'Persecution for Christ's sake enhances joy.' Indeed, St Paul was in prison in Rome when he wrote to the Christians at Philippi to encourage them to 'rejoice in the Lord...Rejoice!' *(Philippians 3:1-4:4)*. **Joy** is a recurring theme in the Bible.

In Acts we read that the Apostles were arrested, imprisoned and flogged for preaching about Jesus and yet they knew joy at that time! *(Acts 5:41)*. Peter tells us to be glad when we go through difficult times: 'rejoice that you participate in the sufferings of Christ, so that you may be overjoyed when his glory is revealed *(I Peter 4:13)*. Peter encourages us that 'you believe in him and are filled with an inexpressible and glorious joy' *(I Peter 1:8)*. Paul served the Church helping people grow faith, writing: 'we work with you for your **joy**' *(II Corinthians 1:24)*. He expects their 'progress and joy in the faith' *(Philippians 1:25)*. Jesus said: 'Ask and you will receive, and your **joy** will be complete' *(John 16:24)*.

---

[183] Joy the meaning of the sacraments, Peter Waddell, Canterbury Press, Norwich, 2012, p. 16, p.10

[184] An Expository Dictionary of Biblical Words: W.E. Vine, Thomas Nelson, Inc, 1984, p.336

Mary's life had times of great joy as well as times of deep sorrow. In the Joyful Mysteries of the Rosary we meditate on five joyful [185]'scenes from the life of Jesus and Mary', recorded in the Bible which are The Annunciation *(Luke 1:26-38)*, The Visitation *(Luke 1:39-56)*, The Nativity *(Matthew 1:18-25, Luke 2:1-20)*, The Presentation *(Luke 2:22-38)* and The Finding of the Child Jesus *(Luke 2:41-51)*. The Five Glorious Mysteries are five joyful events: [186] The Resurrection *(Mark 16:6)*, The Ascension *(Mark 16:19)*, Descent of the Holy Spirit *(Acts 2:4)*, The Assumption of Mary and the Crowning of Mary *(Revelation 12:1)*. Cally Hammond explains: [187]'The first two glorious mysteries are extremely familiar from the Scriptures; they belong to Easter and its aftermath... The last two have traditionally been associated with Mary the mother of Jesus, in the sense of seeing her as standing for us, for redeemed humankind... Between the mysteries ... the Holy Spirit at Pentecost was... to connect divinity and humanity'. These are biblical events of great joy.

Peter Waddell writes more about the joy of Jesus. He explains: [188] 'the primal spring of joy (is) the life of God himself. Christians came to understand Jesus as being straight from the heart of God: being, as John puts it, 'the Word made flesh' *(John 1:14)* ... Jesus embodies the very character of God: he is what God is translated into flesh and blood. So our experience of him becomes our experience of God ... Jesus is experienced primarily as joy: as the one who brings people to life through loving them, as the one who longs for Israel and all humanity to live and love abundantly, as the one who will not leave anyone behind. Jesus rejoiced to share himself with others so all might **rejoice**... To be a Christian is to share in the joy of Jesus. I t is not a matter of believing his teachings, or following his example, so much as of having his life course through ours.'

---

[185] Hail, Holy Queen: Scott Hahn, Darton, Longman and Todd Ltd, London 2010, p. 164-5

[186] Dictionary of Mary 'Behold Your Mother', Catholic Book Publishing Co., New Jersey, 1985, p. 409

[187] Glorious Christianity, Walking by faith in the life to come, SPCK, 2012, p. xiv

[188] Joy the meaning of the sacraments, Peter Waddell, Canterbury Press, Norwich, 2012, p. 16, p.20

Christians experience the joy of Jesus in their hearts and lives, because Jesus is the source or **cause of joy** for them. God, who is the cause and source of joy longs for us to respond to and receive his joy.

Mary experienced much joy. We remembered some joyful occasions for Mary in the Joyful Mysteries. We sing about this in the hymn [189]*Sing we of the blessed Mother.* We see that Mary <u>felt</u> great joy, but the Bible is very clear that <u>God</u> is the <u>cause</u> of our joy. Jesus 'the Word made flesh' *(John 1:14)* continued to show that God is the 'cause of joy' through his healings and ministry. **Jesus is cause of joy**.

How can Mary be described as 'Cause of our joy'?

Jesus is the source of our joy – we can know the joy of forgiveness, the joy of God's presence and help in our lives all through Jesus. We can recognise Mary as the 'cause of our joy', because she said 'yes' to God and so the incarnation happened and Jesus was born. God brought joy to the world through the incarnation of His Son. Mary said to Angel Gabriel 'I am the Lord's servant. May it be to me as you have said' *(Luke 1:38)*. Mary was filled with joy when she said 'yes' to God.

The 15th century [190]*Pynson Ballad* encourages pilgrims to go to Walsingham and remember 'the great **joy**' *(v 5)* of Our Lady's Annunciation. Through Mary's acceptance of God's will for her life she became the means or '**cause of our joy**' because under God she gave us Jesus the Source of all joy. Mary always points us to Jesus so we can know great joy in following Him. The statue of Our Lady of Walsingham shows Mary, '[191]pointing to her son' and showing Jesus to us, because Mary wants us to meet her Son and grow to know Him more. At Cana she said: "Do whatever he tells you" *(John 2:5)*.

---

[189] Celebration for Everyone, McCrimmons, Great Wakering, Essex, England, hymn number 659, verses 1, 3,4, G. B. Timms 1910- 1997

[190] The "Pynson Ballad", Manuscript 1254/6, The Pepys Library, Magdalene College, Cambridge, A transcription of the "Pynson" Ballad

[191] Hail, Holy Queen': Scott Hahn, Darton, Longman and Todd Ltd, London 2010, p. 28

Bishop Kevin Rhoades writes about **Mary, Cause of Our Joy.** [192] 'I chose to celebrate today the Mass of the Blessed Virgin Mary under the title "causa nostrae laetitiae," "Cause of Our Joy." This is a beautiful and very meaningful title of Our Lady. The sorrow brought into the world by Eve's disobedience has been changed into joy by the obedience of the New Eve, the Blessed Virgin Mary. The prophet Zechariah foretold this as he spoke God's words: "Sing and rejoice, O daughter of Zion! See, I am coming to dwell among you, says the Lord." *(Zechariah 2:10)* The angel Gabriel repeated this call to rejoice when he spoke to Mary at the Annunciation *(Luke 1: 26-38)* and told her she was to conceive the Messiah, the Son of God. This great **joy** was communicated by Mary to Elizabeth at the Visitation. At that joyful encounter, even the unborn infant John the Baptist rejoiced *(Luke 1:44)*. And Mary, on that occasion, sang the beautiful canticle of joy, the Magnificat *(Luke 1:47)* ... Our Lord came into the world to bring peace and joy to the human family... What joy we can all experience when we live Our Lord's new commandment of love *(John 16:24)*... Too often we can turn people away from the faith by not showing them the joy of following Jesus, the joy of His Gospel, the joy of salvation. Mary teaches us the surpassing joy of knowing, loving, and serving her Son.'

The joy experienced by all those who surrounded Mary is also a joy to be experienced by us. Mary was the first one to enjoy the presence of Jesus, as His mother feeding and caring for Him. She shared the 'great joy' *(Matthew 28:8)* on Easter Sunday. Mary felt great joy and is the **cause of our joy** because she agreed to be the Mother of Jesus.

What does this mean for us?

We can be thankful and joyful because of the good things God gives us *(I Timothy 6:17)*. What gives you joy? Maybe your family, friends, and beautiful sunny days? All these are gifts from God to give us **joy**, for which we are grateful.

---

[192] https://www.francislittleassisi.com/our-lady-cause-of-joy 9th March 2018 October 3, 2015 – Annual Mass for the Worldwide Apostolate of Fatima, Cathedral of the Immaculate Conception

Mary the Mother of Jesus is seen as a 'type' of the Church. [193]St Ambrose (339-397) said 'Mary is explicitly said to be the type figure of the Church, which in effect means that she is the Church's pattern or model.' As Our Lady is given the title '**Cause of our joy**', this has great significance and challenge for every member of the Church. Mary was the first one to enjoy the presence of Jesus with the joy of feeding and caring for the baby Jesus, later caring for Jesus as a boy, a teenager and a young man. Like Mary, we need to receive the joy of Jesus so that we can share this joy with others. How can you share the joy of the Lord with other people?

Jesus told us how to live in His presence and experience His joy. He said: "If you obey my commands, you will remain in my love… I have told you this so that my **joy** may be in you and that your joy may be complete. My command is this: Love each other as I have loved you" (John 15:9-12). Jesus tells us to love one another, so there is unity and harmony in the Church, then we will remain in His presence and experience fullness of joy. How can you share love and joy?

When we go through difficult times, we must remember that we do not need to lose the joy of the Lord in our hearts (James 1:2-4).

We should abide in Jesus and know Jesus is in our hearts. Jesus said: 'If anyone loves me, he will obey my teaching. My Father will love him, and we will come to him and make our home with him' (John 14:23). Is joy seen in you?

We say to God: 'In Your presence is fullness of joy' (Psalm 16:11). We will recognize the presence of the Lord by praying more in our daily lives, knowing the Lord is always with us. As we grow in a living relationship with the Lord, the fruit of the Holy Spirit, including **joy** will grow in us (Galatians 5:22-23). Will you pray more?

We can feel tired, when it is wonderful to experience 'the **joy** of the Lord is your strength,' (Nehemiah 8:10) because the Lord strengthens and equips us to do whatever He is calling us to do. How is the Lord calling you to serve at this time?

---

[193] MARY the Complete Resource edited by Sarah Jane Boss, Oxford University Press 2007, p. 149

The definition of **joy** in this song, sung to the tune of *Jingle Bells*, is challenging as we need to put 'Jesus first, yourself last and others in-between'? [194]**J-O-Y, J-O-Y** *surely this must be: Jesus first, Yourself last, And Others in-between.*

We experience joy when we praise and worship the Lord. Let us give thanks, praise and worship the Lord alone and with others at Church Services and be filled afresh with the joy of the Lord *(Psalm 34:1)*. There is '**joy** in heaven' *(Luke 15: 7)* when a sinner repents and we can know great joy in receiving forgiveness. Do you need to say 'sorry' to God and repent, so you can then joyfully receive forgiveness?

We experience joy realising the wonderful providential care of God knowing that the Lord arranges situations for us *(Romans 8:28)*. Can you think of examples of when you have known joy because of God's providential care?

At [195]*The Stations of the Cross*, when remembering Jesus' suffering on Good Friday, we can know joy in realising afresh the Lord's love in suffering so much. We will be 'looking unto Jesus, the author and finisher of our faith, who for the **joy** that was set before Him endured the cross, despising the shame' *(Hebrews 12:2)*.

God's provision for us gives us joy. Paul was filled with joy when the Macedonian Christians gave a gift to the poor Christians in Jerusalem. 'Out of the most severe trial, their overflowing joy and their extreme poverty welled up in rich generosity' *(II Corinthians 8:2)*. We rejoice that God provides for us; we can then be a cause of joy for others by being generous, cheerful givers. 'Each man should give what he has decided in his heart to give, not reluctantly or under compulsion, for God loves a cheerful giver' *(II Corinthians 9:7)*. Is the Lord prompting you to be a 'cause of joy' by cheerfully giving some money to your Church, a Christian project or a Charity?

How sad that we can turn people away from faith by not showing them the joy of following Jesus. Do your life, speech and attitudes show the joy

---

[194] Sunday School song available at https://www.dltk-kids.com/bible/joy.htm 3rd January 2022

[195] Walsingham Pilgrim Manual, 2016, p. 20-44

of the Lord? Are you cheerful or too often complaining? Let us be filled afresh with the joy of the Lord and seek to share that joy with the people that we meet by being positive and cheerful. Do you bring joy to others?

The disciples experienced great joy when they returned from preaching the good news of Jesus and praying for people to be healed. They 'returned with joy' *(Luke 10:17a)*. We can share in that **joy** too by sharing our faith with other people *(I Peter 3: 15)*. It is a great joy helping people come to know the Lord. We should be ready to help people come to the **joy** of believing, loving and following Jesus. The Philippians are Paul's 'joy and crown' *(Philippians 4:1)* because it was such a joy for him to see this Christian community grow in love and faith. Whom is Jesus calling you to witness to now, so you can be a **cause of joy** for them?

Just as Mary carried Jesus, so we need to carry the **joy** of the Lord in our hearts and let that **joy** flow out. Then like Mary, as individuals and as Churches we will be a '**cause of joy**' for others by helping them know more of the love of Jesus, who is **the source of joy**. How can you be a '**cause of joy**'? How is the Lord calling you to serve Him now? How can you be a 'cause of joy' for others by sharing the love and joy of Jesus?

[196] 'The Puritans said, "the chief end of man is to glorify God and **enjoy** Him forever." We can pray and ask the Lord to give us joy in our hearts using the words of this hymn: [197] *Give me joy in my heart, keep me praising, Give me joy in my heart, I pray.*

[198] *Lord our God; you were pleased to bring joy to the world through the incarnation of your Son. Grant that we who honour his Mother,* **the cause of our joy***, may always walk in the way of your commandments, with our hearts set on true and lasting joy. Amen.*

[199] Mary, Cause of Joy, *pray for us.*

---

[196] http://davidolatona.com/ezra-6-god-the-cause-of-our-joy/ 9th March 2018

[197] Celebration for Everyone, McCrimmons, Great Wakering, Essex, England, hymn number 190, verse 1 and chorus, Traditional

[198] Marian Missal Mass for 'The Blessed Virgin Mary, Cause of our Joy' p.45

[199] Dictionary of Mary 'Behold your Mother', Catholic Book Publishing Co. New Jersey 1997, 1985, p.241

CHAPTER 9

MARY'S 'VESSEL' TITLES

In the [200]Litany of Loreto there are three titles of Mary about her being a 'Vessel'. They are the 24th **Spiritual vessel**, the 25th title **Vessel of honour** and the 26th title **Singular vessel of devotion**. In the [201]Walsingham Manual this is a suggested Litany for the First Visit to the Holy House, where these titles are **Vessel of the Spirit**, **Vessel of honour** and **Vessel of devotion wondrous**. A vessel is defined as [202]'a receptacle for a liquid or other substance, a person having the function of a vessel, the body as the receptacle of the soul, a ship, tubes containing fluids of the body.'

---

[200] Dictionary of Mary 'Behold your Mother', Catholic Book Publishing Co. New Jersey 1997, 1985, p.241

[201] The Walsingham Pilgrim Manual 2016, p.13

[202] The Shorter Oxford English Dictionary on Historical Principles, H.W. Fowler & J. Coulson, Clarendon Press, Oxford,1973, p 2469

What does the Bible tell us about vessels?

There are three [203]Hebrew words that are translated 'vessel' and two New Testament Greek words. The Hebrew כְּלִי *keli* is used the most frequently for 'vessel and instrument'. This word is used when Jacob told his sons: 'Put some of the best products of the land in your bags' *(Genesis 43:11)*, to take to Egypt. The altar of burnt offering was to have the utensils, pots and bowls made from bronze *(Exodus 27:3)*. The vessels for the table in the tabernacle were made from gold *(Exodus 37:16)*. Moses anointed the basin on the altar to consecrate it *(Leviticus 8:11)*. *Keli* is also used for other vessels, made from 'wood, cloth, hide or sackcloth'; *(Leviticus 11:32)* also the water jar for Boaz's workers *(Ruth 2:9)* and the pots and sprinkling bowls in Solomon's Temple *(1 Kings 7:45)*. *Keli* is used by David when he visited Ahimelech at Nob *(1 Samuel 21:5)* and they were given some holy bread. [204]'David obtained this favour after giving assurances that the young men were ceremonially clean through abstention from sex and that their 'vessels' were clean.' *Keli* is used figuratively when Jeremiah says that Nebuchadnezzar 'has thrown us into confusion, he has made us an empty jar' *(Jeremiah 51:34)*. The 'empty jar' suggests the physical, emotional and spiritual emptiness and desolation that has come upon the people with Nebuchadnezzar's attack on the city of Jerusalem. The exile of so many people to Babylon left that once great City like an abandoned empty vessel.

The Hebrew *man* is used for 'vessel' and 'utensil' for the gold and silver articles that King Cyrus returned to the Temple in Jerusalem *(Ezra 5:14-15)*. These same gold goblets have the word *man* when described by Daniel at Belshazzar's feast *(Daniel 5:2-3, 23)*. Isaiah uses נֶבֶל *nebel*, translated 'vessel' or 'bottle' to describe the broken pottery vessel that he likens to the sin of the people *(Isaiah 30:14)*.

In the New Testament the Greek word *angeion* ἀγγεῖον is used to mean 'vessel, utensil', for the fisherman's net in the Parable of the Net

---

[203] Analytical Concordance to the Holy Bible, Robert Young, United Society for Christian Literature, Lutterworth Press London, 1973, p.1023-1024

[204] The Oxford Bible Commentary, edited by John Barton and John Muddiman, Oxford University Press, 2001, p.210

(Matthew 13:48) and for the jar containing oil taken by the wise virgins in that parable *(Matthew 25:4)*. A 'vessel' contains first fish and then oil. The more frequently used New Testament Greek word for 'vessel' is σκεῦος σκευος meaning [205]'a vessel, utensil for containing anything' and is used for physical objects. A lamp is not lit and then hidden under a jar *(Luke 8:16)*, and 'the jar of wine vinegar' *(John 19:29)* offered to Jesus on the Cross. This word describes 'the large sheet' containing unclean animals that Peter saw in his vision *(Acts 10: 11, 16)*. The vessels (σκεῦοι) in the Temple cleansed by blood, were objects used in worship *(Hebrews 9:21)*. Merchants will no longer bring 'vessels of ivory, and all manner vessels of most precious wood' *(Revelation 18:12 AV)* after the fall of Babylon. The broken clay vessels in the message to the Church at Thyatira, show the authority given to them *(Revelation 2:27)*.

The word σκεῦος is used by God to explain to Ananias that Paul is 'my chosen instrument to carry my name before the Gentiles' *(Acts 9:15)*, describing a person who will carry a message. Later Paul uses the 'vessel' analogy in writing to the Romans *(Romans 9:21-14)*. Paul uses the image of the potter making clay vessels showing that God chooses some people to be 'vessels' of his mercy because they receive divine favour; while others through their decisions are 'vessels' receiving God's punishment. We know that God 'wants all men to be saved' *(I Timothy 2:4)*. Let us help more people come to faith; so they are 'vessels' of his mercy, receiving God's blessings *(Romans 9:23)*.

Women are described by Peter as the 'weaker vessel' σκεῦος *(I Peter 3:7 AV)*. While many women now would not like to be thought of as 'the weaker partner', all wives would like to be treated with respect and consideration. Peter writes to husbands: 'be considerate as you live with your wives, and treat them with respect as the weaker partner and as heirs with you of the gracious gift of life, so that nothing will hinder your prayers' *(I Peter 3:7)*. Consideration and respect are important in all relationships.

Paul uses the 'vessel' imagery to teach Timothy the importance of repentance. 'In a large house there are articles not only of gold and silver,

---

[205] Analytical Greek Lexicon, Samuel Bagster & Sons Ltd, London, 1973, p.368

but also of wood and clay; some are for noble purposes and some for ignoble. If a man cleanses himself from the latter, he will be an instrument for noble purposes, made holy, useful to the Master and prepared to do any good work' *(II Timothy 2:19b-21)*. The Lord wants us to be holy, like the gold vessels. Everyone 'should learn to control his own body in a way that is holy and honourable' *(I Thessalonians 4:4)*. This is σκεῦος for 'vessel': 'every one of you should know how to possess his vessel in sanctification and honour' *(I Thessalonians 4:4 AV)*.

How wonderful that God's light has shone into our hearts 'to give us the light of the knowledge of God in the face of Christ. But we have this treasure in jars of clay (σκεῦος) to show that this all-surpassing power is from God and not from us' *(IICorinthians 4:7)*. The jars of clay are 'earthen vessels' in the Authorized King James Version of the Bible. Our bodies are like 'earthen vessels' or 'jars of clay' and God in his love comes to dwell with us and fill us with the Holy Spirit. Jesus said: 'If anyone loves me, he will obey my teaching. My Father will love him, and we will come to him and make our home with him' *(John 14:23)*. Like the early disciples we can be 'filled with the Holy Spirit' *(Acts 2:4)*. Our 'earthen vessels' can be places where God dwells!

We see that σκεῦος 'vessel' is used to describe people and to encourage us to come to know Jesus, repent of sins, receive his mercy and live with respect, consideration and holiness. Our bodies should be where God dwells and a 'container' of the Holy Spirit. Paul explains this amazing truth to the Corinthians: 'Don't you know that you yourselves are God's temple and that God's Spirit lives in you?' *(I Corinthians 3: 16)*. He also writes: 'Do you not know that your body is a temple of the Holy Spirit, who is in you, whom you have received from God? You are not your own, you were bought at a price. Therefore honour God with your body' *(I Corinthians 6: 19-20)*. 'The price' was the precious blood of Jesus as 'the blood of Jesus, his Son, purifies us from all sin' *(I John 1:7)*.

How can Mary be addressed as Spiritual vessel, Vessel of the Spirit, Vessel of honour, Singular vessel of devotion and Vessel of devotion wondrous?

Fr Canice writes: [206]'Mary's body was, for nine months, the habitation of the Adorable Person of the Son of God made Man: and for the whole of her mortal life it was the temple of the Holy Trinity.' Mary's womb was the 'vessel' or container of baby Jesus as he grew in those months after his conception. The Angel Gabriel told Mary: 'The Holy Spirit will come upon you, and the power of the Most High will overshadow you. So the holy one to be born will be called the Son of God' *(Luke 1:35).* We can see that Mary's womb was therefore a **Spiritual vessel** and a **Vessel of the Spirit** because the Holy Son of God grew in her womb. Her body was honoured to be the vessel that carried baby Jesus for the nine months before his birth; so we can call Mary **Vessel of honour.**

Sarah Boss explains: [207]'The awareness that **vessels** have the capacity to be infused with holiness has permeated Catholic consciousness for many centuries...... all these things are holy objects in themselves, because of the precious contents they bear. Mary's body, therefore, which carried God incarnate, and part of whose very substance became God's flesh is necessarily the most sacred of these vessels.' This enlightens us about why Mary has the **Spiritual vessel, Vessel of the Spirit, Vessel of honour** titles.

Gregory Pearson OP reflects on the title **Singular vessel of devotion** writing: [208] 'Our Lady occupies a special place in Christian devotion. She whom the angel called 'full of grace' *(Luke 1:28)* was so profoundly conformed to God, the ultimate object of all our devotion, that she was chosen to bear within herself the very Word of God made Flesh. Thus

---

[206] Mary: A Study of the Mother of God, Fr Canice O.F.M.Cap, M.H.Gill and Sons Ltd, Dublin, 1950, p. 219

[207] Walsingham Pilgrims and Pilgrimages: Michael Rear, Gracewing, 2019, p. 294 quoting Empress and Handmaid: Boss, p. 30-31

[208] http://english.op.org/godzdogz/litany-of-loreto-singular-vessel-of-devotion 23rd May 2017

she is quite literally a **singular vessel of our devotion.** So it is that the Byzantine Church dares to sing so exultantly in response to the *Magnificat*, Mary's own song of joy:

'More honourable than the Cherubim, and incomparably more glorious than the Seraphim,

Thou who inviolate didst bring forth the Word of God, very Mother of God,

Thee do we magnify!'

Jesus **honoured** his mother. At the age of twelve, when they returned to Nazareth from the Passover in Jerusalem, we are told by Luke: 'he went down to Nazareth with them and was obedient to them' *(Luke 2:51).* Jesus honoured Mary by obeying the 5th Commandment 'Honour your father and your mother' *(Exodus 20:12).* Jesus arranged for John to care for Mary, after his death on the Cross. 'When Jesus saw his mother there, and the disciple whom he loved standing nearby, he said to his mother, "Dear woman, here is your son," and to the disciple, "Here is your mother." From that time on, this disciple took her into his home' *(John 19:26-27).*

[209] Professor Michael Ogunu writes: '**Singular Vessel of Devotion:** The word *devotion* as used in this title exceeds the narrow meaning of devotional practice and refers to total dedication and fidelity in the service of God. Mary's profession of faith, "Behold, the handmaid of the Lord...," most adequately expresses the meaning of this invocation. She was totally dedicated to her Son. Total dedication has not only the meaning of service, it refers primarily to openness and receptivity of God's will and grace. Devotion in its true sense means a cheerful promptness and alacrity in all that relates to God's service. In Mary, we at once see devotion in its true light. God, Her Divine Son, was the one end and aim of her life. She lived simply and wholly for His service.' Thus we see Mary was a 'vessel' who honoured Jesus.

---

[209] http://www.christendom-awake.org/pages/litany-of-loreto/litany+ogunu+article+2. htm 8th June 2017

[210]Saint Gregory reflected on Mary's being called 'Vessel': he said: 'Mary, you are the **vessel** and tabernacle containing all mysteries. You know what the Patriarchs never knew; you have experienced what was never revealed to the Angels; you have heard what the Prophets never heard. In a word, all that was hidden from preceding generations was made known to you; even more, most of these wonders depended on you.' Saint Gregory greatly honoured Mary as a special Vessel; being chosen to be the Mother of Jesus, helping us to see her as **Vessel of devotion wondrous**.

Fr Ray Blake writes [211] 'David could not build the Temple of the Lord, although he was the Lord's Chosen One, he was a sinner, "a man of blood", an adulterer who had stolen Bathsheba and had Uriah killed, and he killed his own people too. A sinner could not build a house for the Lord, lest the House itself was poisoned by sin. It is Solomon who chose wisdom rather than wealth or power who builds the Lord's House, though he himself loses God's favour after the Temple is built.

'The Temple is a type of Mary, who is uncontaminated by sin, she is also the **Spiritual Vessel**, the **Vessel of Honour, Singular Vessel of Devotion**..... She contains Grace himself. She is full of Grace, highly favoured, the Blessed amongst women, the Lord is with Her... She was chosen before all time, and from the first moment of her being was free from all sin, so that she might contain the Body, Blood, Humanity and Divinity of Jesus Christ.... Mary is our model, she alone was worthy to contain Jesus Christ, we at least must be free of all serious sin and must have a real hatred of sin to receive Christ. The Grace she receives is entirely God's gift.' Mary's womb was the vessel of honour for Jesus where Jesus grew.

Mary is seen as **Vessel of honour** and **Singular vessel of devotion** because [212]**'Jesus honoured her before all ages, and will honour her for all ages.** *St. Maximilian Mary Kolbe* **said 'No one comes to Him, nor**

[210] Dictionary of Mary Behold your Mother, Catholic Book Publishing Co, New Jersey, 1997, 1985, p. 530
[211] http://marymagdalen.blogspot.co.uk/2011/12/spiritual-vessel.html 23rd May 2017
[212] https://avemaria.com/2016/05/17/vessel-of-honor-singular-vessel-of-devotion/ 23rd May 2017

even near Him, no one is saved or sanctified, if he too will not honour her. This is the lot of Angels and of men."

It is important to remember, that Mary's status of deserving these titles is all because of God's grace and favour towards her in choosing her to carry Jesus in her womb. So Mary is addressed as **Spiritual vessel, Vessel of the Spirit, Vessel of honour, Singular vessel of devotion** and **Vessel of devotion wondrous.**

What does this mean for us?

We know that God 'wants all men to be saved and to come to a knowledge of the truth' *(I Timothy 2:4)*. We need to help more people come to receive God's love and forgiveness so they are 'vessels' of his mercy, receiving God's favour and blessing in their lives *(Romans 9:23)*. Let us be active in mission and evangelism. Whom does the Lord want you to pray for and witness to; being active in mission, so people come to know Jesus and become a 'vessel' of his mercy and blessing?

The Lord wants us to be holy, like the gold and silver vessels in a house *(II Timothy 2:19b-21)*. Then our bodies will be temples of the Holy Spirit *(I Corinthians 6:19-20)*. 'The price' was the precious blood of Jesus as 'the blood of Jesus, his Son, purifies us from all sin' *(1 John 1:7)*.

We need to repent and grow in holiness. Consider now; what do you need to repent about? Before receiving Communion we should follow St Paul's teaching to examine ourselves, confess and repent of sins. It is good to prepare for the Confession at the beginning of the Service, by being aware of those sins, failings and mistakes that we need to repent and say 'sorry' for. St Paul writes: 'A man ought to examine himself before he eats of the bread and drinks of the cup. For anyone who eats and drinks without recognising the body of the Lord eats and drinks judgment on himself' *(I Corinthians 11:27-30)*.

Our bodies are like 'earthen vessels' or 'jars of clay' *(II Corinthians 4:7)* and God in his love comes to dwell with us and fill us with the Holy Spirit. Jesus said: 'If anyone loves me, he will obey my teaching. My Father will love him, and we will come to him and make our home with him'

(John 14:23). 'Don't you know that you yourselves are God's temple and that God's Spirit lives in you?' *(I Corinthians 3:16).* Like the early disciples we can be 'filled with the Holy Spirit' *(Acts 2:4).* Our 'earthen vessels' can be places where God dwells! Let us pray: [213]*O come to my heart Lord Jesus, there is room in my heart for thee.*

A Collect reminds us about how we should be a holy temple:

[214]*O Almighty God, who hast built thy Church upon the foundation of the apostles and prophets, Jesus Christ himself being the head cornerstone: grant us so to be joined together in unity of spirit by their doctrine, that we may be made a* **holy temple** *acceptable unto thee.' Amen.*

[215] Mary, *Vessel of honour, Singular vessel of devotion, pray for us.*

[213] The New English Hymnal, The Canterbury Press, Norwich, 1987, p. 461, hymn 465 chorus, Emily Elliott

[214] Common Worship Services and Prayers for the Church of England, Church House Publishing, 2000, p. 515, Collect for Simon and Jude

[215] The Walsingham Pilgrim Manual 2016, p.13

CHAPTER 10

MYSTICAL ROSE

In the [216]Litany of Loreto the 27th title of Our Lady is **Mystical Rose** or **Mystic Rose**. 'Mystical' means [217]'having a certain spiritual character by virtue of a connection or union with God. Spiritually allegorical or symbolic.' The rose is 'mystical' in being spiritually symbolic. A rose is a prickly shrub with beautifully fragrant flowers. Roses in bloom give joy with their wonderful colour, the shape of their petals and fragrance.

[216] Dictionary of Mary 'Behold your Mother', Catholic Book Publishing Co. New Jersey 1997, 1985, p.241

[217] The Shorter Oxford English Dictionary on Historical Principles, H.W. Fowler & J. Coulson, Clarendon Press, Oxford, 1973, p.1380

What does the Bible tell us about a rose?

There are only two [218]Biblical references to the word 'rose'. This is the Hebrew word *chăbatstseleth* חֲבַצֶּלֶת, which means 'meadow saffron or narcissus. We read in the Song of Songs the Beloved saying to her Lover: 'I am a **rose** of Sharon, a lily of the valleys' *(Song of Songs 2:1)*. The rose is a beautiful flower suggesting the Beloved's great beauty. [219] 'The biblical "rose of Sharon" is a cultivated Asian shrub or small tree (*Hibiscus syriacus*) having showy bell-shaped rose, purple, or white flowers. Saint Bernard of Clairvaux states that purple signifies humility and white signifies purity.' This symbolism of the colour is significant as we consider how Our Lady can be called **Mystic Rose**. In Isaiah the Authorized Version of the Bible tells us: 'The wilderness and the solitary place shall be glad for them; and the desert shall rejoice and blossom as the **rose**' *(Isaiah 35:1)*. This rose symbolises hope as life and beauty will come to the desert that had been dry and lifeless. Isaiah is prophesying about a future time of joy for the redeemed 'who walk in the Way' of the Lord *(Isaiah 35:8)*. Then 'the ransomed of the Lord will return. They will enter Zion with singing; everlasting joy will crown their heads' *(Isaiah 35:10)*.

How can Mary be addressed as Mystical Rose?

[220] Professor Michael Ogunu writes: 'The rose is regarded as the queen of flowers. Goodness and holiness flower in the saints. Mary, the queen of saints, can be called then the "Mystical Rose." As the rose is considered the queen of flowers, so Mary is invoked as Queen of All Saints. As described by sacred writers, she is the "mystical rose without thorn", the "rose of paradise", and the "rose bringing salvation to all who call upon her".'

---

[218] Analytical Concordance to the Holy Bible, Robert Young, United Society for Christian Literature, Lutterworth Press London, 1973, p. 825

[219] http://taylormarshall.com/2012/06/why-is-mary-is-mystical-rose.html 3rd June 2017

[220] http://www.christendom-awake.org/pages/litany-of-loreto/litany+ogunu+article+2.htm 8th June 2017

Fr Canice explains: [221] 'there are very many beautiful comparisons to be found in Sacred Scripture concerning Our Lady. She is fair and pure as the lily that grows among thorns; she is fragrant like the **rose** of Jericho; she has the majesty and grace of the cedar.' Accordingly, Fr Canice likens the fragrance of the **rose** to Mary.

Taylor Marshall writes: [222] 'The Litany of Loreto invokes our Immaculate and Blessed Virgin Mary as the *Rosa Mystica* or "**Mystical Rose**." What is meant by this phrase? The most beautiful meditation on Our Lady as *Rosa Mystica* is found in the writings of Saint Brigid. "The rose," Mary told Saint Brigid, "gives a fragrant odour; it is beautiful to the sight, and tender to the touch, and yet it grows among thorns, inimical to the beauty and tenderness. So may also those who are mild, patient, beautiful in virtue, be put to a test among adversaries.... Just as the gentle rose is placed among thorns, so this gentle Virgin was surrounded by sorrow." We consider the sorrow and afflictions of Mary in Chapter 18. Mary is beautiful like a rose and experienced many sorrows, symbolised by the thorns.

In his poem *Ash Wednesday*,[223] T.S. Eliot refers to Our Lady as **Mystical Rose**: *Lady of silences Calm and distressed... Rose of memory Rose of forgetfulness.* She was 'life-giving', giving birth to Jesus who came to show God's love.

St John Henry Newman explains this title of Mary, writing: [224] *'Holy Mary, **Mystical Rose**, you are the most beautiful flower created by God, in venerating you we praise God for his holiness and beauty.* She is the Queen of spiritual flowers; and therefore she is called the *Rose*, for the rose is fitly called of all flowers the most beautiful. ...But moreover, she is the *Mystical*, or *hidden* Rose; for mystical means hidden. How is she now "hidden" from us more than are other saints? ..... If her body was not taken into heaven,

[221] Mary: A Study of the Mother of God, Fr Canice O.F.M.Cap, M.H.Gill and Sons Ltd, Dublin, 1950, p. 23

[222] http://taylormarshall.com/2012/06/why-is-mary-is-mystical-rose.html 3rd June 2017

[223] Selected Poems, T.S. Eliot, Faber and Faber, London, 1972, p. 85-86

[224] http://www.cardinaljohnhenrynewman.com/mary-mystical-rose-cardinal-newman 3rd June 2017

where is it? How comes it that it is hidden from us? Why do we not hear of her tomb as being here or there? Is it conceivable that they who had been so reverent and careful of the bodies of the Saints and Martyrs should neglect her—her who was the Queen of Martyrs and the Queen of Saints, who was the very Mother of our Lord? It is impossible. Why then is she thus the *hidden* Rose? Plainly because that sacred body is in heaven, not on earth.' Newman gives us this explanation about 'Mystical' meaning hidden; to teach about the Assumption of Mary into heaven. Chapter 20 explores this.

The hymn [225]*Crown him with many crowns* includes **mystic Rose.**

*Fruit of the **mystic Rose**,*
*As of that **Rose** the stem;*
The Root whence mercy ever flows,
The Babe of Bethlehem.

Jesus is 'fruit of the Mystic Rose', as He is Mary's son, coming from the root of Jesse.

Mary **Mystic Rose** shows us [226]'Because the Blessed Virgin received the Word of God in her womb, because she was the **rose** who bore God at the very centre of her being, it is possible for each human person to receive that Word and be transformed by it, and so come to recognise God at the heart of all created things.' This is a helpful reflection about Mystic Rose as we are encouraged to receive Jesus and grow in a closer relationship with Him. John writes: 'Yet to all who received him, to those who believed in his name, he gave the right to become children of God' *(John 1:12)*. St Paul tells us: 'So then, just as you received Christ Jesus as Lord, continue to live in him, rooted and built up in him, strengthened in the faith as you were taught, and overflowing with thankfulness' *(Colossians 2:6-7)*. We need to receive Jesus and grow in faith.

[225] Walsingham Pilgrim Manual, 2016, page 73, hymn number 2, verse 2, Matthew Bridges 1800-1894

[226] Mary: The Complete Resource, edited by Sarah Jane Boss, Oxford University Press, 2007, p. 393

This Mosaic of Mary as **Mystical Rose** is on the wall behind the outside Altar at Aylesford Friary, near Maidstone, Kent. [227]It was created in pink stone by Adam Kossowski with other ceramics and paintings as an act of thanks for his release from a slave labour camp in Russia. It is displayed there with other mosaics depicting some of the Titles of Mary in *The Litany of Loreto*.

This Carol sung sometimes by Choirs at Christmas shows that Mary is **Mystical Rose** and also helps us understand the doctrine of the Holy Trinity: [228]

> *There is no **rose** of such virtue*
> *as is the **rose** that bear Jesu: Alleluia.*
> *For in this **rose** contained was*
> *heaven and earth in little space: Res Miranda.*

---

[227] Information leaflet about Aylesford Priory from 1242 to the present day
[228] Carols for Choirs 2, Ed David Willcocks and John Rutter, Oxford University Press, 1966, p. 190, Anon c. 1420, transcribed and edited by Jon Stevens

*By that **rose** we may well see*
there be one God in Persons Three: Pares forma.

A hymn[229] refers to Mary as the **rose**; growing from the root and stem of Jesse, thus tracing Jesus' human ancestry back through David to Jesse *(Matthew 1:6)*.

A noble flow'r of Juda
from tender roots has sprung
a rose from stem of Jesse,
as prophets long had sung;

The rose of grace and beauty
of which Isaiah sings
is Mary, virgin mother,
and Christ the flow'r she brings.

The hymn [230]*I'll sing a hymn to Mary* addresses Mary as **Mystic Rose**, expressing the physical and spiritual beauty of Mary:

O Lily of the Valley,
*O **Mystic Rose**, what tree*
Or flower, e'en the fairest,
Is half so fair as thee?

What does this mean for us?

The Bible tells us: 'The wilderness and the solitary place shall be glad for them; and the desert shall rejoice and blossom as the **rose**' *(Isaiah 35:1 AV)*. The rose here symbolises **hope** as life and beauty come to the desert

---

229 Celebration Hymnal for Everyone, McCrimmons, Essex, England, 1994, hymn number 5, German, 15th century, translated by Anthony G. Petti

230 Walsingham Pilgrim Manual, 2016, page 108-9, hymn number 20 verse 2, John Wyse 1825-1898

that had been dry and lifeless. We should bring the love and life of Jesus to places that are spiritually dry. Ask the Lord to show you 'dry' places where he is calling you to let His love, joy and peace flow through you. Then those dry places can become places that are **beautiful** with the love of Jesus.

We should say '**thank you**' to God for the beauty of roses as well as other beautiful plants and all that He has created in the wonderful world. We give thanks for the senses of sight, hearing and smell enabling us to appreciate the beauty in the world.

Reflecting on **Mystic Rose** above we are encouraged to receive Jesus and grow in a closer relationship with Him *(John 1:12, Colossians 2:6-7)*. We need to receive Jesus and grow in faith, praying: [231]*O come to my heart Lord Jesus, there is room in my heart for thee.*

Roses have a beautiful **scent**. This reminds us that we are called to spread the **fragrance** of Christ: 'For we are to God the **aroma of Christ** among those who are being saved and those who are perishing' *(II Corinthians 2:14-16)*. We need to spread 'the fragrance of the knowledge of him' *(v 14)* by telling people about Jesus so they can come to know Him *(I Peter 3:15)*. We should expect the Lord to arrange conversations when we can share our faith, talking about 'the hope we have' in Jesus; so more people come to know Jesus and 'spread the fragrance of Christ' to others. Whom will you witness to?

Our lives can become beautiful if the **fruit of the Holy Spirit** grows in our lives, changing us to be like Jesus *(Galatians 5:22-23)*. As we follow Jesus and keep close to Him, then the fruit of the Holy Spirit will grow more in us. Which of these 'fruits' are you aware that you need <u>more</u> in your life?

[232] *Mystic Rose, pray for us.*

---

[231] The New English Hymnal, The Canterbury Press, Norwich, 1987, p. 461, hymn 465 chorus, Emily Elliott 1836-1897

[232] The Walsingham Pilgrim Manual 2016, p.13

CHAPTER 11

TOWER OF DAVID AND TOWER OF IVORY

In the [233]Litany of Loreto the 28th title of Our Lady is **Tower of David** and the 29th title is **Tower of Ivory**. A tower is [234]'a lofty building used as a stronghold or fortress for purposes of defence' and tower means 'to exalt, to stand high.'

[233] Dictionary of Mary 'Behold your Mother', Catholic Book Publishing Co. New Jersey 1997, 1985, p.241

[234] The Shorter Oxford English Dictionary on Historical Principles, H.W. Fowler & J. Coulson, Clarendon Press, Oxford, 1973, p.2335-6

What does the Bible tell us about the Tower of David and the Tower of Ivory?

This word for 'tower' is the Hebrew [235] מִגְדָּל *migdal*, where the tower was part of the castle in Zion. When David became King of Israel he conquered Jerusalem *(II Samuel 5:6)* and 'took up residence in the fortress and called it the City of David *(II Samuel 5:9a)*. This is where the tower of David was situated.

In the Song of Songs the Lover says to his Beloved: 'Your neck is like the tower of David, built with elegance; on it hang a thousand shields, all of them shields of warriors,' *(4:4)* complimenting the lady about her beautiful neck.

Towers are mentioned many times in the Old Testament. The first tower was the Tower of Babel *(Genesis 11:4)*. The Lord confused the languages of the people and scattered them *(Genesis11:8-9)*. Towers were useful places to look out for advancing enemies. 'The lookout standing on the tower in Jezreel saw Jehu's troops approaching *(II Kings 9:17)*. Later Jotham 'built towns in the Judean hills and forts and towers in the wooded areas' *(II Chronicles 27:4)*. Hezekiah 'worked hard repairing all the broken sections of the wall and building towers on it'; *(II Chronicles 32:5)* so Jerusalem would be protected and defended against attack from Sennacherib of Assyria. At the time of Nehemiah, men worked hard to rebuild the wall of Jerusalem with towers *(Nehemiah 3:25-27)*.

Towers were places of safety, protection and defence. Towers are used as an analogy of the love and protection of God. 'The LORD is my rock, my fortress and my deliverer' *(Psalm 18:2)*. 'The name of the LORD is a strong tower; the righteous run to it and are safe' *(Proverbs 18:10)*. The LORD 'is my loving God and my fortress' *(Psalm 144:2)*.

The phrase 'tower of ivory' is only found in the Song of Songs, when the Lover says: 'Your neck is like an ivory tower' *(Song of Songs 7:4)*. 'Ivory'

---

[235] Analytical Concordance to the Holy Bible, Robert Young, United Society for Christian Literature, Lutterworth Press London, 1973, p.996

is the Hebrew word [236]*shên* שֵׁן. Ivory is made from elephants' tusks and is very expensive. Solomon's great throne was 'inlaid with ivory and overlaid with fine gold' *(I Kings 10:18).* Solomon's trading ships brought ivory to Israel *(I Kings 10:22).* Later Ahab's palace was 'inlaid with ivory' *(I Kings 22: 39).*

In the Song of Songs the Beloved admires the handsome body of the Lover, saying 'His body is like polished ivory decorated with sapphires' *(5:14).* Ivory is mentioned in the Book of Revelation with the New Testament Greek word [237]*elephantinos* ἐλεφάντινος, which means 'elephant's tooth and ivory', referring to articles made from ivory that will not be traded by the merchants of the world after the fall of Babylon *(Revelation 18:12).*

[238]'The **Tower of David** *(Hebrew:* מגדל דוד*, Migdal David, Arabic:* برج داود*, Burj Daud),* also known as the Jerusalem Citadel, is an ancient citadel located near the Jaffa Gate entrance to western edge of the Old City of Jerusalem…..Dan Bahat writes that the original three Hasmonean towers were altered by Herod, and that 'The northeastern tower was replaced by a much larger, more massive tower, dubbed the "Tower of David" beginning in the 5th century C.E.' The name "Tower of David" is due to Byzantine Christians who believed the site to be the palace of King David. They borrowed the name "Tower of David" from the Song of Songs, attributed to Solomon, King David's son, who wrote: "Thy neck is like the Tower of David built with turrets, whereon there hang a thousand shields, all the armour of the mighty men" *(Song of Songs 4:4).'*

---

[236] Analytical Concordance to the Holy Bible, Robert Young, United Society for Christian Literature, Lutterworth Press London, 1973, p.530

[237] Analytical Concordance to the Holy Bible, Robert Young, United Society for Christian Literature, Lutterworth Press, London, 1973, p.530

[238] https://en.wikipedia.org/wiki/Tower_of_David 8th June 2017

How can Mary be addressed as Tower of David?

Fr Canice connects the symbolism of a tower being a place of defence and protection, to explain Mary's title **Tower of David**. He writes: [239]'The Tower of David with its thousand bucklers stood as a powerful defence in Israel. Mary is the protectress of Christians, the support of Holy Church. Against her the enemy is powerless.' Fr Canice recognises the power of Mary's prayers that protect, defend and help Christians, giving them victory; explored in Chapter 16: **Health of the Sick**, Chapter 18: **Comforter of the Afflicted** and Chapter19: **Help of Christians**.

The **Tower of David** is defined as: [240] 'A symbol of the Blessed Virgin occurring in the Litany of Loreto. Mary's Son recognized as the glory of the line of David, whose star often appears in conjunction with the tower when that symbol is used. Mary, too, is a tower of strength against heresy.' Mary always points to Jesus who is the truth. Jesus said: 'I am the way and the truth and the life' *(John 14:6)*. Mary is the Tower of David because she is a descendant of David, full of grace, spiritual beauty and highly favoured by God *(Luke 1:28)*. Her Son Jesus is the glory of David's line, giving Mary this title.

[241]Fr Juan Velez writes that '**Tower of David** is another title of the Virgin Mary that is not self-evident. Blessed John Henry Newman explains its meaning to us. King David is a type of Our Lord, and thus the *Tower of David* is a defence of Our Lord. And Mary is just that defence because all the veneration that she receives reinforces truths about his divinity... Mary is the "*Turris Davidica*," the **Tower of David**. A Tower in its simplest idea is a fabric for defence against enemies. David, King of Israel, built for this purpose a notable tower; and as he is a figure or type of our Lord, so is his tower a figure denoting our Lord's Virgin Mother. She is called the *Tower*

---

[239] A Study of the Mother of God, Fr Canice O.F.M.Cap, M.H.Gill and Sons Ltd, Dublin, 1950, p. 28

[240] http://www.catholicculture.org/culture/library/dictionary/index.cfm?id=36897 8th June 2017

[241] http://www.cardinaljohnhenrynewman.com/mary-tower-of-david-cardinal-newman/ 8th June 2017

of David because she had so signally fulfilled the office of defending her Divine Son from the assaults of His foes.'

This Mosaic of Mary as **Tower of David** is on the wall behind the outside Altar at Aylesford Friary, near Maidstone, Kent. [242] Mosaics of Mary's titles were created in pink stone by Adam Kossowski.

How can Mary be addressed as Tower of Ivory?

Mary's title **Tower of Ivory** *(Song of Solomon 7:4)* is a symbol of her purity. Ivory is known for being precious and pearly white; showing God's love for Mary as the highly favoured one and His grace that makes Mary immaculate. The brightness, purity and exquisiteness of ivory suggest the

---

[242] Information leaflet about Aylesford Priory from 1242 to the present day

great loveliness and gentleness of the Mother of God and the inner beauty of her heart. Ivory is beautiful and pictures of Mary as Tower of Ivory help us to picture her as beautiful, lovely, pure and gentle. The pure white of the ivory reminds us about Mary's purity which I explore in Chapter 5 **Mary's titles about her Virginity** and Chapter 26 **Queen conceived without original sin.**

[243]'The term **ivory tower** was in use since the 12th century Marian revival at least. It occasionally appears in art, especially in depictions of Mary in the hortus conclusus.' This Latin term means an enclosed garden. We can imagine Mary in an enclosed garden with an ivory tower. 'Ivory tower' is used in British English meaning making academic pronouncements. It is [244]'a position of lofty seclusion … used by Sainte-Beuve of Vigny's seclusion in a turret room.' People speaking from 'an ivory tower' are often thought to be detached from the realities of the world.

St John Henry Newman reminds us that when we say a man 'towers' over others, we mean that they look small in comparison with him. We see this quality of greatness in Mary. She suffered most deeply at Jesus's death and crucifixion, yet she stood by the Cross, while all the disciples except John had fled. Mary 'towered' over the Apostles with her love and generosity in suffering, so she is justly imaged as a Tower, in her devotion and support of Jesus. 'Mary is the *"Turris Eburnea,"* the Ivory Tower'.

The hymn [245]*I'll sing a hymn to Mary* addresses Mary as:
O noble **Tower of David**, of gold and **ivory**.

What does this mean for us?

The name of the Lord is our 'strong tower; the righteous run to it and are safe'*(Proverbs 18:10).* Let us remember to 'run' to the Lord and be safe in

---

[243] https://en.wikipedia.org/wiki/Ivory_tower 8th June 2017

[244] The Shorter Oxford English Dictionary on Historical Principals, Clarendon Press, Oxford, 1973, p. 1122

[245] Walsingham Pilgrim Manual, 2016, page 108-9, hymn number 20, verse 3, John Wyse 1825-1898

His loving care and protection; enjoying the 'strong tower' of Jesus' love and protection.

Ivory is white and pure, which reminds us that we are called to be pure and holy. We need to repent of sins, confess our sins and receive forgiveness. We will then be seen by the Lord as white and clean, restored to a 'right' relationship with God and 'righteous'; because if we confess our sins 'the blood of Jesus his Son purifies us from all sin' *(1 John 1:7, 9)*.

A tower is a place of safety and protection; offering shelter and defence for those feeling vulnerable. The Church should offer shelter and protection for those in need. Can you help provide care by helping your Church's outreach to the homeless? Can you give food to a food bank? Ask the Lord to show you ways you can help those in need.

We should pray prayers of protection so that people are safe in the Lord's 'strong tower.' We pray in the Lord's Prayer [246]'deliver us from evil' and so prayers of defence are an important part of our intercessions for family, friends, the world and the Church.

A tower made from ivory would be extravagant and excessive. As we have seen there was no physical tower of ivory; but this can be seen as a symbol of the rich, generous, overflowing and excessive love of God. Let us feel the love of God and be assured of His amazing love for us. Then let us be ready to share with others and talk about our faith; so more people come to experience the wonderful love and grace of the Lord, knowing His peace, protection, comfort, help and presence.

[247] Mary, *Tower of David and Tower of Ivory, pray for us.*

---

[246] Common Worship Services and Prayers for the Church of England, Church House Publishing, 2000, p.106

[247] The Walsingham Pilgrim Manual 2016, p.13

CHAPTER 12

HOUSE OF GOLD

House of Gold is the 30th title of Mary in the Litany of Our Lady, the [248]Litany of Loreto.

What does the Bible tell us about House of Gold?

The Temple built by Solomon was a House of Gold, where the people could worship God *(II Chronicles 3: 3-7)*. This was a magnificent golden building, to honour God and be a place where the people came to worship him. Much gold was used to build the Temple and this **House of Gold** must have been a splendid and amazing sight. The Holy of Holies inside Solomon's Temple, where the Ark of the Covenant was kept, was a special **House of Gold** at the heart of the golden Temple *(II Chronicles 3: 8-10)*. Everything in that house of gold was made from gold: the walls, the nails,

---

[248] Dictionary of Mary 'Behold your Mother', Catholic Book Publishing Co. New Jersey 1997, 1985, p.241

the roof and the cherubim. [249]'In that perfect space, symbolised by its cubic measure of 10 X 10 X 10 cubits, everything was of gold. There the ark, the throne of God, stood behind the veil. That was the place where God dwelt.' This was where the High Priest went once a year.

The writer to the Hebrews tells us: 'Behind the second curtain was a room called the **Most Holy Place**, which had the golden altar of incense and the gold-covered Ark of the Covenant. This Ark contained the gold jar of manna, Aaron's staff that had budded, and the stone tablets of the covenant. Above the Ark were the cherubim of the Glory, overshadowing the atonement cover.... But only the high priest entered the inner room, and that only once a year, and never without blood, which he offered for himself and for the sins the people had committed in ignorance. The Holy Spirit was showing by this that the way into the Most Holy Place had not yet been disclosed as long as the first tabernacle was still standing' *(Hebrews 9:3-8)*. The inner House of Gold had very restricted access: the only person allowed in there was the High Priest; and that was just once a year. God's presence filled the Temple and the Holy of Holies, the House of Gold, when the Ark was brought into the Temple *(II Chronicles 5:13-14)*.

When Jesus died on the Cross, the curtain in the Temple separating the Holy of Holies from the rest of the Temple, was torn in two *(Matthew 27:51)*. This is amazing as through Jesus' death on the Cross, everyone who believes in Him can draw close to God: no longer is this the privilege of the High Priest just once a year! Consequently 'we have confidence to enter the **Most Holy Place** by the blood of Jesus, by a new and living way opened for us through the curtain, that is, his body let us draw near to God with a sincere heart in full assurance of faith, having our hearts sprinkled to cleanse us from a guilty conscience and having our bodies washed with pure water' *(Hebrews 10:19-25)*. All who believe in Jesus have free and open access to the Lord's presence.

Jesus said: 'If anyone loves me, he will obey my teaching. My Father will love him, and we will come to him and make our home with him' *(John 14:23)*. How amazing that just as God used to dwell in the **House**

---

[249] House of Gold, Welcome, Nathaniel Literature Distributors, Canada, 1983, 1984, p.60

of Gold in the Temple; now He wants to make His home in our hearts and abide in us! We are being built into a spiritual house as 'you also, like living stones, are being built into a spiritual house to be a holy priesthood, offering spiritual sacrifices acceptable to God through Jesus Christ... But you are a chosen people, a royal priesthood, a holy nation, a people belonging to God, that you may declare the praises of him who called you out of darkness into his wonderful light *(I Peter 2:4-5, 9)*. As members of the Church we are 'living stones' in that house; praising and serving Jesus.

The Temple was a place where God dwelt and met with the people. Jesus dwelt in Mary's womb so God became man and could meet with people and Jesus became 'the way' for people to find God. Our bodies should be where God dwells. Paul explains this amazing truth to the Corinthians: 'Don't you know that you yourselves are God's temple and that God's Spirit lives in you?' *(I Corinthians 3: 16)*. He also writes: 'Do you not know that your body is a temple of the Holy Spirit, who is in you, whom you have received from God? You are not your own, you were bought at a price. Therefore honour God with your body' *(I Corinthians 6:19-20)*. 'The price' was the precious blood of Jesus as 'the blood of Jesus, his Son, purifies us from all sin' *(I John 1:7)*.

Haggai prophesies that the new Temple will be a place of peace: "... And in this place I will grant peace,' declares the Lord Almighty'" *(Haggai 2:9)*. Jesus says: 'Peace I leave with you; my peace I give you. I do not give to you as the world gives. Do not let your hearts be troubled and do not be afraid' *(John 14:6)*.

We can look forward to heaven and being in that golden city, the Holy City, the New Jerusalem. John tells us: 'I saw the Holy City, the new Jerusalem, coming down out of heaven from God, prepared as a bride beautifully dressed for her husband... The wall was made of jasper, and the city of pure **gold**, as pure as glass. The foundations of the city walls were decorated with every kind of precious stone... The street of the city was of pure gold, like transparent glass' *(Revelation 21:2,15-19a,21)*. What a wonderful future we can look forward to in Heaven. That golden place in the continual close presence of Jesus; with our departed loved ones who have gone before us.

How can Mary be described as House of Gold?

Margaret Barker writes about this title: [250] 'In the *Litany of Loreto*... preceding her title 'Ark of the Covenant' is 'House of gold', *domus aurea*, which in the language of the temple, indicates the holy of holies. In the book of Revelation, the Lady was identified as the holy of holies and as the true Jerusalem. St John saw 'the Bride of the Lamb', 'the holy city of Jerusalem coming down out of heaven' *(Revelation 21:9-10)* and what he saw was a huge holy of holies, a golden cube *(Revelation 21:16)* .... In a way that seems strange to us, these images of the temple identified the Lady with her city / sanctuary.' This reflection supports our addressing Mary as **House of Gold**.

[251] Professor Michael Ogunu writes: 'House of Gold: This is an ancient biblical symbol related to the temple of God in **Jerusalem, which God Himself commanded to be covered with gold so that it would be worthy to be His dwelling place on earth** *(I Kings 6:22)*. So, too, the altar and many of the furnishings were of gold *(1 Kings 7:48-50)*. Mary was the temple of God; her womb "housed" the Lord. She is the "House of Gold." The title denotes Mary's personal perfection and her privilege of divine motherhood. She was the house wherein God dwelt during nine months in her womb, and for his sake she was a house of gold, adorned by the Creator with the most precious virtues.' He explains that, because Mary was the Mother of Jesus and because of her virtues; she should be given this title.

St John Henry Newman writes: [252]'Mary is the "Domus Aurea," the House of Gold. Why is she called a House? And why is she called Golden? Gold is the most beautiful, the most valuable, of all metals.... Therefore it is that Mary too is called golden; because her graces, her virtues, her innocence, her purity, are of that transcendent brilliancy and dazzling

---

[250] The Images of Mary in the Litany of Loreto, Margaret Barker, Usus Antiquior, Vol 1, No. 2, July 2010, p. 126-127

[251] http://www.christendom-awake.org/pages/litany-of-loreto/litany+ogunu+article+2. htm 8th June 2017

[252] http://www.cardinaljohnhenrynewman.com/the-virgin-mary-house-of-gold-cardinal-newman/ 1st July 2017

perfection, so costly, so exquisite, that the angels cannot, so to say, keep their eyes off her any more than we could help gazing upon any great work of gold. But observe further, she is a golden house, or, I will rather say, a golden palace…. Our Lord, the Co-equal Son of God, once dwelt in her. He was her Guest; nay, more than a guest, for a guest comes into a house as well as leaves it. But our Lord was actually born in this holy house. He took His flesh and His blood from this house, from the flesh, from the veins of Mary. Rightly then was she made to be of pure gold, because she was to give of that gold to form the body of the Son of God. She was golden in her conception, golden in her birth. She went through the fire of her suffering like gold in the furnace, and when she ascended on high, she was…. *Standing next to the King in a vesture of gold.'* St John Henry Newman recognises that as the Mother of Jesus and because of her qualities; Mary should be given this title **House of Gold**. In the hymn [253]*Hail, Queen of the heavens, hail Mistress of earth;* we remember the gold of Mary in heaven: *Set next to the King in **a vesture of gold**.*

Rev Richard Klaver explains about how he recognises Mary as **House of Gold**. [254]'The wonders of grace filling the true *Domus Aurea,* the living "House of Gold," are always turned to our benefit. "Know you not that your members are the temple of the Holy Ghost," *(I Corinthians 6:19)* asked St. Paul of the Catholics in Corinth. If such can be said of the followers of Christ, what can we say of she *(sic)* who carried Him within her body? If the Golden Temple of Solomon, an inanimate object, was a fitting "house" for the Lord, how much more fitting was His *living* "house," the Mother who would bear Him, hold Him, nurse Him, carry Him, and give Him that maternal love that all Infants need so much… Our Lady is the Golden Temple of the Blessed Trinity, or the House of Gold, placed among men as a symbol of God's bounty. For in her the Divine Word became incarnate and dwelt among us as an effusion of the eternal light and the source of eternal life, and a revelation of the eternal wisdom of

---

[253] Universalis App, Universalis publishing, 1996-2019, Birthday of BM, Vespers, Office Hymn

[254] http://www.catholictradition.org/Mary/house-gold.htm, Fr. Richard Klaver, *The Litany of Loreto,* 1954 July 1st 2017

God through the maternal activity of Mary, the Mother of God.' Thus Klaver sees Mary as God's house, because she 'housed' Jesus in her womb for nine months; deserving this title.

What does this mean for us?

We are being built into a spiritual house *(I Peter 2:4-5,9)*. As members of the Church we are 'living stones' in that house. Are you an active 'living stone', playing your part in the building up of the Body of Christ? Ask the Lord to show you the projects and activities He is calling you to be actively involved with. Be ready to share your faith; so the 'spiritual house' is built up with more 'living stones' added. The Holy Place is open to all believers in Jesus who now have free and open access to the **House of Gold**; because Jesus opened up the way through His death on the Cross *(Matthew 27:51)*.

How can you 'spur one another on towards love and good deeds' *(Hebrews 10:19-25)*? Let us keep meeting together and encouraging one another. Our bodies are 'temples of the Holy Spirit' *(I Corinthians 6: 19-20)*. 'The price' was the precious blood of Jesus as 'the blood of Jesus, his Son, purifies us from all sin' *(I John 1:7)*. We need to repent and grow in holiness. What do you need to repent of?

Jesus said: 'If anyone loves me, he will obey my teaching. My Father will love him, and we will come to him and make our home with him' *(John 14:23)*. How wonderful that just as God used to dwell in the **House of Gold** in the Temple; now He wants to abide in us! We can grow to know the Lord more as He is with us and in us. We know the Lord's closeness in a special way when we receive Holy Communion, because we receive Jesus sacramentally. In the [255]*Prayer of Humble Access* we pray:

We do not presume to come to this your table, merciful Lord, trusting in our own righteousness, but in your manifold and great mercies. We are not worthy so much as to gather up the crumbs under your table. But you are the same Lord whose nature is always to have mercy. Grant us therefore, gracious

---

[255] Common Worship Services and Prayers for the Church of England, Church House Publishing, 2000, p. 181

*Lord, so to eat the flesh of your dear Son Jesus Christ and to drink his blood, that our sinful bodies may be made clean by his body and our souls washed through his most precious blood, and **that we may evermore dwell in him, and he in us.** Amen.*

The Temple was a place where God dwelt and met with the people. Jesus dwelt in Mary's womb so God became man and could meet with people and Jesus became 'the way' for people to find God. The Lord wants us to meet with Him and grow in a living relationship with Jesus. 'Don't you know that you yourselves are God's temple and that God's Spirit lives in you?' *(I Corinthians 3:16)*. Like the early disciples we can be 'filled with the Holy Spirit' *(Acts 2:4)*. Just as God's presence filled the Temple of Solomon, *(II Chronicles 5: 14)* so we can be filled with the Holy Spirit! Haggai prophesied that the new Temple will be a place of peace: *(Haggai 2:9)*. If you lack peace then come afresh to Jesus, *(John 14:6)* meeting Jesus where you are and receiving His peace. I write more about peace in Chapter 28, the 50th title of Mary **Queen of Peace**. We can pray again: [256]*O come to my heart Lord Jesus, there is room in my heart for thee.*

What a wonderful future we can look forward to in heaven *(Revelation 21)*, that golden place in the continual close presence of Jesus; with our departed loved ones who have gone before us. We are challenged: [257]'Will you be there too? Will you go with us when He comes to bring His own into His **House of Gold**? How tremendous, to be on the journey there! You may come along. You are welcome!'

Here is a prayer to come to Jesus and to give us assurance we are God's children and on our way to heaven. [258]*Lord Jesus Christ, I am sorry for the things I have done wrong in my life. ..... Please forgive me. I now turn from everything that I know is wrong. Thank you that you died on the cross for me so that I could be forgiven and set free. Thank you that you offer me forgiveness*

---

[256] The New English Hymnal, The Canterbury Press, Norwich, 1987, p. 461, hymn 465 chorus, Emily Elliott 1836-1897

[257] House of Gold, Welcome, Nathaniel Literature Distributors, Canada, 1983, 1984, p.62

[258] Why Jesus? Nicky Gumbel, Kingsway Publications Ltd, 2013, p.18

and the gift of your Spirit. I now receive that gift. Please come into my life by your Holy Spirit to be with me forever. Thank you, Lord Jesus. Amen

A Collect reminds us about how we should be a holy **temple:** [259] *O Almighty God, who hast built thy Church upon the foundation of the apostles and prophets, Jesus Christ himself being the head cornerstone: grant us so to be joined together in unity of spirit by their doctrine, that we may be made a* **holy temple** *acceptable unto thee.' Amen.*

[260] Mary, *House of Gold, pray for us.*

---

[259] Op. cit., p. 515, Collect for Simon and Jude
[260] The Walsingham Pilgrim Manual 2016, p.13

CHAPTER 13

ARK OF THE COVENANT

In this chapter I will discuss the 31st title in the [261]Litany of Loreto, '**Ark of the Covenant**'.

What does the Bible tell us about the Ark of the Covenant?

The Ark of the Covenant was a special box, made by the Israelites on their journey to the Promised Land after leaving Egypt with Moses. In the Old Testament in Exodus God gives specific and clear instructions about the Ark. *(Exodus 25: 10-16)*. It was 'a chest of acacia wood', covered inside and out with gold and the exact measurements were 'two and a half cubits long, a cubit and a half wide and a cubit and a half high'. The Lord gave Bezalel the skill and ability to make the Ark and he was chosen to construct it *(Exodus 35:30, 37:1-9)*. God wrote the words of the 10 Commandments,

---

[261] Dictionary of Mary 'Behold your Mother', Catholic Book Publishing Co. New Jersey 1997, 1985, p.241

which were 'the words of the covenant' on two stone tablets *(Exodus 34)* and these were put in the Ark inside a special tent called 'the tabernacle'. There Moses met with God and instructed people.

Fr Peter[262] tells us: 'The presence of those tablets embodied the covenant love of God for his people. In fact, the Ark's presence among the people of Israel came to symbolize God's presence itself.' The Ark carried God's word and also some manna – the miraculous food that God gave the Israelites in the desert. It was a place where God met with His people and spoke to them. [263] 'The Ark of the Covenant was covered within and without with gold. God is so great that even the heaven of heavens cannot contain Him, yet in condescending love, He placed His throne here.'

The Hebrew word for the Ark is [264] אָרוֹן *aron* meaning 'an ark or chest' and בְּרִית *berith* meaning 'Covenant', which is a promise or an agreement: the Israelites were to keep God's laws and then God would continue to be with them to help and protect them. The stone tablets where the Law was written were kept in the Ark. The Ark was in the Holy of Holies in the Tabernacle and was where God met with Moses.

When Joshua led the people into the Promised Land, the Ark of the Covenant led the way *(Joshua 3:17)*. The Ark led the people into the battle of Jericho *(Joshua 6)* and into other battles for their land. When David was King, the Ark was brought into Jerusalem with much celebration and rejoicing *(II Samuel 6)*. King Solomon built the Temple in Jerusalem and the priests 'brought up the ark of the LORD and the Tent of Meeting' *(I Kings 8; II Chron 5:2-10)* when the Temple was dedicated. The Ark was placed in a special area of the Temple called 'the most holy place' *(1 Kings 8:6 AV)* and only the High Priest went in there once a year *(Hebrews 9:6-7)*. The Ark showed the people that God was dwelling with them.

The Israelites, however, did not keep God's laws and Commandments. Much later in 586 BC, when the Babylonians besieged Jerusalem and the city fell, at the time of Jeremiah, the Ark was hidden or destroyed and was

---

[262] Walsingham Review December 2010 'Do you know what the Ark is?' Fr Peter Anthony

[263] House of Gold, Welcome, Nathaniel Literature Distributors, Canada, 1983, 1984, p.53

[264] Analytical Concordance to the Holy Bible, Robert Young, United Society for Christian Literature, Lutterworth Press London, 1973 p. 49 and p. 207

not seen again. Scott Hahn[265] refers to the Jewish tradition recorded in II Maccabees *(New English Bible)*, which tells us that Jeremiah took 'the tent, the ark, and the incense-altar' *(II Maccabees 2:5)* into a cave on 'the mountain from the top of which Moses saw God's Promised Land' *(II Maccabees 2:4)*. I was interested to discover that this was Mount Nebo in Moab. 'Go up into the Abarim Range to Mount Nebo in Moab, across from Jericho' *(Deuteronomy 32:49a)*. [266]Mount Nebo is across the River Jordan from Jericho. Jeremiah 'then blocked up the entrance' and he reprimanded people who tried to find the cave, saying 'the place shall remain unknown until God finally gathers his people together and shows mercy to them' *(II Maccabees 2:6-8)*. That is where the Ark is hidden.

There was much lamentation and sadness that the Ark had gone. Fr Peter writes that the 'people longed for the days when the Ark assured them of God's presence and protection.' The Temple was rebuilt at the time of Ezra, but it no longer contained the Ark of the Covenant with the tablets of stone, given to Moses by God. The Commandments were written on scrolls and kept in the Most Holy Place of the Temple.

Brant Pitre writes about the absence of the Ark of the Covenant in the Temple at the time of Jesus. [267]'King Herod and his successors had spent much of their time and money transforming the second Temple into one of the wonders of the ancient world... But the second Temple also had many problems, not least of which was the fact that the Holy of Holies was *empty*, the Ark of the Covenant having been lost since the destruction of Jerusalem centuries before. As Josephus tells us, during the first century A.D., inside the Holy of Holies was "nothing at all".'

It is interesting that today in Jewish Synagogues the Rabbis still keep the Torah Scrolls in a special cupboard called 'The Ark', to remember back to the original Ark of the Covenant.

---

[265] Hail, Holy Queen, Scott Hahn Darton. Longman + Todd London 2001, reprinted 2010 p.51-52

[266] Oxford Bible Atlas, Ed Herbert G. May, London, Oxford University Press, 1962, p. 69

[267] Jesus and the Jewish Roots of the Eucharist, Brant Pitre, Image, New York, 2016, p. 37, (War 5:219)

In the New Testament we discover that the Ark of the Covenant is a woman, as we read: 'Then the temple of God was opened in heaven, and the ark of His covenant was seen in His temple. And there were lightnings, noises, thunderings, an earthquake, and great hail. Now a great sign appeared in heaven: a woman clothed with the sun, with the moon under her feet, and on her head a crown of twelve stars. Then being with child, she cried out in labour and in pain to give birth' *(Revelation 11:19-12:2)*.

How can Mary be described as 'Ark of the Covenant'?

In the 4th century Ambrose saw this woman in Revelation as Mary[268]'because she is the mother of the Church, for she brought forth Him who is the Head of the Church'. Ambrose thought this woman is Mary who is the **Ark of the Covenant**. Margaret Barker writes agreeing with this. [269]'In the *Akathistos Hymn* Mary is addressed with titles that show she has restored the true temple... In the *Litany of Loreto*, the restoration is summarised by Mary's title 'Ark of the Covenant' which appeared again in the temple when the Lady returned to the holy of holies' *(Revelation 11:19-12:1)*.

[270]'The Ark of the Covenant *(Exodus 26:33, 40:20)* points to Mary in a variety of ways, as set forth by Saint Ambrose: 'The **Ark** contained the Tablets of the Law; Mary contained in her womb the Heir of the Testament. The Ark bore the Law; Mary bore the Gospel. The Ark made the voice of God heard; Mary gave us the very Word of God. The Ark shone forth with the purest gold; Mary shone forth both inwardly and outwardly with the splendour of virginity."

---

[268] Hail, Holy Queen, Scott Hahn Darton. Longman + Todd London 2001, reprinted 2010, p. 65

[269] The Images of Mary in the Litany of Loreto, Margaret Barker, Usus Antiquior, Vol 1, No. 2, July 2010, p. 126

[270] Dictionary of Mary 'Behold your Mother', Catholic Book Publishing Co. New Jersey 1997, 1985, p.307

Scott Hahn explains [271]'Mary's body contained the Word of God enfleshed. If the first ark contained miraculous bread from heaven, Mary's body contained the very Bread of Life that conquers death for ever.' Jesus said: 'I am the bread that came down from heaven' *(John 6:41)*. Fr Peter clarifies that: [272]'Referring to Mary as the **Ark of the New Covenant** isn't over-enthusiastic piety, but rather a beautiful biblical truth found at the heart of the gospels. Just as the Old Ark contained the assurance of God's presence and the signs of his covenant love, so the womb of Mary would contain a new assurance of the abiding presence of God with his people – her Divine Son Jesus.' Thus, we can recognise Mary as Ark of the Covenant because she carried Jesus, who is 'the Word made flesh' *(John 1:14)* in her womb.

Jeffrey John[273] said that just as the presence of God was over the Ark in the Temple, so, because of Mary's obedience, she became the **Ark of the New Covenant**, as the new dwelling place of the physical presence of God was within her womb. Mary is therefore the new Ark of the new Covenant. John's Gospel tells us that Jesus is 'the Word' *(John 1:1)* and that 'the Word became flesh and made his dwelling among us' *(John 1:14)*. The Ark of the Covenant originally contained and carried God's word written on tablets of stone, while the womb of Mary was the Ark of the New Covenant, because Jesus who is the Word made flesh, was carried in her womb.

At the Annunciation the Angel Gabriel told Mary 'thou shalt conceive in thy womb, and bring forth a son, and shalt call his name Jesus. He shall be great, and shall be called the Son of the Highest' *(Luke 1:31-32 AV)*. At the Visitation, when Mary visited Elizabeth, Elizabeth was amazed that 'the mother of my Lord should come to me' *(Luke 1:43 AV)* and she said the words that we say in the 'Hail Mary': 'Blessed art thou among women, and blessed is the fruit of thy womb' *(Luke 1:42 AV)*. The events of the Annunciation and the Visitation closely parallel when David brought the

[271] Hail, Holy Queen, Scott Hahn Darton. Longman + Todd London 2001, reprinted 2010, p. 61

[272] Walsingham Review, December 2010, 'Do you know what the Ark is?' Fr Peter Anthony, p. 10

[273] Talk at St Alban's Cathedral, March 5th 2011, 'Mary in the New Testament', Jeffrey John

Ark into Jerusalem in II Samuel 6. Hahn[274] sees that this points to Mary as the new Ark: 'Luke's language seems to echo the account, in the second book of Samuel, of David's travels as he brought the Ark of the Covenant to Jerusalem.' David *(II Samuel 6:2)* and Mary *(Luke 1:39)* 'arose and went'. On their journeys they both went to the hill country of Judah. David feels unworthy to receive the ark *(II Samuel 6:9)* just as Elizabeth echoes his words asking 'Why is this granted me, that the mother of my Lord should come to me?' *(Luke 1:43)*. David danced before the Ark *(II Samuel 6:14, 16)* while the baby leapt in Elizabeth's womb as Mary, the new Ark, approached. The Ark *(II Samuel 6:11)* and Mary *(Luke 1:56)* remained in the hill country for three months. Scott Hahn comments[275]: 'Was Luke, in his quiet way, showing Mary to be the ark of the new covenant? The evidence is too strong to explain credibly in any other way.' This is a biblical argument for Mary's having the title **Ark of the Covenant**.

Michael Rear clarifies: [276]'The Ark contained the Word of God in stone, but the womb of Mary contained the Word made flesh. Mary is the **Ark of the New Covenant**. She is covered with purest gold within and without because she is sinless, pure and incorruptible. We explore more about Mary's purity in Chapter 26: **Queen conceived without original sin**.

The **Rosary** has Bible verses that are used to support the belief in the Assumption of Mary and Mary's being the new **Ark of the Covenant**. [277]The Fourth Glorious Mystery of the Rosary is The Assumption of Mary. Two verses about Mary's being the Ark of the Covenant are included here. 'Arise, O Lord, and come to your resting place, you and the ark of your might' *(Psalm 132:8)*. The Ark of the Covenant is seen in heaven and so this supports the belief that Mary was taken up into heaven: 'Then God's temple in heaven was opened, and within his temple was seen the ark of his

---

[274] Hail, Holy Queen, Scott Hahn Darton. Longman + Todd London 2001, reprinted 2010 p. 64

[275] Hail, Holy Queen, Scott Hahn Darton. Longman + Todd London 2001, reprinted 2010 p. 65

[276] Walsingham Pilgrims and Pilgrimage: Michael Rear, Gracewing, 2019, p. 87

[277] The New Rosary In Scripture, Edward Sri, Charis Servant Books, Cincinnati, Ohio, 2003, p. 173

covenant' *(Revelation 11:19a)*. Then: 'A great and wondrous sign appeared in heaven: a woman clothed with the sun' *(Revelation 12:1a)*. When praying and reflecting on this Mystery of the Rosary we imagine Mary as the new **Ark of the Covenant** in Heaven.

The hymn [278]*I'll sing a hymn to Mary* addresses Mary as "The **ark** of God's own promise".

Michael Rear refers to a homily attributed to St Athanasius of Alexandria where Mary is addressed as Ark of the Covenant: [279]'… To whom among all creatures shall I compare you, O Virgin? You are greater than them all O **Ark of the Covenant**, clothed with purity instead of gold! You are the Ark in which is found the golden vessel containing the true manna, that is, the flesh in which Divinity resides.'

Our Lady is given the title '**Ark of the Covenant**' because she carried God's Word made flesh in her womb: Jesus who was to announce the New Covenant. Jesus was born, lived, died and rose again to bring us into the New Covenant.

What does this mean for us?

Mary the Mother of Jesus is seen as a 'type' of the Church. So as Our Lady is given the title 'Ark of the New Covenant' this has great significance for every member of the Church. The curtain in the Temple separating the Most Holy Place from the Holy Place in the Temple in Jerusalem 'was torn in two from top to bottom' *(Mt 27:51)* when Jesus died on the cross, because through Jesus' death He opened up a new way for us to know God and experience His peace and love. Through Jesus' birth, life and death we can receive forgiveness and come to know the Lord, 'by a new and living way opened for us through the curtain, that is his body' *(Hebrews 10:20)*.

At the Last Supper Jesus told the disciples: 'this cup is the new covenant in my blood, which is poured out for you' *(Luke 22:20)*. We can then enjoy

---

[278] Walsingham Pilgrim Manual, 2016, page 108-9, hymn number 20, verse 3, John Wyse 1825- 1898

[279] Walsingham Pilgrims and Pilgrimage: Michael Rear, Gracewing, 2019, p. 88

the New Covenant when the Lord puts his laws in our hearts and on our minds and we **know** Him. Jeremiah *(Jeremiah 31:31-34)* prophesied about the time of this new covenant, when people would **know** the Lord. Hebrews tells us: 'This is the new covenant I will make with my people on that day, says the Lord: I will put my laws in their **hearts** so they will understand them, and I will write them on their minds so they will obey them' *(Hebrews 10:16 NLT)*. God's laws are in our hearts – so we <u>want</u> to follow them, rather than being written on stone. Fr Peter writes: [280]'We participate in that great mystery through baptism, when we are made one with Jesus. Through baptism, every human **heart** becomes an **Ark** for God.'

This is an amazing thought! Just as long ago God's word was written on tablets of stone and put in a box, and at the incarnation Jesus the living Word was in Mary's womb; now we can know Jesus living in our **hearts**, so our **hearts** become **Arks** knowing the peace and presence of Jesus! Jesus told his disciples: 'If anyone loves me, he will obey my teaching. My Father will love him, and we will come to him and make our home with him' *(John 14:23)*. We sing: [281] *O come to my heart, Lord Jesus; there is room in my heart for thee.*

Jesus used the picture of the vine to show that we need to abide and remain in Him, saying 'Remain in me and I will remain in you' *(John 15:4)*. Jesus gave us a wonderful way to help us 'remain in him' as He said: 'Whoever eats my flesh and drinks my blood **remains** in me and I in him.' *(John 6: 54)* When we receive the bread and wine at Communion we are receiving the 'body of Christ' and 'the blood of Christ', so we can **know** the Lord more nearly and deeply in our lives. When we receive Holy Communion, we grow into a closer relationship with the Lord and know His presence and closeness with us. We receive Jesus afresh sacramentally and know Jesus is living in our heart. We can reflect on the amazing fact that our hearts are now **Arks** of the Lord's presence.

Paul wrote about this wonderful truth to the Ephesians, praying that the Holy Spirit would strengthen them 'so that Christ may dwell in your

---

[280] Walsingham Review, December 2010, 'Do you know what the Ark is?' Fr Peter Anthony, p. 10

[281] The New English Hymnal, The Canterbury Press, Norwich, 1987, p. 461, hymn 465 chorus, Emily Elliott 1836-1897

hearts through faith' *(Ephesians 3: 17)*. He told the Colossians the amazing mystery, 'which is Christ **in** you, the hope of glory' *(Colossians 1:27)*. St Paul understood about our hearts' being the new **ark** as he wrote to the Corinthians: 'Clearly, you are a letter from Christ prepared by us. It is written not with pen and ink, but with the Spirit of the living God. It is carved not on stone, but on human hearts' *(II Corinthians. 3:3 NLT)*. God's word is on and in our hearts.

The film *Raiders of the lost Ark* is a story about searching for the Ark. If the writers of the film script had read II Maccabees' telling us where Jeremiah hid the Ark, then they would have written a different story! Fr Peter encourages us that [282]'if you want to locate the Ark of the Covenant … you don't need to rush off with Indiana Jones… You just have to look into your own **heart** and find Christ alive in you. And once you've found him, let others know.' This is really significant, encouraging us to share this wonderful good news, that we can know Jesus walking and talking to us each day, because *He lives within my heart.*

The Old **Ark** was carried and Our Lady carried Jesus in her womb. We are called to <u>carry</u> the peace and presence of Jesus in our hearts, and then to carry and share this good news of the love of Jesus with other people, so they come to know Him too. Scott Hahn sees that Mary represents the Church [283]'which labours to give birth to believers in every age.' This is once more the calling to be a missionary congregation, reaching out to people who do not yet believe and helping them on their spiritual journey to know the Lord. Whom is the Lord calling you to pray for and witness to at this time?

Let our **hearts** be **Arks** so we know the peace and presence of Jesus in our hearts and carry and share the good news of the love of Jesus with other people.

[284] *Mary, Ark of the Covenant, pray for us.*

---

[282] Walsingham Review, December 2010, 'Do you know what the Ark is?' Fr Peter Anthony, p. 10

[283] Hail, Holy Queen, Scott Hahn, Darton. Longman + Todd London 2001, reprinted 2010 p. 55

[284] The Walsingham Pilgrim Manual 2016, p.13

CHAPTER 14

GATE OF HEAVEN

Gate of Heaven is the 32nd title of Mary in the Litany of Our Lady, the [285]Litany of Loreto. A gate is the way into a place. 'Gate' is defined as an [286]'opening in a wall of a city, enclosure or large building, made for entrance and exit and capable of being closed with a barrier.'

What does the Bible tell us about Gate of Heaven?

The '**gate of heaven**' is first mentioned in the Bible when Jacob had a dream, when he was travelling to his Uncle Laban. This is the Hebrew word [287] שַׁעַר *sha'ar*, meaning gate. 'When Jacob awoke from his sleep, he thought, "Surely the LORD is in this place, and I was not aware of it." He

---

[285] Dictionary of Mary 'Behold your Mother', Catholic Book Publishing Co. New Jersey 1997, 1985, p.241

[286] The Concise Oxford Dictionary, Oxford University Press, 1985, p. 408

[287] Analytical Concordance to the Holy Bible, Robert Young, United Society for Christian Literature, Lutterworth Press London, 1973, p.382

was afraid and said, "How awesome is this place! This is none other than the house of God; this is the **gate of heaven**'" *(Genesis 28: 12-17)*. Jacob saw the angels and heard God speak clearly to him, affirming His Covenant with Jacob; he realised he had been very close to God and surely at the gate of heaven.

John records his Revelation, which includes a description of the **gates of heaven**. Here the New Testament Greek word is [288]*pulōn* πύλων, meaning 'gate' or 'gateway'. John writes that an angel 'carried me away in the Spirit to a mountain great and high, and showed me the Holy City, Jerusalem, coming down out of heaven from God.... It had a great, high wall with **twelve gates**, and with twelve angels at the gates. On the gates were written the names of the twelve tribes of Israel. There were three gates on the east, three on the north, three on the south and three on the west... The twelve gates were twelve pearls, each gate made of a single pearl... On no day will its gates ever be shut, for there will be no night there.... "Blessed are those who wash their robes, that they may have the right to the tree of life and may go through the gates into the city"'. *(Revelation 21:10-13,21-25; 22:14)* This is a wonderful description showing the beautiful gates in heaven are always open *(21:21)*. How wonderful for those 'who wash their robes' *(22:14)* and are welcomed through the **gate of heaven** because they have been cleansed in the blood of the Lamb.

Jesus told His followers that He is the way to Heaven; He said: 'I am the way and the truth and the life. No one comes to the Father except through me' *(John 14:6)*. Earlier Jesus called Himself the 'gate'. This is the New Testament Greek word [289]*thura* θυρα, also translated 'door'. Jesus said, '**I am the gate** for the sheep... I am the gate, whoever enters through me will be saved' *(John 10:7,9)*. Through faith in Jesus we are saved and receive the assurance of forgiveness and eternal life in heaven. St Paul explains: 'Therefore, since we have been justified through faith, we have peace with God through our Lord Jesus Christ through whom we have

---

[288] Analytical Concordance to the Holy Bible, Robert Young, United Society for Christian Literature, Lutterworth Press London, 1973, p.383

[289] Analytical Concordance to the Holy Bible, Robert Young, United Society for Christian Literature, Lutterworth Press London, 1973, p.269

gained access by faith into this grace in which we now stand' *(Romans 5:1-2).* We now have access to God through Jesus and the assurance that we will enter through the gate of heaven to be with the Lord for ever. Jesus told Martha "'I am the resurrection and the life. He who believes in me will live, even though he dies; and whoever lives and believes in me will never die. Do you believe this?'" *(John 11:25).*

Jesus is the Way and **Gate of Heaven** and we are all invited to come to Jesus. Jesus tells us: 'Enter through the **narrow gate**. For wide is the gate and broad is the road that leads to destruction, and many enter through it. But small is the gate and narrow the road that leads to life, and only a few find it' *(Matthew 7:13-14).* Let us enter through that 'narrow gate' *(pulē πύλή)* meaning [290]'gate or wing of a double gate'.

Ezekiel had a vision of Jerusalem when he was an exile in Babylon: he saw the new Temple with the **gates** *(Ezekiel 40:1-43:27).* The **east gate** remained shut *(Ezekiel 44:1-3).* [291]A Bible commentary suggests the permanently locked door symbolises the permanence of God's presence in the Temple, and the special holiness attributed to God's private entrance. We will discover later that Marian theologians have a different interpretation of this passage.

The word 'gate' is used many times in the Bible and I will now move to more times in the New Testament when we read the word **gate**. The book of Hebrews tells us: 'And so Jesus also suffered outside the **city gate** *(πύλή) (Hebrews 13:12).* The brutal and horrific crucifixions happened outside the city. We give thanks for the wonderful love of Jesus in dying on the Cross so we can be forgiven and receive eternal life.

The word πύλή is used for 'the **temple gate** called Beautiful', where the lame man was healed *(Acts 3:1-10).* That Gate was a place of healing and salvation for that lame man, where he entered into the joy of believing and following Jesus. The **city gate** *(πύλή)* was a gateway to freedom for Peter when the angel rescued him from prison *(Acts 12:10).*

[290] Analytical Concordance to the Holy Bible, Robert Young, United Society for Christian Literature, Lutterworth Press London, 1973, p.383

[291] The Oxford Bible Commentary, ed by John Barton and John Muddiman, Oxford University Press, 2001, p. 561

Jesus tells the parable of the rich man who had a gate *(πύλή)* to his house where Lazarus lay *(Luke 16:20)*. When each of them dies, Lazarus is welcomed through the **gate of heaven**, but the rich man is in hell. Through our faith and the good works that God leads us to do; may we be welcomed into the **gate of heaven**. 'For we are God's workmanship, created in Christ Jesus to do good works, which God prepared in advance for us to do' *(Ephesians 3:10)*.

Jesus stands at the door of our lives (θυρα) and knocks. 'Here I am! I stand at the door and knock. If anyone hears my voice and opens the door, I will come in and eat with him, and he with me' *(Revelation 3:20)*. Holman Hunt's painting[292] is a very powerful image of this verse.

There is no handle on the outside of the door; as it is each person's individual choice to 'open the door' and ask Jesus into their lives. This painting has helped many people on Alpha, Confirmation and Baptism Preparation Courses that I have led. Many people have responded to this invitation and asked Jesus to come into their lives; realising that Jesus died

---

[292] roaringwaterjournal.com/2017/02/05/the-first-viral-sensation-how-a-pre-raphaelite-painting-inspired-a-generation/ 28th June 2021

on the Cross so they can be forgiven and wanting to come into a personal relationship with God through Jesus.

When we open this door, we enter through the 'gate of heaven' and have the assurance of God's presence and help in our lives now; as well as knowing we will go to heaven, through the **Gate of Heaven** when our life here is ended.

How wonderful that Jesus' death on the Cross unlocked the gate of heaven and let us in! [293] *He only could unlock the gate of heaven and let us in.*

How can Mary be described as Gate of Heaven?

The Bible verses from Ezekiel 44:1-3 that I referred to above are used by Marian theologians to explain how Mary can be given the title Gate of Heaven; as they apply these verses to Mary. They recognise that Mary's womb was the 'gateway' and she became the way through which Jesus entered the world, and became man; this therefore entitles Mary to be addressed as **Gate of Heaven**.

The hymn [294]*I'll sing a hymn to Mary* addresses Mary as *The gate of Heav'n to me.*

[295]Professor Michael Ogunu writes about Mary's title **Gate of Heaven**: 'This refers to the fact that Jesus passed through the womb of Mary. So, Mary is like the Gate of Heaven that gives us the Messiah and the King of all. Mary is thus called the Gate of Heaven, because it was through her that our Lord passed from heaven to earth. The Prophet Ezekiel, prophesying of Mary, says, "This gate shall be shut. It shall not be opened and no man shall pass through it: because the Lord the God of Israel hath entered in by it. And it shall be shut for the Prince. The Prince Himself shall sit in

---

[293] The New English Hymnal, Melody, The Canterbury Press, Norwich, 16th Impression, 2004, p. 155, number 92, verse 4, Mrs C.F. Alexander 1818- 1895

[294] Walsingham Pilgrim Manual, 2016, page 108-9, hymn number 20 verse 3, John Wyse 1825-98

[295] http://www.christendom-awake.org/pages/litany-of-loreto/litany+ogunu+article+2. htm 8th June 2017

it…" *(Ezekiel 44:2-3).*' Thus, Mary is seen to be **Gate of Heaven** because she gave birth to Jesus. She was the 'gateway' for God to become man and draw people to know God.

Fr. Juan Velez tells us about St John Henry Newman's understanding of how Mary can be addressed as **Gate of Heaven**, which is similar to the idea of Ogunu, with more detail. [296]'Blessed John Henry Newman tells us that the title *Gate of Heaven* is given to Mary because "it was through her that our Lord passed from heaven to earth." The title alludes to a prophecy about Mary by Ezekiel: "the gate shall be closed; it shall not be opened, and no man shall pass through it." Six or so decades after Newman wrote this, the Virgin Mary, Gate of Heaven, appeared on May 13 in Fatima to open our eyes and ears to heaven. Newman urges us to imitate the example of the Virgin Mary's response to the Angel Gabriel; like her "we must be obedient, and pure in our minds."'

Margaret Barker writes: [297]'In the *Litany of Loreto*, Mary is the Door of Heaven, *ianua Coeli*, which may refer to Bethel, the Gate of Heaven where Jacob saw the ladder up to heaven and the Lord upon it… In the *Akathistos Hymn*, Mary is… the 'Heavenly Ladder by which God came down'. This refers to the time when Jacob saw the ladder and the gate of heaven in his dream *(Genesis 28:12-17).* If we think of Mary as a 'ladder' and a 'door'; we see these are more images that help us to recognise her as **Gate of Heaven**.

Therefore we can recognise that Mary's womb was the 'gateway' and that she became the way through which Jesus entered the world, and became man, and then through His death on the Cross Jesus opened up the way for everyone to come to know God. This therefore entitles Mary to be addressed as **Gate of Heaven**.

[296] http://www.cardinaljohnhenrynewman.com/mary-gate-of-heaven-cardinal-newman/ 4th July 2017

[297] The Images of Mary in the Litany of Loreto, Margaret Barker, Usus Antiquior, Vol 1, No. 2, July 2010, p. 128-129

What does this mean for us?

We have read "'Blessed are those who wash their robes, that they may have the right to the tree of life and may go through the gates into the city" *(Revelation 22:14)*. How wonderful for those 'who wash their robes' *(22:14)* and our welcomed through the gates of heaven because they have been cleansed in the blood of the Lamb. We need to confess our sins to God and turn from them in repentance. Then 'the blood of Jesus, his Son, purifies us from all sin.' *(I John 1:7)* Let us be in that great number who are welcomed through the **gate of heaven** because our sins have been washed away and we are clothed in white robes. Do you need to say 'sorry' to God and repent of anything?

Jesus says to you: 'Here I am! I stand at the door and knock. If anyone hears my voice and opens the door, I will come in and eat with him, and he with me' *(Revelation 3:20)*. Have you opened the door and asked Jesus to come into your life? When leading Alpha Courses and doing baptism and confirmation preparation as a Reader and Licensed Lay Minister, it has been a great joy to lead people to the Lord with the prayer below. This is a prayer to pray so we can enter through the narrow gate of Salvation *(Matthew 7:13-14, John 10:7,9)* and then have the assurance that we are one of God's children and on our way to heaven to enter through the **Gate of Heaven.**

[298]*Lord Jesus Christ, I am sorry for the things I have done wrong in my life... Please forgive me. I now turn from everything that I know is wrong. Thank you that you died on the cross for me so that I could be forgiven and set free. Thank you that you offer me forgiveness and the gift of your Spirit. I now receive that gift. Please come into my life by your Holy Spirit to be with me forever. Thank you, Lord Jesus. Amen*

---

[298] Why Jesus? Nicky Gumbel, Kingsway Publications Ltd, 2013, p.18

We have this framed writing: *'The house of God. The gate of Heaven'* *(Genesis 18:19).* This is displayed in our home because we want our home to be a 'gate of heaven'; a place where people feel and know the love of Jesus, know the presence of the Holy Spirit and come closer to Jesus. Is your home a 'gate of heaven'? Do you share your faith, pray, encourage people to know the love of Jesus in their lives?

The Church should be a **Gate of Heaven** for people; where people encounter Christ through the welcome, word, sacraments, liturgy and the worship. Churches should be the **Gate of Heaven** where everyone meets with Jesus and receives His love. The words over the Chancel Arch in the Church at St Peter's Speightstown, Barbados, reminds about this, as we see: 'This is none other than the House of God and this is the Gate of Heaven Allelujah'. Is your Church a **Gate of Heaven** for the congregation and visitors? Do you go to church to go through the **gate of heaven** and meet with Jesus?

In her book [299] *Within the Gates*, Rebecca Springer gives a very moving account of a 'remarkable vision of paradise'. She had a near-death experience when she passed through the **Gate of Heaven** *(John 14:2-3)*. There is a moving scene of the recently dead being welcomed into heaven by people who knew them *(pp 58-59)*. If you would like to imagine more about Heaven then I recommend this book.

Through our faith and the good works that God leads us to do; may we be welcomed into the **gate of heaven**; like Lazarus *(Luke 16:19-31)*. 'For we are God's workmanship, created in Christ Jesus to do good works, which God prepared in advance for us to do' *(Ephesians 3:10)*. What 'good works' is God calling you to do at this time?

[300]Mary, *Gate of heaven, pray for us.*

[299] Within the Gates, Rebecca Springer, Christ for the Nations, Dallas, Texas, 1984
[300] The Walsingham Pilgrim Manual 2016, p.13

CHAPTER 15

MORNING STAR

'**Morning Star**' is the 33rd title of Mary in the Litany of Our Lady, the [301]Litany of Loreto.

What does the Bible tell us about 'Morning Star'?

There are just five Bible verses that tell us about the **morning star**, when the Hebrew in the original text is [302] כּוֹכָב *kokab* and the New Testament Greek word is *aster* ἀστήρ meaning 'star, luminous meteor'; except in II Peter 1:19 when *phosphorus* φωσφόρος meaning 'light bearer, morning star' is used. The Lord said to Job: 'Where were you when I laid the earth's foundation... while the **morning stars** sang together and all the angels shouted for joy?' *(Job 38:4-7)*. Lucifer had been honoured in heaven as

---

[301] Dictionary of Mary 'Behold your Mother', Catholic Book Publishing Co. New Jersey 1997, 1985, p.241

[302] Analytical Concordance to the Holy Bible, Robert Young, United Society for Christian Literature, Lutterworth Press London, 1973, p.932

'**morning star**, son of the dawn' *(Isaiah 14:12)*, but this former angel rebelled against God and was cast out of heaven *(Revelation 12:7-8)*.

In the New Testament Peter writes: 'And we have the word of the prophets made more certain, and you will do well to pay attention to it, as to a light shining in a dark place, until the day dawns and the **morning star** rises in your hearts' *(II Peter 1:19)*. It is interesting to reflect that: [303]'The light provided by the prophetic message is vital but only partial... Eventually however the eschatological age will arrive and bring complete light because the knowledge of God is in view.' We can come to know God now through Jesus who is the **Morning Star**. Jesus gave the Revelation to John to encourage the Church to be faithful in witness to the nations. "I, Jesus, have sent my angel to give you this testimony for the churches. I am the Root and the Offspring of David, and the bright **Morning Star**" *(Revelation 22:16)*. The Lord will give the Morning Star, who is Jesus, to those who overcome. 'To him who overcomes and does my will to the end, I will give authority over the nations- ... I will also give him the **morning star**' *(Revelation 2:26-29)*. Those who keep close to Jesus will be given the **Morning Star**. It is significant that it is [304]'the brightest of stars, the morning star that accompanies the sun's rising.'

How wonderful that Jesus gives Himself the title **Morning Star** so we can know the love, light and presence of Jesus with us. St Paul prays 'that Christ may **dwell** in your hearts through faith' *(Ephesians 3:17a)*. Jesus, the **Morning Star,** can dwell in our hearts when we receive Him! A hymn praises Jesus, the Word of God who is the Morning Star:

> [305]*Almighty God, we bring You praise*
> *for Your Son, the Word of God.*
> *Morning Star, the Father's glory*
> *we now worship and adore You:*

---

[303] The Oxford Bible Commentary, edited by John Barton and John Muddiman, Oxford University Press, 2001, p.1272

[304] *Ibid* p.1305

[305] http://higherpraise.com/lyrics/love/love852920.htm 25th June 2017 © **1983 Kingsway Thankyou Music**

in our hearts Your light has risen;
Jesus, Lord, we worship you.

What does the Bible tell us about some other stars?

In the beginning God created the world and 'He also made the stars' *(Genesis 1:16b)*. There are many other references to stars, so I will refer to some significant stars here in our reflections on **Morning Star**. After Abraham was tested in being prepared to sacrifice his son, Isaac, God said: 'I will surely bless you and make your descendants as numerous as the stars in the sky' *(Genesis 22:17a)*. The stars then became a symbol of the Jewish people. Joseph's dream had 'the sun and moon and eleven stars bowing down' *(Genesis 37:9-10)* to him; which Isaac interpreted as his parents and eleven brothers bowing down to him. Here the eleven stars represented the tribes of Israel. This dream came true later in Egypt *(Genesis 43:26)*. Moses told the people 'The LORD your God has increased your numbers so that today you are as many as the stars in the sky' *(Deuteronomy 1:10)*, fulfilling God's promise to Abraham. Psalm 148 proclaims praise: 'Praise the LORD.... praise him, all you shining stars' *(v. 1,3)*. When Nehemiah was organising the re-building of the wall of Jerusalem 'we continued the work with half the men holding spears, from the first light of dawn till the stars came out' *(Nehemiah 4:21)*. They started work at dawn, when the **morning star** was seen.

A star guided the Wise Men to find baby Jesus *(Matthew 2:9)*; as Margaret Barker tells us: [306]'The *Book of the Cave of Treasures* says that the magi saw a brilliant star in which was a virgin carrying a child, and the child wore a crown... as the magi saw the star 'in the east', that is, at its rising, this would have been a Morning Star' *(Matthew 2:2)*. The morning star led the magi to find Jesus who is the **Morning Star.**

In his revelation John saw one like a Son of Man with seven stars in his right hand *(Revelation 1:16)*. 'The seven stars are the angels of the

---

[306] The Images of Mary in the Litany of Loreto, Margaret Barker, Usus Antiquior, Vol 1, No. 2, July 2010, p. 114

seven churches' *(Revelation 1:20)*. Messages are then written to the angels of the seven churches. Stars are now seen to represent the Church. Later: 'A great and wondrous sign appeared in heaven: a woman clothed with the sun, with the moon under her feet and a crown of twelve stars on her head. She was pregnant and cried out in pain as she was about to give birth… She gave birth to a son, a male child, who will rule all the nations with an iron sceptre' *(Revelation 12:1-2, 5a)*. This woman is recognised by some as Mary. Others see [307]'Jesus' mother Mary is scarcely in view in the symbolic, not historical, account of his birth…; rather, as her crown of twelve stars shows, the woman in the sky is the people of God, both Israel and the Church.' However, Edward Sri [308]writes: 'the woman in Revelation 12 should be understood as *both* an individual (Mary) *and* a symbol for the People of God'.

Then how can Mary be described as 'Morning Star'?

Fr Canice writes: [309] 'Mary is the Star that arose out of Jacob whose rays illumine the whole universe. And the star is placed over the spacious sea of this world, shining by its merits and giving light by its examples.' Fr Canice develops the imagery of the stars representing Israel to apply to Mary the name of the brightest star, because of her world-wide influence in the Church.

Professor Michael Ogunu writes: [310] '**Morning Star:** This is the star which precedes the rising of the Sun just as Mary preceded the coming of the Son of God. And just as the Morning Star precedes the sun, announcing the dawn of day, so the Blessed Virgin Mary preceded Christ

[307] The Oxford Bible Commentary, edited by John Barton and John Muddiman, Oxford University Press, 2001, p.1296

[308] The New Rosary In Scripture: Edward Sri, Charis Servant Books, Cincinnati, Ohio, 2003, p. 223

[309] Mary: A Study of the Mother of God, Fr Canice O.F.M.Cap, M.H.Gill and Sons Ltd, Dublin, 1950, p.229

[310] http://www.christendom-awake.org/pages/litany-of-loreto/litany+ogunu+article+2.htm 8th June 2017

the Son of Justice, announcing the day of salvation. Through Her coming, the whole world was enlightened. Mary was truly the bright Morning Star of that blissful day when the world saw the divine sun of its redemption arise upon it.' This is an explanation of how Mary can be seen as Morning Star, because she preceded Jesus, the light of God coming into the world.

St John Henry Newman writes: [311]'It is Mary's prerogative to be the *Morning Star*, which heralds in the sun. She does not shine for herself, or from herself, but she is the reflection of her and our Redeemer, and she glorifies Him. Mary is the "*Stella Matutina*," the Morning Star—after the Dark Night, but always Heralding the Sun.' Newman explains that, just as heavenly bodies that are planets reflect the light of the sun, so the **Morning Star** can be seen as a perfect title for Mary because she shines with reflected glory from Jesus, rather than shining for herself. Art shows Mary as **Morning Star**, and she is often depicted with a crown of twelve stars *(Revelation 12:1)*.

[312] 'But the most common "Star" figure, which all the spiritual writers have used, is "Star of the Sea," the guide to man who is sailing on the sea of life. 'She is called Mary, which name signifies Star of the Sea, for as sailors steer their ship to port by watching the stars, so Christians are brought to glory by the intercession of Mary. This is Dante's thought: "If thou follow but thy star, thou canst not miss at last a glorious haven."' Reflections about Mary as Star of the Sea show the intercession, guidance and direction of Mary as the **Morning Star** who lights our way.

The example of Mary's life can be inspirational to us, showing us how to live. [313] 'Mary is the noble Star rising from the house of Jacob, whose rays illuminate the whole world. ... Let us follow her. If we want to see this Morning Star rising, we must imitate the ten Virtues of the Virgin Mary. For just as a star once led the three wise men to Jesus, so will this **Morning**

---

[311] http://www.cardinaljohnhenrynewman.com/mary-the-morning-star-cardinal-newman/ 18th June 2017

[312] http://www.salvemariaregina.info/SalveMariaRegina/SMR-169/Star.htm 18th June 2017

[313] http://www.thedivinemercy.org/news/Mary-the-Morning-Star-Who-Lights-Our-Way-3382 18th June 2017

Star, shining with the ten rays of these evangelical virtues, lead us to Jesus sitting at the right hand of the Father in the heavenly kingdom. Let us look at each of the 10 rays of this **Morning Star**, and see how Mary's example of virtue lights the way for us. The first is purity.... Mary's example was very important to St Maria Faustina in her struggle to become a true disciple of Christ.' The other virtues seen in Mary, like the rays of a star are prudence, humility, faith, devotion to God by spending more time in prayer and worship, obedience, realising our need of God, showing mercy and charity to those in need and turning to God in our sorrows.

St Ignatius reflects: [314]"A **star** shone forth in heaven brighter than all the stars; its light was indescribable and its strangeness caused amazement.'" This star, the **Morning Star,** shone physically for the Wise Men to follow and it can be seen as Mary as well as Jesus.

The Church of England Lectionary connects Mary's title **Morning Star** to the belief in her Immaculate Conception, which I explore in Chapter 26: **Queen conceived without original sin**. [315] 'As a result of our study, the Commission offers the following agreements, which we believe significantly advance our consensus regarding Mary. We affirm together.... that in view of her vocation to be the Mother of the Holy One, Christ's redeeming work reached 'back' in Mary to the depths of her being and to her earliest beginnings... In the night of the Advent expectation, Mary began to shine like a true Stella Matutina. For just as the Morning Star, together with the Dawn, precedes the rising of the Sun, so Mary from the time of her Immaculate Conception preceded the coming of the Saviour, the Sun of Righteousness.' This is interesting as we see Mary's Immaculate Conception preceded the coming of Jesus; just as the Morning Star precedes the coming of the Sun. This title **Morning Star** helps to explain the doctrine of the Immaculate Conception.

---

[314] *Silence, A Christian History:* Diarmaid MacCulloch, Penguin, 2014, p.50

[315] Order for the Eucharist and for Morning and Evening Prayer in the Church of England 2017, Tufton Books, p. xxxiv

The hymn [316]*Mary immaculate, **star of the morning***, addresses Mary by this title.

The hymn [317]*I'll sing a hymn to Mary* calls Mary **Morning Star**:

> *When troubles dark afflict me in sorrow and in care,*
> *Thy light doth ever guide me O beauteous **Morning Star**.*

This hymn reminds us that through her prayers, Mary gave guidance, help and protection to people who asked her to pray for them when they were in times of sorrow and danger. People then felt the light of Jesus shine on the darkness of their difficult situations.

What does this mean for us?

The Lord will give the Morning Star, who is Jesus, to those who overcome. 'To him who overcomes and does my will to the end.... I will also give him the **morning star**' *(Revelation 2:26-29)*. Those who keep close to Jesus will be given Jesus, the **Morning Star**. It is significant that this is the brightest of stars that shines when the sun rises. How wonderful that Jesus gives Himself the title **Morning Star** so we can know the love, light and presence of Jesus with us.

Jesus calls us to be lights in the world. Jesus said: 'You are the light of the world... Let your light shine before men, that they may see your good deeds and praise your Father in heaven' *(Matthew 5:14-16)*. What are your 'good deeds' that people see?

Let us keep following Jesus and be 'overcomers' in difficult situations as we allow Jesus, the Morning Star to guide us. We do not need to be overwhelmed by darkness, depression and difficulties, but rather look to Jesus to shine His light into our hearts. Jesus said 'I am the light of the world' *(John 9:5)*. We need to let the light of Jesus shine in our hearts and

---

[316] Celebration Hymns for Everyone, McCrimmons, Great Wakering, Essex, England, 1994, hymn number 483, F.W. Weatherell 1829-1903

[317] Walsingham Pilgrim Manual, 2016, page 108-9, hymn number 20 verse 4, John Wyse 1825-1898

lives and follow Jesus who is the light. John tells us: 'if we walk in the light, as he is in the light, we have fellowship with one another, and the blood of Jesus, his Son, purifies us from all sin' *(I John 1:7)*. Let us say sorry to God for our sins, failings and mistakes; receiving cleansing and forgiveness; in this way, we continue to live in the light.

At our Baptism we are given the light of Christ from the Paschal Candle and the priest says: [318]'You have received the light of Christ; walk in this light all the days of your life.' Just as the Olympic flame is passed on, so the light of Christ is given to the newly baptised. In the Baptism Service everyone tells the newly baptised: 'Shine as a light in the world to the glory of God the Father.' How can you be a 'light' in your home? How can you be a 'light' in your Church? How can you be a 'light' in the world?

The star guided the wise men giving them light and direction *(Matthew 2:9)*. If you need direction and guidance, then may the light of Jesus, the **Morning Star**, guide you making the way clear before you. We pray words from an Epiphany hymn:

[319]*As with gladness, men of old*
did the guiding star behold;
as with joy they hailed its light
leading onward, beaming bright;
so, most gracious God, may we
evermore be led to Thee.

We can seek to develop the ten virtues of Mary listed above, which are seen to be represented by the ten rays of the **Morning Star**. We can follow the example of Mary's life so that our lives shine more with the love of Jesus. Mary reflected the light of Jesus in her life. We should do this, too, by growing in these ten 'virtues': purity, prudence, humility, faith, devotion to God by spending more time in prayer and worship, obedience,

---

[318] Common Worship, Services and Prayers for the Church of England, Christian Initiation, Church House Publishing, 2006, p. 77
[319] The New English Hymnal, The Canterbury Press, Norwich, 1987, p. 50, hymn 47, v. 1, W. Chatterton Dix 1837- 1898

realising our need of God, showing mercy and charity to those in need and turning to God in our sorrows. Then our lives will become increasingly filled with the light of Christ and we will be like a star shining brightly, bringing joy to others.

St Paul tells us to shine like stars by being cheerful. He tells us to stop complaining. How easy it is to join in complaining, negative and cynical conversations. St Paul tells us to be different and: 'Do everything without complaining or arguing, so that you may become blameless and pure, children of God without fault in a crooked and depraved generation, in which you shine like **stars** in the universe' *(Philippians 2:14)*. Let us try to be cheerful and positive in our conversations so we shine like stars. Can you shine like a star in your conversations at work, at home and at Church?

The hymn *Shine Jesus Shine*, by Graham Kendrick, reminds us about the light and love of Christ and how Jesus shines.[320]

> *Lord, the light of Your love is shining,*
> *in the midst of the darkness, shining:*
> *Jesus, Light of the world, shine upon us...*
> *shine on me, shine on me!*
>
> *Shine, Jesus, shine,*
> *fill this land with the Father's glory;*
> *blaze, Spirit, blaze,*
> *set our hearts on fire.*

Let us be open to receive the love and light of Jesus, who is **Morning Star**, the brightest star. Then let us be channels of that light and love to other people.

[321] *Mary, Morning Star, pray for us.*

---

[320] Celebration Hymnal for Everyone, McCrimmons, Essex, England, 1994, hymn number 388, Graham Kendrick 1950 -

[321] The Walsingham Pilgrim Manual 2016, p.13

CHAPTER 16

HEALTH OF THE SICK

In the [322]Litany of Loreto the 34th title of Mary is **Health of the Sick.**

What does the Bible tell us about 'Health of the Sick'?

The Old Testament tells us about the healing love and power of God. After the crossing of the Red Sea, God said: "If you listen carefully to the voice of the LORD your God and do what is right in his eyes…. I will not bring on you any of the diseases I brought on the Egyptians, for **I am the LORD, who heals you**" *(Exodus 15:26)*. The Lord revealed that He wants to protect and heal His people.

The Psalms tell us about the healing love of the Lord 'who forgives all your sins and heals all your diseases' *(Psalm 103:3)*. 'He heals the broken-hearted and binds up their wounds' *(Psalm 147: 3)*, giving emotional

---

[322] Dictionary of Mary 'Behold your Mother', Catholic Book Publishing Co. New Jersey 1997, 1985, p.241

and physical healing. If we 'fear the Lord' and try to live to please the Lord: 'This will bring health to your body and nourishment to your bones' *(Proverbs 3:8)*. Isaiah prophesies about how Jesus' death on the cross will achieve our forgiveness and healing, as 'he was pierced for our transgressions, he was crushed for our iniquities; the punishment that brought us peace was upon him, and by his wounds we are healed' *(Isaiah 53:5)*.

The New Testament tells us much about the wonderful healing ministry of Jesus. The Gospels contain many accounts of Jesus' healing the sick, the blind, the lame, lepers and all who came to Him. Jesus shows the compassion and love of God in healing the sick. [323]'Jesus comes into the midst of the world and heals *with his hands*. There are numerous stories to document this part of Jesus' ministry, so that we have no excuse to miss the important point: in touching people's lives with power and feeling, Jesus healed them by God's love. Whether blind or lame, leper or paralytic, Jesus embraced their physical condition totally and without limit.' Jesus showed God's love and compassion in healing the sick.

In the Synagogue at Nazareth, Jesus read verses from the scroll of the Prophet Isaiah *(Isaiah 61:1-2)* "The Spirit of the Lord is on me..." *(Luke 4:18-19)*. On that Sabbath day Jesus claimed to be the fulfilment of this prophecy in Isaiah, proclaiming his manifesto at the beginning of his ministry. How marvellous that Jesus came to bring freedom and healing in proclaiming 'good news' to the poor. At the beginning of his ministry at Capernaum, Jesus healed the man with an evil spirit in the synagogue *(Mark 1:21-27)*; Simon's mother-in-law *(Mark 1:30-31)*; and in the evening 'Jesus healed many who had various diseases' *(Mark 1:32-34)*. 'One day as he was teaching... the power of the Lord was present for him to heal the sick' *(Luke 5:17)*. Jesus then healed the paralytic who had been brought to the house by friends who carried him on his mat and then lowered him through the roof' *(Luke 5:20-25)*. The man received forgiveness and physical healing: he was set free and made whole.

---

[323] Time to heal: A Contribution towards the Ministry of Healing, Report to the House of Bishops, Church House Publishing, 2000, p. 19

'Jesus went through all the towns and villages, teaching in their synagogues, preaching the good news of the kingdom and healing <u>every</u> disease and sickness' *(Matthew 9:35)*. This showed God's love. Jesus healed the sick woman who had suffered from bleeding for many years *(Mark 5:25-34)*. Jesus said to her: "Daughter, your faith has healed you. Go in peace and be freed from your suffering" *(Mark 5:34)*. Jesus healed the elderly crippled woman in the synagogue *(Luke 13:10-17)*. How wonderful for that woman, that after eighteen long years of suffering, she was free from pain.

Jesus healed men with the dreaded skin disease leprosy *(Luke 5:12-15)*. Here we see the compassion and love of Jesus reaching out to <u>touch</u> the leper and make him clean; giving him wholeness and healing. Later Jesus healed ten lepers *(Luke 17:11-19)*; only one of them came back to thank Jesus *(vv 17-19)*. This is a reminder for us to remember to give thanks to the Lord when he answers prayers.

Jesus healed the blind. He healed blind Bartimaeus who was begging by the road near Jericho *(Mark 10:47-52)*. How marvellous that Bartimaeus was healed and then he followed Jesus. In Jerusalem there was a man who had been born blind *(John 9:3-7)*. How amazing that Jesus 'the light of the world' gave light and healing to that man. Later 'the man said, "Lord, I believe," and he worshipped him' *(John 9:38)*. The man received physical and spiritual sight and came to believe and worship Jesus.

Jesus healed children. The miracle of Jairus's daughter is amazing as she was restored to life and healed *(Luke 8:40-41,49-56)*. The Roman official asked Jesus to heal his son *(John 4:50-53)*. Jesus showed God's love to these children and their families, by restoring the sick children to health.

Jesus healed all these suffering men, women and children, and he healed many more. John wrote near the end of his Gospel: 'Jesus did many other miraculous signs in the presence of his disciples, which are not recorded in this book. But these are written that you may believe that Jesus is the Christ, the Son of God, and that by believing you may have life in his name' *(John 20:30-31)*. Jesus' healing miracles show us God's love and power and help us to believe that Jesus is the Son of God. It is good to read through the Gospels in the Bible and discover all the recorded healings of Jesus. How amazing that he healed many more people who are not recorded.

Jesus told his disciples to 'Heal the sick, raise the dead, cleanse those who have leprosy, drive out demons. Freely you have received, freely give' *(Matthew 10:8)*. When Jesus sent out the seventy-two he told them: 'Heal the sick' *(Luke 10:8-9)*. Jesus later said of his followers: 'they will place their hands on sick people and they will get well' *(Mark 16:18)*. This is why we have the Church's ministry of laying-on hands and praying for the sick. Jesus' healing ministry continues today in the Church. [324]'The mission of the Church, therefore, is nothing less than to continue Jesus' own mission, the proclamation of the kingdom, the good news that suffering may end, that health may be freely given.' James writes, 'Is any one of you sick? He should call the elders of the church to pray over him and anoint him with oil in the name of the Lord' *(James 5:14)*. That is why priests anoint the sick and pray for their healing. We can all pray for the sick in the Intercessions at a Church service and in our own prayers at home.

Jesus showed God's love in healing the sick; the Early Church continued Jesus' loving healing ministry that we can read about in Acts. Jesus said, 'I tell you the truth, anyone who has faith in me will do what I have been doing. He will do even greater things than these, because I am going to the Father' *(John 14:12)*.

After the healing of the lame man, Peter said: 'By faith in the name of Jesus, this man whom you see and know was made strong. It is Jesus' name and the faith that comes through him that has given this complete healing to him, as you can all see' *(Acts 3:16)*. How wonderful that: 'The apostles performed many miraculous signs and wonders among the people' *(Acts 5:12a)*.

Jesus equips the Church to continue His ministry of healing now.

---

[324] Time to heal: A Contribution towards the Ministry of Healing, Report to the House of Bishops, Church House Publishing, 2000, p. 23

How can Mary be called 'Health of the Sick'?

There are many written records of healing miracles given by Mary after Jesus' Resurrection and Ascension. [325]Smith Lewis writes about 'the power of Marian intercession' that it 'is a frequent theme of the Six Books narratives, which extensively describe the numerous miracles worked by the Virgin in the days prior to her death... Women travelled from all over the Christian world seeking Mary's miraculous assistance... And whoever had an affliction, she healed it.' Mary was associated with healing from those early days of the Church. However, the healings were from Jesus as Mary was just an intercessor and she would have felt the same as Peter after the healing of the lame man that Jesus has given the healing. We can think of Mary as **'Health of the Sick'** because she prays for us, and Jesus in His love brings healing.

Cyril Vollert has a contrasting opinion about Mary and healing. Maybe he had not read the records of healing miracles studied by Smith Lewis. Vollert writes that [326]'The working of miracles was not for her during her lifetime, because at that period the teachings of Christ was (*sic*) to be confirmed by miracles, and so it was fitting that only Christ and his disciples, who were the bearers of his doctrine should work miracles. On the basis of such sound reasoning, we should be slow to ascribe to Mary gifts of grace that are not in accord with the purpose of divine maternity or that are proper to authoritative officials of the Church.' He thinks that healing was only through the men who were the Apostles and Church leaders.

However, I do not agree with this opinion because as a mother I want my children to be free from hurt and pain. Healing is part of a mother's love as we bathe wounds, give medicines, hugs, walk rocking our teething babies and pray for our children to be healed. We can see that Mary as a Mother can be described as **'Health of the Sick'** because like any mother she wants her children to be well and happy.

---

[325] MARY The Complete Resource, edited by Sarah Jane Boss, Oxford University Press 2007, quotes Smith Lewis 1902 p.33-4, p.136

[326] A Theology of Mary: Cyril Vollert SJ, Herder and Herder, 1965, p. 205

Mary can be described as **'Health of the Sick'** because there are many examples of people who prayed to Mary and received healing through her intercession to Jesus. [327]'In the 'Miracles of Our Lady of Chartres' we read of a Lady of Audignecourt who is cured of a skin disease by praying to the Virgin.' It is important that we glorify Jesus for these healings and remember that Mary has prayed to Jesus for them. We can thank Mary for praying; as we would thank any friend for praying for us.

Pope Innocent VIII was glad for the intercessions of Our Lady when he was in great pain and distress. Here is an account of the recovery of Pope Innocent VIII: [328]'One of the most miraculous and worthy of mention is the cure of his Holiness Pope Innocent VIII. This Pope had been lying ill for a long time in great agony and the doctors could not in any way appease his sufferings. Already he had given up all hope and was awaiting death from hour to hour, when there came to visit him the Cardinal Protector of the Servite Order, John Micheli, who began to narrate to him the marvellous favours granted by the Santissima Annunziata at Florence to her devout servants. The Cardinal then encouraged the Pope to trust in Mary, who is truly called 'health of the sick' and to ask her to deliver him from his painful malady. When Innocent heard this he felt in his heart a lively trust in the protection of our blessed Lady. He vowed to dedicate himself especially to her service, if she could be pleased to free him from his grievous sufferings. How great was the amazement of the doctors and the joy when, after a short time Innocent was found to be perfectly cured. Full of gratitude for this unexpected deliverance he ordered a skilled artist to depict the tragic scene of his mortal illness and he sent this painting to Florence in testimony of the grace granted to him.' The Alpha Course[329] tells the story of the healing of Pope Innocent as an example of God's healing people through the prayers of the Church in the past, but it does not mention Mary.

Walsingham in Norfolk, England, is a place of healing where people think of Mary as **Health of the Sick**. This is explored more in Chapter 30:

---

[327] Boss, op. cit., p.399, quoting p.120

[328] Mary Health of the Sick website information, October 28th 2016

[329] The Alpha Course, DVD Talks, Session 9, Niki Gumbel, 2003

Our Lady of Walsingham. [330]'In 1061 according to tradition' the Virgin Mary appeared in a vision to Lady Richeldis de Faverche at Walsingham asking her 'to build a replica of Mary's house in Nazareth, the house where Gabriel appeared to Mary.' *The Pynson Ballad* records that Richeldis was *'a noble widow'*. [331]'The Ballad goes on to tell of the miraculous building of the house, by angels, beside a pair of wells in a location chosen by Mary herself... Records indicate that Walsingham rapidly acquired huge popularity as a place of pilgrimage. As England's Nazareth' many pilgrims including monarchs came.

> [332]*The Pynson Ballad* tells us:
> *'Many sick been here cured by our Lady's might*
> *Dead again revived of this is no doubt*
> *Lame made whole and blind restored to sight*
> *Deaf wound and lunatic that hither have fought*
> *And also lepers here recovered have be*
> *By our Lady's grace of their infirmity.'*

Walsingham continues to be a place where pilgrims seeking healing come to the daily services of sprinkling with water from the holy well; and to the healing services with anointing and laying-on of hands on Tuesday and Saturday evenings. The daily Shrine Prayers for healing include the prayer requests written by pilgrims for those in need of healing. It is important to emphasise that at Walsingham Mary points us to Jesus. We ask for Mary to pray for us in the 'Hail Mary', but our prayers for healing are addressed to God. The prayer for the sick is a prayer to God: [333] *'Father, your Son Jesus Christ brought healing in body and soul to those who turned to him in faith. Hear our prayers for all the sick: restore them to health and*

---

[330] The Shrine of Our Lady of Walsingham booklet, Jarrold Publishing and Guardians of the Shrine of Walsingham 2002, p.2

[331] Ibid., p.2

[332] A transcription of the "Pynson Ballad", Manuscript 1254/6 The Pepys Library Magdalene College Cambridge

[333] The Walsingham Pilgrim Manual 2016, p.49

strength, comfort them with the presence of your Holy Spirit, and lead them to
know and do your will. We ask this through Christ our Lord. Amen.

When focussing on this title, Mary **Health of the Sick**, it is paramount
that the healings happen because Jesus loves the sick and brings His
healing love and power to them. Mary's role is as an Intercessor. She does
not heal but prays for the sick.

Lourdes in France is another place where the Virgin Mary appeared,
this time to [334]'the peasant girl Bernadette Soubirous, a poverty-stricken,
pure-hearted adolescent, who saw a vision of a 'Beautiful Lady' near her
home town of Lourdes in 1858.' The healing water at Lourdes is where
many pilgrims have visited and continue to visit to receive healing. They
recognise Mary there as **'Health of the Sick'** because they ask her to pray
to Jesus to bring them healing. The healing waters at Lourdes are a special
place where Mary wanted people to experience and receive the healing
love of Jesus.

Andrea Dahlberg tells us more about the healing ministry at Lourdes
from her study of three English Pilgrimages to Lourdes in the 1980s. She
writes: [335]'The shrine at Lourdes centres upon its healing spring and is
particularly associated with prayer for the sick… The focus of devotion at
Lourdes is care for those who are suffering illness or injury, and prayer for
physical healing… The cult of a healing spring is founded upon the belief
that divine power may work through material things.'

The Sacraments of the Church show that God's power does work
through material things. The bread and wine at Communion become
the body and blood of Christ. The oil used for anointing brings the
healing love and power of Jesus to the sick. The holy water at Lourdes
and Walsingham can bring healing to the sick when Mary is **'Health of**
the Sick' because she is interceding for those sick people asking Jesus to
heal them.

We can picture Mary as a Mother wanting her children to be well,
happy, healed and loved. Sometimes when people feel really ill, even as

---

[334] Writing on the case of the Video 'The Song of Bernadette'

[335] MARY The Complete Resource, edited by Sarah Jane Boss, Oxford University Press
2007, p. 232

adults they long for their mother to be with them and help them. Mary in her role as 'Health of the Sick' can be a comfort to people when they feel poorly. Scott Hahn appreciates Mary's motherly role, writing [336]'Mary then is a mother to the family of God', and can be seen as a mother wanting the sick to be healed.'

What does this mean for us?

We should pray for the sick. I have written prayer lists that I use, praying for some people every day and others twice a week. We pray for the sick at Church services. We can ask Mary to pray for the sick and be encouraged by the examples about how Jesus heard and answered Mary's prayers leading to her title **'Health of the Sick'**. We can pray and ask Jesus to heal the sick remembering that Jesus said: "Ask and it will be given to you" *(Matthew 7:7)*. We ask Jesus to bring His healing love and power to the sick. How wonderful that we pray to God the Father, in the name of Jesus in the power of the Holy Spirit. 'Let us then approach the throne of grace with confidence, so that we may receive mercy and find grace to help us in our time of need' *(Hebrews 4:16)*.

Read through the Gospels in the Bible where there are so many recorded accounts of Jesus' healing the sick. Enjoy reading the Book of Acts where Jesus' followers prayed for the sick and they were healed. Rejoice that so many people received the healing love of Jesus.

Be encouraged that God heals today! Can you write a list of the sick known to you and pray regularly for their healing?

Do you need to receive prayer for healing? You can ask friends and family to pray for you. Also you can ask at Church for prayer with laying-on of hands for healing and ask the Priest to pray and anoint you with the holy oil for the sick that is blessed by the Bishop every Holy Week at the Cathedral.

Let us ask **Mary Health of the Sick** to pray for us:

---

[336] Hail, Holy Queen: Scott Hahn, Darton, Longman and Todd Ltd, London 2010 p.142

[337]*O Mary, recall the solemn moment when Jesus, your divine Son, dying on the cross, confided us to your maternal care. You are our mother: we desire ever to remain your devout children. Let us therefore feel the effects of your powerful intercession with Jesus Christ. Make your name again glorious in this place, once renowned throughout our land by your visits, favours and many miracles. Pray, O holy Mother of God, for the conversion of England, **restoration of the sick**, consolation for the afflicted, repentance of sinners, peace to the departed. O blessed Mary, Mother of God, our Lady of Walsingham, intercede for us. Amen.*

[338] Mary, *Health of the sick, pray for us.*

---

[337] Walsingham Pilgrim Manual, 2016, p. 75

[338] Ibid., p.13

CHAPTER 17

REFUGE OF SINNERS

'**Refuge of sinners**' is the 35th title of Mary in the [339]Litany of Loreto. A **refuge** is [340] a 'shelter or protection from danger or trouble; a place of safety or security.' A **sinner** [341]'one who sins, a transgressor against divine law'.

What does the Bible tells us about 'Refuge of sinners'?

The phrase **'Refuge of sinners'** is not in the Bible. However, the Bible does tell us about sinners and refuge. The Bible tells us that 'all have sinned' *(Romans 3:22)*; we are all sinners in need of refuge. I explore sin and original sin in Chapter 26.

---

[339] Dictionary of Mary 'Behold your Mother', Catholic Book Publishing Co. New Jersey 1997, 1985, p.241

[340] The Shorter Oxford English Dictionary on Historical Principles, H.W. Fowler & J. Coulson, Clarendon Press, Oxford, 1973, p.1780

[341] Ibid., p.2003

In the Old Testament there are six [342]Hebrew words for refuge. God gave clear instructions about **Cities of Refuge**, where people accused of crimes would be safe and take refuge *(Numbers 35:9-15)*. This is מִקְלָט *miqlât*, which is 'asylum, refuge, restricted place'. These instructions are repeated, showing the importance of these cities *(Deuteronomy 19:2-11)*. This illustrates God's mercy and love in wanting there to be 'space' for the accused to be safe. Joshua followed God's instructions and arranged for the cities of refuge *(Joshua 20:1-9, 21:13,21,27,32,38)*. These cities were places of safety and refuge; giving time for the sinner to repent and make restitution while awaiting trial.

God is our refuge. This is the Hebrew מַחֲסֶה *machseh* meaning 'a refuge. A place of refuge.' 'God is our refuge and strength, an ever-present help in trouble' *(Psalm 46:1)*. We say to the Lord 'you are my strong refuge' *(Psalm 71:7)*. We proclaim: 'I will say of the LORD, 'He is my refuge and my fortress' *(Psalm 91:2)*. God is a refuge for the poor and needy *(Isaiah 25:4)*. There are other Hebrew words for refuge to show how God is our refuge. Twice in the Bible we have מָנוֹס *mânôs* meaning a 'place of flight', which David used in his Song of Praise to God: *(II Sam 22:3)* and 'you are my fortress, my refuge in times of trouble' *(Psalm 59:16b)*. A 'habitation or den' is מְעוֹנָה *me'ônâh* that was a place of safety used to say: 'The eternal God is your **refuge**' *(Deuteronomy 33:27)*. We should make God our 'habitation' or dwelling place. God is a refuge like a high place or a tower is מִשְׂגָּב *misgâb*. 'The LORD Almighty is with us; the God of Jacob is our fortress' *(Psalm 46:7&11)*. 'To take refuge' is חָסָה *châsâh* when we pray to God: 'O God, have mercy on me, for in you my soul takes refuge. I will take refuge in the shadow of your wings until the disaster has passed' *(Psalm 57:1)*. These six words for refuge all show that **God is our refuge**.

Sinners commit sins. The [343]Hebrew words include חֵטְא *chêt'* meaning 'sin, error, failure'. David prayed for cleansing from sin *(Psalm 51:7-10)*. He praises God for compassion and forgiveness, 'as far as the east is from the west, so far has he removed our transgressions from us *(Psalm 103:8-12)*.

[342] Analytical Concordance to the Holy Bible, Robert Young, United Society for Christian Literature, Lutterworth Press London, 1973, p.800
[343] Ibid., p.890

The Lord says 'Come now, let us reason together, though your sins are like scarlet, they shall be as white as snow' *(Isaiah 1:18)*. Isaiah prophesies about Jesus' suffering and death for our sins *(Isaiah 53)*. Sin separates us from God; in the Old Testament there are instructions about guilt offerings and sin offerings חַטָּאת *chaṭṭâ'th*, so people could be cleansed of sin and be close to God again *(Leviticus 4 & 5)*. The Old Testament is a long story of God's wanting His chosen people to be close to Him, while so often they sinned and separated themselves from his loving help and presence. God says 'turn from your wicked ways' *(Ezekiel 33:11)*. God sent prophets to turn the people back him, which we explore more in Chapter 23: **Queen of Prophets**. God told Ezekiel about how good it would be if the people turned back to the Lord: 'They will be my people, and I will be their God' *(Ezekiel 14:11)*. God wanted the people to follow Him and receive blessings. Moses said 'If you fully obey the LORD your God …. You will be blessed in the city and blessed in the country… You will be blessed when you come in and blessed when you go out' *(Deuteronomy 28:1,3,6)*.

Jesus is a refuge for sinners. The New Testament Greek word ἁμαρτία *hamartia* means [344] 'to miss a mark, to be in error, to sin, to be guilty of wrong'. We recognise that all have sinned. The wonderful news is that through Jesus' death on the Cross sinners can be forgiven. We realise that 'all have sinned and fall short of the glory of God, and are justified freely by his grace through the redemption that came by Christ Jesus' *(Romans 3:23-25a)*. The angel told Joseph that Jesus will 'save his people from their sins' *(Matthew 1:21b)*. John the Baptist said when he saw Jesus: 'Look, the Lamb of God who takes away the sin of the world!' *(John 1:29)*. Jesus healed and forgave the paralytic *(Mark 2:5)*.

We need to come to God to confess our sins and receive cleansing, forgiveness and peace as 'the blood of Jesus, his Son, purifies us from all sin. If we claim to be without sin, we deceive ourselves and the truth is not in us. If we confess our sins, he is faithful and just and will forgive us our sins and purify us from all unrighteousness' *(I John 1:7-9)*. Peter told the crowd on the Day of Pentecost: 'Repent and be baptised, every one of you, in the name of Jesus Christ for the forgiveness of your sins' *(Acts 2:38)*.

---

[344] Analytical Greek Lexicon, Samuel Bagster & Sons Ltd, London, 1973, p.17

Repentance means 'turning around', so we need to turn from sin. 'For the wages of sin is death, but the gift of God is eternal life in Christ Jesus our Lord' *(Romans 6:23)*. How wonderful that Jesus 'gave himself for our sins to rescue us from the present evil age' *(Galatians 1:4)*. We give thanks to God: 'For he has rescued us from the dominion of darkness and brought us into the kingdom of the Son he loves, in whom we have redemption, the forgiveness of sins *(Colossians 1:13-14)*.

The Old Testament system of sacrifices could not take away sin, 'because it is impossible for the blood of bulls and goats to take away sins' *(Hebrews 10:4)*. Only through Jesus can we receive forgiveness as 'Christ was sacrificed once to take away the sins of many people' *(Hebrews 9:28)*. Peter tells us 'He himself bore our sins in his body on the tree' *(1 Peter 2:24)*. John explains that Jesus Christ 'is the atoning sacrifice for our sins, and not only for ours but also for the sins of the whole world' *(I John 2:2)*. How amazing that Jesus Christ 'loves us and has freed us from our sins by his blood' *(Revelation 1:5b)*. We therefore see that **Jesus is a refuge for sinners** and only through His death on the Cross can we receive forgiveness, freedom and peace.

Jesus invites us to come to Him and find that He is our **refuge**. Jesus says: "Come to me, all you who are weary and burdened, and I will give you **rest**" *(Matthew 11:28-30)*. Horatius Bonar found that Jesus was his refuge and place of safety and his resting place. He wrote about that in this lovely hymn:

> [345]*I heard the voice of Jesus say, "Come unto Me and rest;*
> *Lay down, thou weary one, lay down thy head upon My breast."*
> *I came to Jesus as I was, weary and worn and sad;*
> *I found in Him a **resting place**, and He has made me glad.*

Some other Hymns remind us that **Jesus is a refuge for sinners** and encourage us to respond to Jesus' invitation that we come to him:

---

[345] *The New English Hymnal*, The Canterbury Press, Norwich, 1987, page 379, hymn 376, verse 1, Horatius Bonar 1808 - 1889

346Just as I am, without one plea,
but that thy blood was shed for me
and that thou bidst me come to thee,
O Lamb of God I come, I come.

Jesus is a refuge for sinners and a place of safety:

347Rock of Ages, cleft for me,
*let me **hide** myself in Thee;*
let the water and the blood,
from Thy wounded side which flowed,
be of sin the double cure:
save from wrath and make me pure.

We should pray to Jesus, a **refuge for sinners**:

348What a friend we have in Jesus, all our sins and griefs to bear!
What a privilege to carry everything to God in prayer!

Are we weak and heavy laden, cumbered with a load of care?
*Jesus only is **our refuge**, take it to the Lord in prayer!*

When we sing and listen to these hymns; we are reminded that **Jesus is our refuge**, a **refuge for sinners** and we can come to Jesus to receive forgiveness and peace.

Every **Church** should be a **refuge for sinners**; places where sinners can be reconciled to God and reconciled to other people through confession and receiving absolution. Church services have a prayer of confession and an absolution, which people who come to Church regularly as well as

---

346 *The New English Hymnal*, The Canterbury Press, Norwich, 1987, page 305, hymn 294, verse 1, Charlotte Elliott 1789- 1871

347 *Ibid.*, page 443, hymn 445, verse 1, Augustus Toplady 1740 - 1778

348 *Hymns Old & New*, Anglican Edition, Kevin Mayhew Ltd, Bury St Edmunds, Suffolk, 1996, hymn 541, verses 1 and 3, Joseph Medlicott Scriven 1819 - 1886

occasional visitors can benefit from. At Holy Communion we may pray this Prayer of Confession or a similar one:

[349]*Almighty God, our heavenly Father, we have sinned against you and against our neighbour in thought and word and deed, through negligence, through weakness, through our own deliberate fault. We are truly sorry and repent of all our sins. For the sake of your Son Jesus Christ, who died for us, forgive us all that is past and grant that we may serve you in newness of life to the glory of your name. Amen.*

The Priest will then give the absolution: *Almighty God, who forgives all who truly repent, have mercy upon you,* ✠ *pardon and deliver you from all your sins, confirm and strengthen you in all goodness, and keep you in life eternal; through Jesus Christ our Lord. Amen.*

Jesus gave authority to his apostles to forgive sins: 'If you forgive anyone his sins, they are forgiven; if you do not forgive them, they are not forgiven' *(John 20:23).* James asks: 'Is any one of you sick? ... If he has sinned, he will be forgiven. Therefore confess your sins to each other and pray for each other so that you may be healed *(James 5:14-16).* It is helpful to understand that the **Church is a refuge for sinners**, a place where everyone should feel welcomed and accepted; where the needy receive healing, forgiveness, acceptance and peace.

The Church should be a **refuge for sinners**, by giving everyone the same <u>welcome</u>; whatever their social or economic background. James is very clear on his teaching that we should not show favouritism and treat wealthy visitors better than the poor *(James 2:1-9).*

How can Mary be described as 'Refuge of sinners'?

Father Canice explains how we can think of Mary as Refuge of sinners because Mary prays for sinners and understands. [350]'Mary is our constant **refuge** at the hour of temptation; from her we all implore assistance and

---

[349] *Common Worship Services and Prayers for the Church of England,* Church House Publishing, 2000, p. 169-170

[350] A Study of the Mother of God, Fr Canice O.F.M.Cap, M.H.Gill and Sons Ltd, Dublin, 1950, p. 82-83

protection. Her help will be all the more authorised and efficacious if she has been similarly tempted in her lifetime… In order that her heart might be penetrated with more tender compassion, it behoved her to have known and felt the miseries she was appointed to relieve.' Fr Canice wrote that Mary is a: [351]'sovereignly devoted Protectress, an Advocate whose pleadings are always heard, a **Refuge** that is always available and always secure. In Heaven she ever intercedes for us, protects us…' Fr Canice encourages us to ask Mary to pray for us and appreciate her being a refuge of sinners.

Thomas Rooke proposes that many Old Testament passages refer to the Mother of Jesus, her life, her personality and her role in the history of salvation. He suggests that Ruth prefigures Mary as **refuge of sinners**. [352]'Ruth acted as a type or figure of our Lady… By 'type' is meant that what is done in part and imperfectly in the Old Testament is brought to fulfilment and perfection in the Gospel and forms part of the economy of salvation. So, Ruth sets out to glean the ears of corn which the reapers leave behind in order to be able to feed Naomi her mother-in-law and herself. When, in the Gospels, Jesus speaks of harvesting, He usually means gathering in souls to the kingdom of heaven. Since He speaks through the Old Testament as well as the New it is worth considering the possibility that references to the same subject in the one will have the same purpose as in the other… It seems then legitimate to read this passage as an allusion to the role played by the Mother of God in bringing into the kingdom those who escape from the hands of the reapers … The despairing can turn to her and she will raise them from the earth, gather them in her arms and present them to her Divine Son who can refuse nothing from the hands of His most beloved mother.' This explanation of a typological link between Ruth and Mary is helpful in seeing Mary as **Refuge of sinners.** Mary's love for sinners and wanting them to know her Son; connects with Ruth's concern to gather the rejected ears of corn.

---

[351] Ibid., p. 286

[352] http://catholicscot.blogspot.co.uk/2015/01/mary-refuge-of-sinners.html, 18th January 2015, 23rd July 2017

More Marian theologians write about Mary's being Refuge of Sinners. [353]'No one could have yearned for the return of sinners as much as Jesus yearns. He died on the Cross for them… He is our ultimate refuge. So when we give to Our Lady that consoling title, "**Refuge of Sinners**," we see in Her one who loves the lost sheep, as Jesus loves them. We see Her as the great intercessor with Him, as She prays for them in conformity with the Divine Will. We know that Mary has great power with Jesus, and that She loves us because God loves us, and intercedes continually that not one of us may be lost. … It is in this sense that Our Lady is the "**Refuge of Sinners**," wanting to save us, pleading with Jesus to save us, ever ready to come to our help, ever ready to cover us with Her mantle of love, a mother's love. St. John Damascene calls Mary a city of refuge to all who flee to Her.' We can recognise that Mary prays for sinners and can be a refuge for them.

St Alphonsus de Liguori tells us more about why Mary is addressed as Refuge of sinners: [354]'There are several sources for our knowledge of and devotion to Our Lady, **Refuge of Sinners**. St John Bosco was given a vision wherein it was revealed that Our Lady is the resort of sinners… St Alphonsus Liguori had a tremendous devotion to the Mother of God and … has promoted devotion to Our Lady as the hope or refuge of sinners and in his book, *The Glories of Mary*, he has … almost as a running theme within the overall theme St. Alphonsus instructs us regarding confidence in Mary as the **refuge of sinners**. Our Blessed Lady told St. Bridget that there are no sinners, however far from God's grace, from whom the devils are not forced to flee immediately when they invoke her holy name with a firm resolution to repent. And on another occasion our Lady said to her: "Just as the devils fly from sinners who invoke my name, so do the Angels come nearer."' Mary prays for sinners with love and can be seen as their refuge.

---

[353] http://www.salvemariaregina.info/SalveMariaRegina/SMR-171/Refuge.htm 23rd July 2017

[354] https://www.trinitystores.com/store/read-more/our-lady-refuge-sinners *Excerpts From The Glories of Mary; St. Alphonsus de Liguori Redemptorist Fathers, 1931 with Nihil Obstat and Imprimatur,* 23rd July 2017

What does this mean for us?

'God is our **refuge** and strength, an ever-present help in trouble' *(Psalm 46:1)*. 'The eternal God is your **refuge**' *(Deuteronomy 33:27)*, meaning a dwelling-place. God's presence can be our dwelling-place. We need to abide in Jesus and keep close to him. Does Jesus dwell in your heart? *(John 14:23)*. Does 'Christ dwell in your heart through faith'? *(Ephesians 3:17a)*. You may like to pray the *Prayer of Confession* above to confess your sins to God, remembering that Jesus is the **refuge for sinners**, ready to welcome and forgive you. Some people find it helpful to make their confession before a priest and receive absolution.

You can pray to commit your life afresh to Jesus and ask Jesus to come and live in your heart: [355] *O come to my heart Lord Jesus, there is room in my heart for thee.*

Jesus invites us to come to Him and find that He is our **refuge**. Jesus says: 'Come to me, all you who are weary and burdened, and I will give you rest' *(Matthew 11: 28-30)*. Do you feel 'weary and burdened'? Then come afresh to Jesus today. Remember that Jesus Christ 'loves us and has freed us from our sins by his blood' *(Revelation 1:5b)*.

Is your **Church** a **refuge for sinners**? Is it a place where sinners can be reconciled to God and reconciled to other people through confession and receiving absolution? Do people who come to Church regularly as well as occasional visitors benefit from the prayer of confession and receiving absolution? Do you welcome all people to your Church? Do you welcome the needy, the homeless and the hungry? Is your Church overflowing with the love and compassion of Jesus? Do people from any background receive welcome, acceptance and affirmation? Do you give a genuinely warm welcome to all who come to your Church?

Are you a **refuge for sinners** by being welcoming and accepting of all? [356] Mary, *Refuge of sinners, pray for us.*

---

[355] The New English Hymnal, The Canterbury Press, Norwich, 1987, p. 461, hymn 465 chorus, Emily Elliott 1836-1897

[356] The Walsingham Pilgrim Manual 2016, p.13

CHAPTER 18

COMFORTER OF THE AFFLICTED

'**Comforter of the Afflicted**' is the 36th title of Mary in the[357]Litany of Loreto. In the [358]Walsingham Manual this 36th title is called '**Consoler of the afflicted**'. 'Consoler' is a synonym of 'Comforter' and so I will use both of these nouns in my exploration of the title. The word 'consoler' suggests a deep emotional empathy. The New Testament Greek word is from the verb [359]παρακαλέω *parakaleō*, which means to encourage, comfort, console and solace. The 'afflicted' are those who suffer affliction, which is the New Testament Greek word [360]θλίβω *thlibō*, which means to squeeze, press, encumber, distress, afflict, with distressing circumstances, trial and affliction. In affliction people can feel squeezed and distressed

---

[357] Dictionary of Mary 'Behold your Mother', Catholic Book Publishing Co. New Jersey 1997, 1985, p.241

[358] The Walsingham Pilgrim Manual 2016, p.13

[359] Analytical Greek Lexicon, Samuel Bagster & Sons Ltd, London, p. 303

[360] Ibid., p. 195

by upsetting circumstances and trials and need to receive comfort, help and strength.

What does the Bible tell us about 'Comforter of the Afflicted'?

David asks God to help him in a time of distress and affliction: 'Look upon my affliction and my distress… rescue me' *(Psalm 25:16-20)*. David turns to God in his time of affliction, which may be [361]illness and also enduring the many attacks from his enemies.

Paul boasts about his sufferings and the afflictions that he has endured while preaching and proclaiming the Gospel as an Apostle and a servant of Christ, compared to the other Apostles: 'I have worked much harder, been in prison more frequently, been flogged more severely, and been exposed to death again and again. Five times I received from the Jews the forty lashes minus one. Three times I was beaten with rods, once I was stoned, three times I was shipwrecked, I spent a night and a day in the open sea, I have been constantly on the move. I have been in danger from rivers, in danger from bandits, in danger from my own countrymen, in danger from Gentiles; in danger in the city, in danger in the country, in danger at sea; and in danger from false brothers. I have laboured and toiled and have often gone without sleep; I have known hunger and thirst and have often gone without food; I have been cold and naked. Besides everything else, I face daily the pressure of my concern for all the churches' *(II Corinthians 11:23-28)*. This list of afflictions is almost overwhelming. We can, however, be encouraged through this that, just as God comforted, helped, consoled and strengthened Paul through all of these terrible dangers and difficulties, so the Lord will help us too, when we go through times of affliction. Paul writes about his discovery of God's grace, recording how the Lord spoke to him: 'But he said to me, "My grace is sufficient for you, for my power is made perfect in weakness"' *(II Corinthians 12:9)*. In times of suffering afflictions, Paul received God's grace, strength and help. In our times of

---

[361] Glo Computer Commentary for Psalm 25

weakness and affliction; we can also receive God's grace and strength in afflictions.

In his letter to the Romans, Paul urges them: 'Be joyful in hope, patient in affliction, faithful in prayer' *(Romans 12:12)*. Paul is thankful that God has helped him in his afflictions. He praises God who 'comforts us in all our troubles ... so that we can comfort those in any trouble with the comfort we ourselves have received from God' *(II Corinthians 1:3-4)*. This is hugely significant, as we will only have real understanding and empathy for others who are suffering affliction if we have gone through times of affliction in our lives *(II Corinthians 1:5-11)*. Paul is thankful to have suffered afflictions as he has then experienced God's consolation and help and he is able to encourage and help other people who are suffering affliction. Paul seems glad to have suffered so he can help others. He urges people to continue to pray for the afflicted. Jesus consoles and comforts us *(II Corinthians 1:5)* because he has suffered and understands *(Hebrews 4:15)*. We can pray knowing that Jesus understands all that we feel and suffer. Jesus told us that the Holy Spirit will come as our Comforter: saying: 'And I will pray the Father, and he shall give you another Comforter, that he may abide with you for ever; even the Spirit of truth ... for he dwelleth with you, and shall be in you' *(John 14:15-16 AV)*. Jesus tells us that the Holy Spirit will be with us and in us to give us comfort in our times of affliction. Paul praised God, writing: 'Praise be to the God and Father of our Lord Jesus Christ, the Father of compassion and the God of all comfort'. God the Father is 'the Father of compassion and the God of all comfort'. Thus, God the Father, the Son and the Holy Spirit give us compassion, comfort, consolation and strength in our times of affliction. 'Let us then approach the throne of grace with confidence, so that we may receive mercy and find grace to help us in our time of need' *(Hebrews 4:16)*.

In the Holy Communion Service, the priest prays: [362]'we most humbly beseech thee of thy goodness, O Lord, to comfort and succour all them, who in this transitory life are in trouble, sorrow, need, sickness, or any

---

[362] The Book of Common Prayer, Collins Sons & Co., Ltd, Glasgow, The Lord's Supper or Holy Communion, p. 168

other adversity.' This prayer of intercession includes prayers to God for those suffering and enduring affliction.

The Psalmist says: 'My comfort in my suffering is this: 'Your promise preserves my life' *(Psalm 119:50)*. We too can discover [363]'God's word is my comfort and my guide whatever my circumstances.' The Bible shows us that God is the **Comforter of the Afflicted** and we should pray asking for God's help in our times of affliction as well as praying asking God to console others in their sufferings and afflictions.

Then how can Mary be described as 'Comforter of the Afflicted'?

Mary can console and comfort people because she suffered afflictions. We can ask Mary to pray for us, knowing that she will empathise with our suffering. Some people are helped to think of Mary as a loving Mother who cares for them by praying for them with understanding when they are enduring affliction. This prayer, the *Salve Regina*, asks for Mary to be the **Comforter of the Afflicted:**

[364]*Hail, holy Queen, Mother of Mercy, our life; our sweetness and our hope! To you do we cry, poor banished children of Eve; to you do we send up our sighs, mourning and weeping in this valley of tears. Turn then, most gracious advocate, thine eyes of mercy toward us; and after this our exile show us the blessed fruit of your womb, Jesus. O clement, O loving, O sweet Virgin Mary.*

We will now reflect on some of the times of affliction in Mary's life, times of trial and distress that people can identify with when they are going through similar suffering. Mary suffered affliction and distress with the misunderstanding and rejection in her life when people realised she was expecting a baby, when Joseph 'had in mind to divorce her quietly' *(Matthew 1:19)*. After the visit from the angel, Joseph 'took Mary home as his wife' *(Matthew 1:24)*. Mary and Joseph suffered the affliction of being homeless in Bethlehem; Jesus' birth in a dirty, cold stable in Bethlehem would have been a time of trial and difficulty for Mary. Mary's baby only

---

[363] Glo Computer Bible Commentary for Psalm 119: 50

[364] Walsingham Pilgrim Manual, 2016, p. 15

had a manger, where the animals ate straw, for her precious baby to sleep *(Luke 2:7)*. At the presentation of Christ in the Temple, Simeon warned Mary that she would suffer, saying 'a sword will pierce your own soul too' *(Luke 2:35)*: as well as Jesus, she would suffer deep anguish. Mary was warned and prepared by Simeon's words to realise that she would suffer many afflictions.

Mary suffered the affliction of being a refugee in Egypt after the visit of the Wise Men. The Holy Family had to leave Bethlehem and escape to Egypt, so Jesus would be safe *(Matthew 2:13-15)*. [365] Juan Felez recognises that 'the Blessed Virgin is the comforter of the afflicted' because along with many other afflictions 'when our Lord was an Infant, she had to flee across the desert to the heathen Egypt... And she especially can console us because she suffered more than mothers in general'. Mary can be seen as **Comforter of the Afflicted** for the homeless, those who fear for the safety of their families, for refugees, asylum seekers and those suffering the distress of having to flee their homes.

What terrible suffering for Mary when she stood by the cross watching her Son die, as 'Near the cross of Jesus stood his mother' *(John 19:25)*. Mary suffered appalling sorrow watching Jesus suffering cruelty, mocking and death on the Cross. Mary can comfort the afflicted because she has suffered so much. We remember this at the twelfth *Station of the Cross* when Jesus died on the Cross. We can imagine more of Mary's affliction at the Cross through some word from one of the [366] *Office Hymns in the Walsingham Breviary for the Feast of the Compassion of Our Lady*:

> *Watching as they rudely drag Him*
> *Who can count her tears that fall?*
> *There she sees the Flesh she gave Him*
> *Bruised and torn with bitter blows,*
> *And the thorn-crown crushed upon Him*

---

[365] http://www.maryqueenofallsaints.com/MarysTitles/37ComforterOfAfflicted/
37AfflictedTextPage.htm 14th November 2016

[366] Walsingham Pilgrims and Pilgrimage: Michael Rear, Gracewing, 2019, p. 341, v. 2 and 3, translated by Fr W.H. Sandell

Till the blood in torrents flows
Down His face defiled with spittle,
Till His eyes in anguish close.

This 13th century Latin hymn [367]*Stabat mater* helps us understand more of the depths of sorrow and affliction suffered by Mary when she saw her beloved Son Jesus suffer and die on the Cross. We see here how she can comfort the afflicted because she has experienced affliction.

At the Cross her station keeping,
Stood the mournful Mother weeping,
Close to Jesus at the last,
Through her soul, of joy bereavèd,
Bowed with anguish, deeply grievèd,
Now at length the sword hath passed.

Mary is **Comforter of the Afflicted** for parents who suffer the terrible sorrow of the death of a child. The thirteenth [368]*Station of the Cross*, 'Jesus is taken down from the Cross', is one of immense sadness as we see Mary holding the dead body of her beloved Son. Often at the 13th Station of the Cross we pray for parents who have suffered the death of a child: [369]'We pray for all who cannot see beyond the darkness of grief, and for all who mourn – especially parents mourning the death of a child. May Mary, who knew the pain of grief, pray with them and for them.'

[370] 'Blessed Claude Bernard had great devotion to Our Lady as **"Comforter of the Afflicted."** That was the constant theme of his preaching in hospitals, in prisons, everywhere. He was filled with charity for the afflicted because he sought to imitate Her kindness.' He comforted the afflicted, following Mary's example.

---

[367] The New English Hymnal, Canterbury Press, Norwich, 1987, p. 104, Hymn 97, verses 1-5, 13th century Latin, translation by various hands

[368] The Walsingham Pilgrim Manual 2016, p. 40

[369] Ibid., p. 41

[370] http://www.salvemariaregina.info/SalveMariaRegina/SMR-172/Comforter.htm 14th Nov 2016

[371]'St. Jerome Emilianus was a patrician of Venice—a soldier. While he was in prison, crushed by unhappiness, he resolved to change his sinful life and begged Mary for the courage to do so. Our Lady appeared to him, broke his chains, and released him from his prison tower. He devoted the rest of his life to the care of orphans. Our Lady had comforted him; he in turn comforted others. St Jerome could well call Her, as did St. Laurence Justinian—"the Hope of malefactors."' They were comforted in affliction and gave comfort to others who suffered.

[372] 'Blessed John Henry Newman ... signals out one particular type of suffering, namely that of travel to foreign lands with little means and exposed to many dangers, such as that faced by the Virgin Mary, first to Egypt and after Jesus' death to Ephesus. In spite of all St. John's care of her, which was as great as was St Joseph's in her younger days, she, more than all the saints of God, was a stranger and a pilgrim upon earth.' Mary can understand the afflictions of travelling and those of being a refugee.

In 1876 Mary appeared to four children and revealed herself as **Comforter of the Afflicted** at Mettenburg in Germany. [373]'In 1876, four children were visited by the Virgin, the Lord and several angels from December 1st to 21st. 130 years later, a small Chapel testifies to this appearance... They saw the child sitting on the lap of his mother, who in turn sat on a chair. Our Lady showed a face full of joy unspeakable and was wrapped in a robe of blue, bluer than the sky, with white socks and gold shoes, a white veil fell from head to half of the tunic. She told them: "I am the **Comforter of the Afflicted**."' Mary revealed herself to these children as **Comforter of the Afflicted**. They were blessed by these visions and reminded of Mary's consolation. Mary experienced much sorrow, so she is able to comfort others who suffer affliction. We sing this hymn:

---

[371] Ibid.

[372] http://www.maryqueenofallsaints.com/MarysTitles/37ComforterOfAfflicted/37AfflictedTextPage.htm 14th November 2016

[373] http://www.mariancalendar.org/mary-comforter-of-the-afflicted/ 14th November 2016

[374] *Sing we, too, of Mary's sorrows,*
of the sword that pierced her through
when beneath the cross of Jesus
she his weight of suffering knew.

In times of affliction, we can **pray** asking Mary to intercede for us.

What does this mean for us?

When we go through times of affliction we should pray and receive God's grace, help and strength in our difficulties. We should pray for patience in our afflictions *(Romans 12:12)*; remembering Jesus is with us *(Matthew 28:20)*. We should also pray intercessory prayers asking the Lord to help others who are suffering affliction.

We can be thankful for difficult times, in retrospect, so like Paul, so we can help other people. Paul is thankful to have had afflictions as he then experienced God's comfort, consolation and help. He is then able to help other people who are suffering affliction. Real empathy is only possible when someone has suffered. Indeed, Paul seems glad to have suffered so he can help others *(II Corinthians 1:6)*.

We are thankful that God gives us consolation and comfort *(II Corinthians 1:3-4)*. This is hugely significant, as we will only have real understanding and empathy for others who are suffering affliction if we have gone through times of affliction in our lives. What are the painful experiences that you have suffered, that have then helped you to show empathy and care to others? Can you thank the Lord for bringing you through those difficult times?

In our times of weakness and affliction; we can receive God's grace, strength and help in our times of need, just as St Paul encourages us to do *(Romans 12:9)*. Are you in a situation of affliction now? Turn to the Lord and Jesus will meet you where you are and help you.

---

[374] Celebration for Everyone, McCrimmons, Great Wakering, Essex, England, hymn number 659, verses 2, G.B. Timms 1910 -1997

155

We should listen with great empathy to other people who are going through times of affliction which we have experienced. We can be inspired by St Paul to give consolation and comfort to other people who suffer afflictions that we have endured *(II Corinthians 1:3-11)*. Do you listen attentively with compassion when people are talking to you about their times of suffering? How can you give them comfort and help?

Paul is grateful for the prayers that have been prayed for him *(II Corinthians 1:11)* and urges the people to continue to pray for the afflicted. Let us keep praying for the afflicted. Do you know someone who is suffering affliction now? Will you keep praying for them in their time of need?

Jesus says: "Ask and it will be given to you; seek and you will find; knock and the door will be opened to you" *(Matthew 7:7)*. We ask Jesus to help us in affliction and intercede directly praying to God for others who suffer. 'Let us then approach the throne of grace with confidence, so that we may receive mercy and find grace to help us in our time of need' *(Hebrews 4:16)*.

As I complete this Chapter, we are suffering the Coronavirus Crisis of 2020-22. When I lead Intercessions at Mass during this unparalleled time, before the *Hail Mary* I say: 'We ask the Blessed Virgin Mary, **Comforter of the Afflicted** to unite our prayers with hers.' This is a time of affliction for many suffering fear, anxiety, loneliness, illness, exhaustion and bereavement. This is a time when many people are praying much for the afflicted. These prayers[375] were written for this time of the Coronavirus pandemic and can be used to pray in other times of affliction too.

God of healing and hope, in Jesus you meet us in our places of pain and fear. Look with mercy on those who have contracted the new virus, on any who are vulnerable, and on all who feel in danger. Through this time of global concern, by your Holy Spirit bring out the best, not the worst in us. Make us more aware of our interdependence on each other, and of the strength that comes from being one body in you. Through Christ our wounded healer. **Amen.**

---

[375] Praying at Home, A resource for those praying at home as a result of the Coronavirus pandemic, produced by The Church Union and The Society, 2020

Keep us, good Lord, under the shadow of your mercy. Sustain and support the anxious, be with those who care for the sick, and lift up all who are brought low; that we may find comfort knowing that nothing can separate us from your love in Christ Jesus our Lord. **Amen**

We have been exploring Mary's titles of **Consoler of the Afflicted** and **Comforter of the Afflicted** and so we can ask Mary to pray for us and others, just as we can ask our family and friends to pray for us in times of affliction. Mary can be **Comforter of the Afflicted** for the homeless, those who fear for the safety of their families and for refugees. Many people at the time of the Coronavirus pandemic were concerned about the safety of their families. Social-distancing separated close families, because they were not allowed to be together.

Mary suffered bereavement when Joseph died. Mary experienced terrible sorrow watching Jesus suffer and die on the Cross *(John 19:25)*. She could not hold his hand. Mary can be **Comforter of the Afflicted** for parents who suffer the death of a child. We pray for all who mourn, asking Mary, who knew the pain of grief, to pray with and for them. Thousands of people at this time in 2020 to 2022 were mourning the death of a loved-one with Coronavirus. Mary can be the **Comforter of the Afflicted** for those suffering that terrible grief. Let us pray: [376] *O Mary, recall the solemn moment when Jesus, your divine Son, dying on the cross, confided us to your maternal care…. Pray, O holy Mother of God, for the restoration of the sick,* ***consolation for the afflicted****, repentance of sinners, peace to the departed. O blessèd Mary, Mother of God, our Lady of Walsingham, intercede for us.* **Amen**.

[377] Mary, *Comforter of the Afflicted, pray for us.*

---

[376] Walsingham Pilgrim Manual, 2016, p. 75

[377] Ibid., p.13

CHAPTER 19

HELP OF CHRISTIANS

In this chapter I explore the 37ᵗʰ title in the [378]Litany of Loreto, **Help of Christians**.

What does the Bible tells us about Help of Christians?

As the phrase 'help of Christians' is not in the Bible, we will turn to verses about 'help'. The Hebrew words for 'help' mean 'safety'. There are several Hebrew and New Testament Greek words for help.[379] I refer to some of them below.

There are many Psalms that make clear to us that **God is our helper**. The Psalmist writes: 'God is our refuge and strength, an ever-present **help** in trouble' *(Psalm 46:1)*. That is the Hebrew word עֶזְרָה *'ezrâh*. God is

---

[378] Dictionary of Mary 'Behold your Mother', Catholic Book Publishing Co. New Jersey 1997, 1985, p.241

[379] Analytical Concordance to the Holy Bible, Robert Young, United Society for Christian Literature, Lutterworth Press London, 1973, p.476

always with us and ready to help in our troubled times. This theme is a recurring one: 'My help comes from the LORD' *(Psalm 121:1-2)*. This is the Hebrew word עֵזֶר *'êzer* meaning 'help', which is used in this Psalm: 'We wait in hope for the LORD; he is our **help** and our shield' *(Psalm 33:20)*. The Psalmist writes: 'In my distress I called to the LORD; I cried to my God for help. From his temple he heard my voice' *(Psalm 18:6)*. The Psalms express praise and thanks to God for the help and protection that He has given *(Psalm 30:1-3, Psalm 10:17-18)*. We can be encouraged that in the past God helped those in trouble, danger and need.

My favourite verse about God's help is, 'So do not fear, for I am with you; do not be dismayed, for I am your God. I will strengthen you and **help** you; I will uphold you with my righteous right hand' *(Isaiah 41:10)*. This reassures us in times of difficulty that God will strengthen, uphold and help us so we do not need to be afraid. This is the Hebrew word עָזַר *'âzar* for 'help', which is also used in these prayers asking for God's help: 'Help me, O LORD my God' *(Psalm 109:26)*; and, 'May your hand be ready to help me' *(Psalm 119:173)*.

The Hebrew word is תְּשׁוּעָה *t^eshû'âh*, meaning 'safety'; it is used when David wrote 'Give us aid against the enemy, for the **help** of man is useless' *(Psalm 60:10-11a)*. God gave help, safety and protection to David. Help can mean 'to strengthen' as with the Hebrew word חָזַק *châzaq* in: 'the Levites helped them until the task was finished'; *(II Chronicles 29:34)* giving 'strength' by practically helping the priests.

The image of the Lord's being our **Shepherd** is a powerful picture of God's love and care. The Psalmist says: '**Help** us, O God our Saviour... Then we your people, the sheep of your pasture, will praise you for ever' *(Psalm 79:7,13)*. David recognises 'The LORD is my shepherd, I shall not be in want....' *(Psalm 23:1-6)*. This Psalm speaks of God's provision, care, guidance, protection, **help**, healing and blessing.

Later, Jesus tells us that he is the Good Shepherd who finds the lost sheep *(Luke 15:4)*. How wonderful that 'He calls his own sheep by name and leads them out' *(John 10:3)*. Jesus said: 'I am the good shepherd. The good shepherd lays down his life for the sheep' *(John 10:11)*. Jesus loves, cares and **helps** us just like a Good Shepherd cares for his sheep. Jesus knows us by name, leads, guides, feeds and care for us. This 'Shepherd' image would have been special for the people who first heard this message; and also for us picturing the care, help and protection given by the Shepherd.

The New Testament Greek word βοηθέω *boētheō*, means [380]'to run to the aid of those who cry for help, to advance to the assistance of anyone, **help**, aid, succour.' This is the word used here: 'So we say with confidence, "The Lord is my helper; I will not be afraid. What can man do to me?" *(Hebrews 13:6)*.

People asked Jesus to help them. The father of the demon-possessed boy asked for Jesus' help *(Mark 9:22, 24)*. This word βοηθέω is used here and by the Canaanite woman who asked Jesus to heal her daughter: '"Lord, **help** me!" she said' *(Matthew 15:25)*. How wonderful that Jesus gave those distressed parents the help they asked for, by healing their children.

The disciples asked Jesus to help them in the terrible storm on the lake and Jesus was sleeping on a cushion *(Mark 4:39)*. Jesus will **help** and calm 'storms' in our lives. Jesus **helped** the family at the Wedding at Cana when they ran out of wine, because his Mother asked him to help *(John 2:1-11)*. This shows the love and kindness of Jesus helping in this family crisis.

βοηθέω is used when Paul is called to Macedonia with the dream: 'a vision of a man of Macedonia standing and begging him, "Come over to Macedonia and **help** us"' *(Acts 16:9)*. Paul went to preach in Macedonia where people came to faith, including Lydia and her household *(Acts 16:11-15)*, and the jailor and his family *(Acts 16:29-34)*. Later Paul wrote them his Epistle to the Philippians. Paul helped the people in Macedonia to come to know and follow Jesus. Paul told King Agrippa: 'But I have had **God's help** to this very day...' *(Acts 26:22-23)*. This is the New Testament Greek word ἐπικουρία *epikouria*, which means help, aid and assistance. Paul says God has given him help to enable him to preach the good news of Jesus' death and resurrection.

In the Parable of the sheep and the goats *(Matthew 25:31-46)*, Jesus tells us to give practical **help** and care to those in need. The Parable of the Good Samaritan *(Luke 10:25-37)* teaches us to help and care for anyone in need as Jesus says 'Go and do likewise' *(Luke 10:37)*.

---

[380] Analytical Greek Lexicon, Samuel Bagster & Sons Ltd, London, 1973, p. 72

Many hymns, based on Bible verses about God's help, contain encouragement about how God has helped us in the past and so we can trust God's continuing help for the future. [381]*The Lord's my Shepherd* is based on Psalm 23 and reminds us that Jesus is our Good Shepherd giving us love and help.

> *The Lord's my shepherd, I'll not want;*
> *He makes me down to lie*
> *in pastures green; he leadeth me*
> *The quiet waters by.*

In [382]*O God our help in ages past*, Isaac Watts writes about God's help, protection and God's faithfulness, encouraging us to be thankful for God's help in the past and ask for God's help now and in the years to come:

> *O God, our **help** in ages past,*
> *our hope for years to come,*
> *our shelter from the stormy blast,*
> *and our eternal home....*
> *be Thou our guard while troubles last,*
> *and our eternal home.*

The hymn *Rock of Ages* pictures us hiding close to Jesus and being safe in Jesus' care and protection, where [383]*the helpless look to thee for grace.*

The Bible tells us to come with confidence to God to ask for and receive the Lord's help: 'Let us then approach the throne of grace with confidence, so that we may receive mercy and find grace to **help** us in our time of need' *(Hebrews 4:16).* This is the New Testament Greek word meaning [384]'to take hold of, to support, help, aid'. This word is also used for

---

[381] Common Praise, Canterbury Press 2001, p.525, hymn number 594, Scottish Psalter 1650

[382] Ibid., p.473, hymn number 537, Isaac Watts 1674 - 1748

[383] Common Praise, Canterbury Press 2001, p.498, hymn number 565, v. 3, Augustus Toplady 1740 -1748

[384] Analytical Greek Lexicon, Samuel Bagster & Sons Ltd, London, 1973, p. 386

'help' in a verse that tells us that the Holy Spirit helps us to pray *(Romans 8:26)*: the Holy Spirit 'takes hold of' us and guides our prayers.

How wonderful that we can pray directly to God, remembering that Jesus says: "Ask and it will be given to you; seek and you will find; knock and the door will be opened to you" *(Matthew 7:7)*. We can ask Jesus to help us and intercede to God for others who need help. The Bible shows us clearly that **God is the source of our help**. We have seen how God who is Father, Jesus the Son and the Holy Spirit are the '**help of Christians**'.

Then how can Mary be described as 'Help of Christians'?

[385] 'There are two inscriptions of the first centuries of Christianity in <u>Greek</u> related to the Virgin Mary: θεοτοκος (Theotokos, Mother of God) and βοηθεια (Boetheia, the Helper). The <u>Fathers of the Church</u> referred to Mary as "βοηθεια". <u>John Chrysostom</u> used the title in a homily of 345, <u>Proclus</u> in 476 and Sebas of <u>Caesarea</u> in 532... <u>John of Damascus</u> in 749 and German of Constantinople in 733.' Mary was given the title 'Helper' from these early times, as Christians asked her to pray and they received help.

Pilgrims to Walsingham experienced Mary **Help of Christians'** being a help for them by her prayers. [386] *The Pynson Ballad* tells us that those early pilgrims to Walsingham appreciated Mary's help as through her prayers: *Mariners vexed with tempest safe to port brought*. People in danger and peril asked Mary to pray for them and they were helped and kept safe in times of trouble and danger.

This title is explained because[387]: 'from the very beginning, Christians have taken refuge in our Lady in times of adversity... Pope Leo XIII explained "since Mary's greatest joy is to grant her help and assistance to those who call upon her, there is no reason to doubt not only that she

---

[385] https://en.wikipedia.org/wiki/Mary_Help_of_Christians 4th November 2016

[386] A transcription of the "Pynson Ballad", Manuscript 1254/6 The Pepys Library Magdalene College Cambridge

[387] Dictionary of Mary 'Behold your Mother', Catholic Book Publishing Co. New Jersey 1997, 1985, p.297

wishes to answer the prayers of the universal Church but also that she is eager to do so." Hence it was altogether natural for Mary to be given the title **Help of Christians** by the faithful of every century. It became an official title of Mary when it was inserted in the Litany of Loreto in 1571 by Pope Pius V in gratitude for the Christian victory over the Turkish forces at the Battle of Lepanto.'

Jacques Bur writes about Mary, the Help of Christians. [388]'By her maternal intercession, Mary communicates her own 'yes' to us so that it welcomes the grace of Christ in us, just as formerly her consent welcomed the divine Word when he became incarnate in her womb.' He sees Mary's intercessions **help** us when we sin and are 'closed to grace by our hardness, our feebleness, or our indifference, the more need we have of Mary, 'the help of Christians', to remedy the inadequacies of our dispositions.' We can be thankful for Mary's prayers, which draw us back into a close relationship with Jesus. Scott Hahn appreciates Mary's motherly role, writing, [389]'Mary, then, is a mother to the family of God', and can be seen as a mother wanting the children to be helped.

[390]'The feast of **Our Lady, Help of Christians** was instituted by Pope Pius VII. By order of Napoleon I of France, Pius VII was arrested on June 5, 1808, and detained a prisoner... In January 1814, after the battle of Leipzig, he was brought back to Savona and set free on March 17... The pontiff, attributing the victory of the Church after so much agony and distress to the Blessed Virgin, visited many of her sanctuaries on the way and crowned her images. The people crowded the streets to catch a glimpse of the venerable pontiff... He entered Rome on May 24, 1814, and was enthusiastically welcomed. After the Congress of Vienna and the battle of Waterloo, the Pope returned to Rome on July 7, 1815. To give thanks to God and Our Lady, on 15 September 1815 he declared 24 May, the anniversary of his first return, to be henceforth the feast of **Our Lady, Help of Christians**.'

---

[388] How to understand the Virgin Mary: Jacques Bur, SCM Press Ltd, Translation 1994 John Bowden & Margaret Lydamore, p. 106

[389] Hail, Holy Queen: Scott Hahn, Darton, Longman and Todd Ltd, London 2010 p.142

[390] https://en.wikipedia.org/wiki/Mary_Help_of_Christians 4th November 2016

We can ask Mary to pray for us just as we can ask a friend to pray for us when we are in need of God's help. We can think of Mary's being 'the help of Christians' because through her 'yes' to God *(Luke 1:38)* Jesus our Saviour and helper was born.

[391]Mary **Help of Christians** is the Patron Saint of Australia. It became the patronal feast of Australasia, after the reforms of the Second Vatican Council; it was designated a Solemnity, to be kept on the first available Sunday on or after 24th May.

There are **hymns** that address Mary as **Help of Christians**. In [392]*Hail Holy Queen enthroned above* we sing asking Mary to pray for us so Jesus will help us:

> *To thee we cry, poor sons of Eve, O Maria!*
> *to thee we sing, we mourn, we grieve, O Maria!*
> *turn then most gracious advocate, O Maria!*
> *t'ward us thine eyes compassionate, O Maria!*

In the hymn, [393]*Hear thy children* we are asking Mary **Help of Christians** to pray for us:

> *Hear thy children, gentlest Mother,*
> *prayerful hearts to thee arise;*
> *hear us while our evening Ave*
> *soars beyond the starry skies.*

The hymn[394]*Maiden yet a Mother* asks Mary to pray for us:

> *Lady, lest our vision,*
> *striving heavenward, fail,*

---

[391] Ibid.

[392] The Walsingham Pilgrim Manual 2016 p. 100, v. 3, 4, Hermannus Contractus 1013-1054

[393] Ibid., p. 103, v. 1, Francis Stanfield 1835-1914

[394] Ibid., p. 11, v. 4, a translation of a poem by Durante (Dante) degli Alighieri (c.1265–1321)

still let thy petition
with thy Son prevail.

Mary can be seen to be **Help of Christians** by her help at the Wedding at Cana for that family in their time of need when they realised that the wine had gone. 'His mother said to the servants, "Do whatever he tells you"' *(John 2:5)*. Mary pointed them to Jesus who can help them. Mary's advice to "Do whatever he tells you" is a recommendation for us all to follow. In times of need we need to pray and listen to Jesus and "Do whatever he tells us." Hilda Graf comments on this that [395] 'Mary must not only have counted on a miracle but must even have known that it would involve the assistance of servants.' Then the miracle happened as Jesus changed the water into wine and all the guests enjoyed celebrating the wedding! Jesus showed his love and care by helping those people practically in their time of need.

What does this mean for us?

We can pray asking the Lord to help us; confident in his loving kindness *(Matthew 7:7)*. We can be encouraged that, as in the past God helped those in trouble, affliction and in need; so we can pray trusting that God will help us our times of suffering and distress. We should pray listening to Jesus and "Do whatever he tells us" *(John 2:5)*. Let us [396]'turn to him instinctively whenever we are confronted by sorrow, perplexity or fear.' 'Let us then approach the throne of grace with confidence, so that we may receive mercy and find grace to **help** us in our time of need' *(Hebrews 4:16)*.

Jesus will help and calm 'storms' in our lives *(Mark 4:35-41)*. We must remember to ask Jesus to help us. We can ask friends to pray for us when we are going through times of suffering. We can ask Mary **Help of Christians** to pray for us: she will intercede for us by asking Jesus to help us. We should also intercede for others who need help.

---

[395] Mary A History of Doctrine and Devotion: Hilda Graf, Christian Classics Westminster, 1987

[396] The Way of Love': Brother Ramon SSF, Marshall Pickering, 1994, p. 70

The Parable of the Good Samaritan *(Luke 10:25-37)*, teaches us to give help and care to anyone in need as Jesus says 'Go and do likewise' *(Luke 10:37)*. We should give help like Dorcas 'who was always doing good and helping the poor' *(Acts 9:36)*. 'Those able to **help** others' are listed in the teaching about the Church's being Christ's body and how we should all be active parts *(I Corinthians 12: 28)*. What gifts has God given you to help others and build up the Church? In the Parable of the sheep and the goats *(Matthew 25:31-46)*, Jesus tells us to give **help** and care to the hungry, the thirsty, strangers, those in need of clothes, the sick and those in prison. How can you give practical help to those in need? We need to be open and ready for God to call us to help people who need our help. God may call us through a dream like Paul's calling to Macedonia *(Acts 16: 9)*. Where and how is God calling you to **help** others?

I am an Anna Chaplain, because I have been called by God to share his love with older people, especially those living in Care Homes and living alone. Care Home ministry has been an increasingly important part of my ministry as a Reader and Licensed lay Minister since 2013. I was commissioned as an Anna Chaplain at Canterbury Cathedral in September 2019. Anna Chaplaincy is affiliated to The Bible Reading Fellowship. During the coronavirus crisis I helped residents in Care Homes to be reminded that Jesus is with them and loves them, by leading many individual telephone services and Skype services for three Care Homes. I will continue to visit Care Homes and housebound parishioners after the pandemic to lead Church services, talk and listen to these older people; reassuring them of the love and presence of Jesus.

We can be encouraged by these words from the Letter to the Hebrews: 'God will not forget your work and the love you have shown him as you have **helped** his people and continue to help them' *(Hebrews 6:10-11)*. How wonderful that God notices and appreciates all those acts of love, help and kindness that you do, that other people may not see! Let us all **'continue to help'**.

We finish our reflections on **Mary Help of Christians** by asking her to pray for us with Saint John Bosco's prayer: [397] *Mary, powerful Virgin, you are the mighty and glorious protector of the Church. You are the marvellous* **help of Christians**.... *In the midst of our anguish, our struggle, and our distress, defend us from the power of the enemy, and at the hour of death receive our soul in heaven.*

[398] Mary, *Help of Christians, pray for us.*

---

[397] Dictionary of Mary 'Behold your Mother', Catholic Book Publishing Co. New Jersey 1997, 1985, p.297, p.538

[398] The Walsingham Pilgrim Manual 2016, p.13

CHAPTER 20

QUEEN ASSUMED INTO HEAVEN

When I visited Walsingham in September 2016, I asked 'Why do 13 of the titles of Our Lady in the [399]Litany of Loreto begin with 'Queen'? Here I explore the title **'Queen'** and focus on the 47th title **Queen assumed into heaven**, which is **Queen taken up to heaven** in the [400]Walsingham Manual. Later Chapters discuss the other **'Queen'** titles.

What does the Bible tell us about assumption into heaven and the title 'Queen'?

The Bible does not record the assumption of Mary into heaven, although many refer to when: 'a great and wondrous sign appeared in heaven: a woman clothed with the sun, with the moon under her feet and a **crown**

---

[399] Dictionary of Mary 'Behold your Mother', Catholic Book Publishing Co. New Jersey 1997, 1985, p.241

[400] The Walsingham Pilgrim Manual 2016, p.14

of twelve stars on her head' *(Revelation 12:1)*. Some commentators[401] see here that 'Jesus' mother Mary is scarcely in view', as the crown with stars 'is the people of God'. It is nevertheless significant that there were three men in the Old Testament who were taken up into heaven at the time of their deaths. That is also the glorious promise for Christians who are alive when Jesus returns. These Biblical texts are significant when we focus on the 'assumption of Mary' as we see a Scriptural precedent and pattern of '**assumption**'.

Enoch lived for 365 years *(Genesis 5:18-23)*; 'And Enoch walked with God: and he was not; for God took him' *(Genesis 5:24 AV)*. That must have been such a shock for Enoch's family that suddenly 'God took him' so 'he was not'. Enoch's life was very well-pleasing to God so at the time of his death, Enoch was taken up or 'assumed' into heaven. The New Testament tells us: 'By faith Enoch was taken from this life, so that he did not experience death; he could not be found, because God had taken him away. For before he was taken, he was commended as one who pleased God'. *(Hebrews 11:5)*

Moses led the people out of Egypt across the desert to the Promised Land. He gave and taught them God's laws. They reached Moab and 'Moses the servant of the LORD died there in Moab... but to this day no-one knows where his grave is' *(Deuteronomy 34:5-6)*. As Moses' grave was not found; the people thought the Lord buried him. Others assumed that as in the case of Enoch, God had taken him into heaven.

Elijah was a great Prophet who served God and turned people back to the Lord. Later Elisha was with Elijah and: 'suddenly a chariot of fire and horses of fire appeared ... and Elijah went up to heaven in a whirlwind' *(II Kings 2:11)*. It is significant that [402] 'Elijah, like Enoch before him was taken up to heaven bodily without experiencing death; like Moses, Elijah was outside the Promised Land when he was taken away.' Later **Moses** and **Elijah** met with Jesus on the Mount of Transfiguration *(Matthew*

---

[401] The Oxford Bible Commentary, edited by John Barton and John Muddiman, Oxford University Press, 2001, p. 1296

[402] Glo Computer Commentary for 2 Kings 2:11

17:1-9). [403] 'Moses appears as the representative of the old covenant and the promise of salvation, which was soon to be fulfilled in the death of Jesus. Elijah appears as the appointed restorer of all things' *(Malachi 4:5-6).*

Christians who are alive when Jesus returns will be taken up into heaven, as we read 'we who are still alive and are left will be caught up together with them in the clouds to meet the Lord in the air' *(I Thessalonians 4:15-18).* This is sometimes called the 'rapture' and will be a wonderful time when many Christians will be 'assumed' into heaven. This is [404]'the only place in the New Testament where a "rapture", from the Latin Vulgate rendering, is clearly referred to. Some hold that this will be secret, but Paul seems to be describing something open and public, with loud voices and a trumpet blast.' This is a wonderful hope for Christians who are alive when Jesus comes again.

The **Rosary** has Bible verses that are used support the belief in the **Assumption of Mary.** [405]The Fourth Glorious Mystery is **The Assumption of Mary**. Ten Bible verses can be read before the *Hail Mary*, when praying this decade of the Rosary. There is no <u>explicit</u> description similar to Elijah's being taken up into heaven, but these verses are <u>implicit</u> of Mary's assumption. These verses are seen to apply to Mary: "Arise, my darling, my beautiful one, and come with me" *(Song of Songs 2:10).* 'All beautiful you are, my darling; there is no flaw in you' *(Song of Songs 4:7).* 'Who is this that appears like the dawn, fair as the moon, bright as the sun?' *(Song of Songs 6:10)* One of Mary's titles is **Ark of the Covenant**, which is seen in heaven and so this supports the belief that Mary was taken up into heaven; 'and within his temple was seen the ark of his covenant' *(Revelation 11:19a, Psalm 132:8).* I explored this in Chapter 13: **Ark of the Covenant**. Also: 'A great and wondrous sign appeared in heaven: a woman clothed with the sun' *(Revelation 12:1a).* Three verses from St Luke's Gospel show Mary is well-pleasing to God: The angel said "Greetings, you who are highly favoured!" *(Luke 1:28).* Elizabeth rejoiced: 'Blessed are you among women'

---

[403] Ibid., for Matthew 7: 3

[404] Glo Computer Commentary for 1 Thessalonians 4:17

[405] The New Rosary in Scripture: Edward Sri, Charis Servant Books, Cincinnati, Ohio, 2003, p. 173

(Luke 1:42). Mary praises God, 'all generations will call me blessed, for the Mighty One has done great things for me' *(Luke 1:48-9).* This verse suggests Mary's assumption: 'You are the exultation of Jerusalem you are the great glory of Israel, you are the great pride of our nation!' *(Judith 15:9)*

Now we will explore **Queens** in the Bible. In the Old Testament the Hebrew word for 'Queen' is [406] *g^{e}bîyrâh* גְּבִירָה, which means 'mighty one and mistress'. This word is used for the Egyptian Queen Tahpenes *(I Kings 11:19).* Also *g^{e}bîyrâh* is used for wicked Queen Mother Maacha whom Asa removed from her position because she tried to turn people away from the Lord *(I Kings 15:13 & II Chronicles 15:16).* Jeremiah prophesied the fall of King Jehoiachin and the queen mother, *g^{e}bîyrâh (Jeremiah 13:18, 29:2).* Another Hebrew word for 'A Queen' is [407] *malkah* מַלְכָּה and this is used for the Queen of Sheba *(I Kings 10 & II Chronicles 9),* Vashti *(Esther 1),* Esther *(Esther 2-9)* and King Belshazzar's mother, the queen who recommended Daniel to interpret the writing on the wall *(Daniel 5:1).* Solomon gave his mother a throne *(I Kings 2:19),* so here the Queen is the King's mother and not his wife.

The New Testament Greek word [408] *basilissa* βασίλισσα means [409] 'Queen' and it is used for 'the Queen of the South', whom Jesus says will judge and condemn this generation for not recognizing Him *(Luke 11:31). Basilissa* is used for the Ethiopian Queen Candace, whose treasury official met Philip on the desert road *(Acts 8:26-40).* The wicked boastful Queen *(Revelation 18:7,9),* with whom the kings of the earth committed adultery is *Basilissa.* Some other Queens were wicked, such as Jezebel *(I Kings 21),* and Athaliah *(II Kings 11).* Herodias, the wife of King Herod cruelly arranged the beheading of John the Baptist *(Mark 6:14-29).* King Agrippa's wife Queen Bernice listened to Paul speaking about his journey of faith *(Acts 26).* Some Queens in the Bible were the King's mother and others were the King's wife. Some Queens were good and others were not.

---

[406] Analytical Concordance to the Holy Bible, Robert Young, United Society for Christian Literature, Lutterworth Press London, 1973, p. 789

[407] Ibid., pp. 789-790

[408] Young, op. cit., p. 790

[409] Analytical Greek Lexicon, Samuel Bagster & Sons Ltd, London, 1973, p.67

There were good Queens like **Esther** who was encouraged by her Uncle Mordecai that 'who knows but that you have come to royal position for such a time as this?' *(Esther 4:14)* Queen Esther risked her own comfort and safety so that she could help her people by interceding and influenced the King to keep them safe and show compassion to them *(Esther 5-8)*. Esther bravely used her privileged access to the King to help others.

Scott Hahn explains[410] 'In most Near Eastern cultures...the woman ordinarily honoured as queen was not the wife of the king, but the mother of the king... The office of queen mother was well established among the gentiles by the time the people of Israel began to clamour for a monarchy... David's first successor, Solomon, reigns with his mother **Bathsheba**, at his right hand'.

'When Bathsheba went to King Solomon to speak to him for Adonijah, the king stood up to meet her, bowed down to her and sat down on his throne. He had a throne brought for the king's mother, and she sat down at his right hand' (II Kings 2:19). Scott Hahn says 'This makes the **queen mother** unique among the royal subjects' as 'even the king's wives were required to bow before him *(I Kings 1:16)*. ...Yet Solomon rose to honour Bathsheba. Moreover, he showed further respect by bowing before her and by seating her in the place of greatest honour, at his right hand... As a political adviser and even strategist, as an advocate for the people, and as a subject who could be counted on for frankness, the queen mother was unique in her relationship to the king.' Bathsheba and also other King's mother-Queens above, give a Biblical precedent for Mary the Mother of King Jesus, to be given the title 'Queen'.

The **Rosary** Bible verses that are used to support the belief in Mary as **Queen**. [411] The Fifth Glorious Mystery is **The Crowning of Mary** in heaven. Ten Bible verses can be read when praying this decade of the Rosary. There is no <u>explicit</u> verse where Mary is given the title 'Queen' in the Bible, but these verses are <u>implicit</u> of Mary's being Queen. The first

---

[410] 'Hail, Holy Queen': Scott Hahn, Darton, Longman and Todd Ltd, London 2010, p.78 – 82

[411] The New Rosary In Scripture: Edward Sri, Charis Servant Books, Cincinnati, Ohio, 2003, p. 174

four Bible readings connect Mary to Bathsheba's being the Queen Mother *(I Kings 2:19a, & 2:1b)*. "I have one small request to make of you" *(I Kings 2:20a)*. 'The king replied, "Make it, my mother; I will not refuse you."' *(I Kings 2:20b)*. The Angel told Mary her son would be King: 'the Lord God shall give unto him the throne of his father David' *(Luke 1:31-32)*. Elizabeth recognizes Mary as: "'the mother of my Lord'" *(Luke 1:43)*, which implies a queenly status for her. **The Crowning of Mary** includes verses from Revelation 12, which a commentary I referred to earlier[412] felt the woman here meant the people of God. However, Edward Sri [413] explains: 'the woman in Revelation 12 should be understood as *both* an individual (Mary) *and* a symbol for the People of God'. 'A great and wondrous sign appeared in heaven: a woman clothed with the sun, with the moon under her feet' *(Revelation 12:1a)*, 'and a crown of twelve stars on her head' *(Revelation 12:1b)*. 'She gave birth to a son, a male child, who will rule all the nations with an iron sceptre' *(Revelation 12:5a)*. 'And her child was snatched up to God and to his throne' *(v. 5b)*. These verses are <u>implicit</u> of Mary's being **assumed into Heaven** and then crowned **Queen** in heaven, sharing the triumph and joy of her Son.

After the Fall of Jerusalem when some of the people went to live in Egypt; Jeremiah prophesied disaster for them *(Jeremiah 44:18)*, because they turned away from the Lord and 'burned incense to the Queen of Heaven *(Jeremiah 44:18)*. [414] 'Here women are the chief practitioners and defenders of idolatrous practices.' They turned from trusting God. In contrast Mary is Queen in Heaven who encourages us to trust God and do what Jesus tells us *(John 2:5)*.

How can Mary be addressed as Queen Assumed into Heaven?

We have seen that there were several Old Testament Queens who were the mother of the King: Queen Bathsheba was King Solomon's mother,

---

[412] The Oxford Bible Commentary, edited by John Barton and John Muddiman, Oxford University Press, 2001, p. 1296

[413] Sri, op. cit., p. 223

[414] Barton and Muddiman, op. cit., p. 521

King Asa's mother was Queen Maacha, King Jehoiachin's mother and the mother of King Belshazzar. This is important as we see a Biblical precedent for the King's mother's being recognized as **Queen**, which can extend to Mary, the mother of Jesus who is Christ the King. On the last Sunday before Advent we celebrate Christ the King. In [415]Year C the Epistle *(Colossians 1:11-20)*, tells us that Jesus is King who created 'all things', whose kingdom we have been 'transferred' to by faith because 'in him we have redemption, the forgiveness of sins'.

The Biblical texts about Enoch, Moses, Elijah and Christians who are alive when Jesus returns are significant because they give a Biblical pattern for those who are very well-pleasing to God being taken up into heaven. Mary was very well pleasing to God, she was full of grace and 'highly favoured' *(Luke 1:28)*; giving a Biblical precedent for the assumption of Mary.

[416]'The title of **Queen** is given to Mary by Christian Tradition from the beginning of the 4th Century as an indication of her pre-eminence and power… It enters progressively into the usage of the people of God and eventually finds expression in the *Litany of the Hours' Hail Holy Queen*; *Queen of Heaven*; in popular piety in the Litany of the Blessed Virgin, the Rosary and in Christian iconography that frequently depicts Mary's coronation. Attribution of the title of Queen goes on to become a common and accepted practice within the Church, to the point that Pope Pius XII, in 1954 institutes the liturgical Feast of the Queenship of Mary.'

The Angel Gabriel spoke to Mary at the Annunciation, saying of Jesus that: 'He will be great and will be called the Son of the Most High. The Lord God will give him the throne of his father David, and he will reign over the house of Jacob for ever; his kingdom will never end" *(Luke 1:32-33)*. Pope Pius XII taught [417]'these texts show clearly that because of her Son's royal dignity, Mary possessed a greatness and an excellence that set her apart.' This supports Mary's title as **Queen**.

---

[415] The Common Worship Lectionary, NRSV Anglicized Edition, Oxford University Press, 1999, p.1087

[416] Dictionary of Mary "Behold your Mother", Catholic Book Publishing Co, New Jersey 1997, 1985, p. 387

[417] Ibid., p.388

Scott Hahn sees Mary as a 'queen mother', like Bathsheba, writing: [418]'Thus we can confidently approach the queen mother of heaven not just because she condescends, in her great mercy, to hear us, but because we are her children, of royal birth, of noble blood. We can go to her not only because she is Christ's queen mother but because she is ours.' Scott Hahn refers to teaching of Pope Pius and Saint Irenaeus that we are 'brothers and sisters of Christ'.

[419]'The **Assumption of Mary into Heaven**, often shortened to the **Assumption** and also known as the Falling Asleep of the Blessed Virgin Mary, according to the beliefs of the Catholic Church, Eastern Orthodoxy, Oriental Orthodoxy, and parts of Anglicanism, was the bodily taking up of the Virgin Mary into Heaven at the end of her earthly life. The Catholic Church teaches as dogma that the Virgin Mary "having completed the course of her earthly life, was assumed body and soul into heavenly glory". This doctrine was dogmatically defined by Pope Pius XII on 1 November 1950, in the apostolic constitution *Munificentissimus Deus* by exercising papal infallibility.'

---

[418] 'Hail, Holy Queen': Scott Hahn, Darton, Longman and Todd Ltd, London 2010, p.123

[419] https://en.wikipedia.org/wiki/Assumption_of_Mary 3rd November 2016

This painting shows [420] Mary being assumed into heaven. We see people are looking up and watching as Mary is taken up into heaven. It is because of God's grace and favour that Mary is now in a place of honour in heaven as Queen. Mary is seen as a type of the Church so Jacques Bur understands that the Assumption of Mary and her place in heaven are a pre-shadowing of what will happen to the Church. He writes [421]'This glorious assumption of Mary, realised at the end of her earthly life, was a privilege for her... The glorification of the body which will be ours at the end of time was anticipated for Mary at the end of her earthly life.' This is the glorious hope of Christians.

St John Henry Newman writes about Mary's Assumption: [422]"Is it conceivable that they who had been so reverent and careful of the bodies of the Saints and Martyrs should neglect her... who was the very Mother of our Lord? It is impossible. Plainly because that sacred body is in heaven, not on earth." There is no grave for us to visit. [423]'The Assumption completes God's work in her since it was not fitting that the flesh that had given life to God himself should ever undergo corruption. The Assumption is God's crowning of His work as Mary ends her earthly life and enters eternity. The feast turns our eyes in that direction, where we will follow when our earthly life is over.' [424]Mary is a type of the Church and we can be encouraged by her Assumption to know that we will be with the Lord in heaven too.

The **Assumption** on August 15th is [425]'the feast of Mary's destiny of fullness and blessedness, of the glorification of her immaculate soul and

---

[420] Ibid.

[421] How to understand the Virgin Mary: Jacques Bur, SCM Press Ltd, Translation 1994 John Bowden and Margaret Lydamore, P. 75

[422] http://www.cardinaljohnhenrynewman.com/mary-mystical-rose-cardinal-newman/ 3rd June

[423] https://www.ewtn.com/library/ANSWERS/AOFMARY.HTM Fr Clifford Stevens 4th August 2017

[424] MARY the Complete Resource edited by Sarah Jane Boss, Oxford University Press 2007, p. 149

[425] Dictionary of Mary 'Behold your Mother', Catholic Book Publishing Co., New Jersey, 1997, 1985, p. 506-507

of her virginal body, of her perfect configuration to the Risen Christ; a feast that sets before the eyes of the Church and of all mankind the image and consoling proof of the fulfilment of their final hope.' Mary is a type of the Church[426] and so Mary's assumption can encourage Christians to know that we will be taken to heaven at the end of our earthly lives. The **Queenship** of Mary is celebrated on August 22nd. [427]'The solemnity of the Assumption is prolonged in the celebration of the **Queenship** of the Blessed Virgin Mary, which occurs seven days later. On this occasion we contemplate her who, seated beside the King of Ages, shines forth as **Queen** and intercedes as Mother.' Erasmus writes that Mary is [428]'the human woman who gives her body to divinity, becomes Mother of God and is thereby exalted to a position which is higher even than that of the all-spiritual angels, for she is enthroned as Queen of Heaven.' [429]Michael Rear rejoices that 'Our destiny is to be crowned, like Mary, in the Kingdom of God.'

We read of 'The Virgin's **Queenship**' that [430]'throughout the early and high Middle Ages, the Virgin's queenship was a central aspect of her cult. This had a political aspect to it, since earthly rulers associated their own authority with hers.' [431] 'In the high Middle Ages ... Mary's queenship was firmly established and flourishing in Western Christendom. The many visual representations of Mary as queen bear witness to this. Pope Innocent III called her '**Queen of Heaven**' and at that time the *Salve Regina* was becoming increasingly popular in the Latin Church'.

Mary is addressed as Queen in many Hymns. These hymns address Mary as **Queen Assumed into Heaven** so they are helpful both to encourage and support that belief.

---

[426] 'Hail, Holy Queen': Scott Hahn, Darton, Longman and Todd Ltd, London 2010, p. 24

[427] Dictionary of Mary op. cit., p. 507

[428] Walsingham Pilgrims and Pilgrimage: Michael Rear, Gracewing, 2019, p. 92

[429] Ibid., p. 92

[430] MARY the Complete Resource edited by Sarah Jane Boss, Oxford University Press 2007, p. 156

[431] Ibid., p. 159

[432]*Hail!* ***Queen of heaven,*** *the ocean Star,*
guide of the wanderer here below!
[433]In *Holy light on earth's horizon* we sing:
Thou who now art ***crowned*** *in glory.*

We sing[434]*Hail,* ***holy Queen*** *enthroned above…*

Salve, Salve ***Regina.***
In [435]*Daily, daily sing to Mary* we:
Sing the world's ***majestic Queen*** *…*
While we sing her awful ***glory.***
[436] ***Chosen by God*** by Thomas Pestel refers to Mary from
Revelation 12:
High in the heavens John's eagle vision found you,
the blazing sun enfolds you in its light;
to make your ***crown*** *the* ***stars*** *are shining round you;,*
beneath your feet the ***silver moon*** *is bright.*

In [437]***Hail, Queen of the heavens,*** and the following hymns we can
imagine Mary as Queen in heaven when we sing:

Hail, Queen *with the stars as a diadem crowned;*
Above all the angels in glory untold,
Set next to the King in a vesture of gold.
[438]*In splendour arrayed,*

---

[432] Walsingham Manual 2016, p. 102, Hymn 14, verse 1, John Lingard 1771 - 1851

[433] Ibid., p. 105, Hymn 17, verse 3, Edward Caswall 1814-1878

[434] Ibid., p. 99, Hymn 11, verse 1 and chorus, Contractus Hermannus 1013-1054

[435] Ibid., p. 94 -95, Hymn 6. verses 2 and 4, St. Casimir 1458- 1484, translator Henry Bittleston

[436] Walsingham Manual 2016, p. 93, Hymn 5, verse 5, Thomas Pestel 1586 - 1667

[437] Universalis App, Universalis publishing, 1996-2019, Birthday of BM, Vespers, Office Hymn, Edward Caswall 1814-1878

[438] Walsingham Manual 2016, p. 109, Hymn 21, verse 1, St John Henry Newman 1801- 1890

*in vesture of **gold**,*
the Mother of God
*in **glory** behold!*
O daughter of David,
*thou **dwellest on high**,*
excelling in brightness
the hosts of the sky.
[439]*Joy to thee **Queen**! within thine ancient dowry –*
*Joy to thee **Queen**! .....*
Ladye of Walsingham! ....
*England's protectress – our Mother and **our Queen**.*

[440]This is one of four Marian antiphons, traditionally said after night prayer, from the end of Eastertide until the beginning of Advent:

Hail, holy Queen, *Mother of mercy, our life, our sweetness and our hope.*

We sing [441]*Joy to thee **O Queen of Heaven*** at Eastertide in the *Regina Coeli*.

[442]From the 7th century Roman churches had images of Popes standing or kneeling 'before a sovereign Virgin wearing a massive crown'. Mary was depicted as a 'truly regal type with attributes of supreme majesty.' Paintings showing The Coronation of Mary and those depicting her as Queen were powerful images that helped people to imagine Mary in Heaven as Queen. The **Coronation of Our Lady**, which is the fifth of The Glorious Mysteries of the Rosary, gives time for reflection about this as: [443] 'We see Our Lady as Queen of Heaven, sharing the triumph and joy of her Son and God who has rewarded her faithfulness.'

---

[439] Ibid., p. 110, Hymn 22, verse 1, Edward Caswall 1814-1878

[440] Ibid., p. 15

[441] The Order of the Mass, St Michael & All Angels Maidstone p. 10

[442] MARY the Complete Resource edited by Sarah Jane Boss, Oxford University Press 2007, p. 547

[443] The Walsingham Pilgrim Manual 2016, p. 56

[444] 'In ancient and medieval art, she is always enthroned and has a regal bearing with her Son seated on her lap... A statue of this type is known as Virgin in Majesty, or Seat of Wisdom.' In the Chapter 7: **Seat of Wisdom** we explore this title. The photograph of Our Lady of Walsingham on the front cover shows Mary as 'Seat of Wisdom'. [445] As a mother Mary supports her Son in her lap, yet as the Mother of God she serves as a throne for the incarnation of Divine Wisdom, whom she is holding and presenting to the world.' Paintings and statues show Mary's regal status shown by her portrayal as **Queen**. [446] 'The highest honour is given to Mary 'to conceive and bear God in her very body. So in the traditions of both the Catholic and Eastern Orthodox Churches, the Virgin is said to be higher than the angels, and is crowned and enthroned as **Queen of Heaven**. It would be hard to overstate the extent of Mary's power and majesty in the culture of Western Europe in the eleventh and twelfth centuries... Mary is associated both with queenship and the figure of wisdom.' The picture of a statue of Our Lady of Walsingham on the front cover shows Mary as Queen sitting on a throne.

Father Mateo writes [447]'Catholics believe she is indeed our Queen and that her spiritual royalty flows from and is subordinate to Christ's kingship.... Her role is to draw people to acknowledge and follow Jesus as their Lord and King. The Bible prefigures her role in her instructions to the waiters at the Wedding feast in Cana *(John 2:5)*; in her acceptance of the beloved disciple as her Son, a type of all Christ's disciples in every age *(John 19:26)*; and in her presence and prayer as a member of the tiny Church in the upper room, where the first Christians waited for the Holy Spirit to enliven them *(Acts 1:14, 2:1-41)*. Mary's queenship is spiritual leadership... exercised by holy example and all-embracing intercession.' She is seen as a caring **Queen** who intercedes to the King.

---

[444] Boss, op. cit., p. 547

[445] 'Mary throne of Wisdom': Catherine Combier-Donovan

[446] MARY the Complete Resource edited by Sarah Jane Boss, Oxford University Press 2007, p. 159

[447] Refuting the attack on Mary: Father Mateo, Catholic Answers, San Diego, 1999, p. 63-64

In Chapter 16: **Health of the sick**, Chapter 18: **Comforter of the afflicted** and Chapter 19: **Help of Christians** we explored Mary's role as 'Intercessor'. We can now picture Mary as Queen in heaven, bringing these requests to Jesus, just as Queen Esther brought requests to the King *(Esther 5-8)*. Mary is in an exalted position in heaven because she found favour with God and was obedient to Him, in agreeing to become the mother of Jesus *(Luke 1:28,38)*. If we accept that Mary is **Queen Assumed into Heaven**, then this will help our understanding of the other Queen titles, which I explore in the following Chapters, except the 44th title **Queen of Virgins** is included in Chapter 5: Mary's titles about her Virginity.

What does this mean for us?

Queen Esther was encouraged by her Uncle Mordecai, 'who knows but that you have come to royal position for such a time as this?' *(Esther 4:14)* Sometimes we find ourselves in situations when we can influence decisions in such a way that many people could be helped. We need to pray for wisdom to say and do what is right in that situation. Are you in such a situation now? Queen Esther had access to the King and could bring her requests to him. We have privileged access into Jesus' presence and we should bring with us intercessions for those in need as well as our own concerns *(Hebrews 4:16)*.

Let us learn from Enoch who was taken up into heaven *(Hebrews 11:5)*. Jude tells us that Enoch said that God would judge sinners who: 'are grumblers and fault-finders' *(Jude 14-16)*. Do you need to repent of grumbling? John writes: 'when he appears, we shall be like him, for we shall see him as he is. Everyone who has this hope in him purifies himself, just as he is pure' *(I John 3:2-3)*. The hope of seeing God *(I Thessalonians 4:15-18)*, should cause us to want to grow in purity. We should be open for the Holy Spirit to convict us of sin, so we grow in purity' *(II Corinthians 3:18)*. How is the Lord changing you?

Let us follow the good example of Queen Bernice and be ready to listen attentively to other people talk about their faith journey and how Jesus has helped them. We should learn from the experiences of others and offer appreciation and encouragement. Mary is honoured by God because she said 'yes' *(Luke 1:38)*. We should say 'yes' to what God is calling us to do. Mary points us to Jesus and says to us as she said long ago in Cana: 'Do whatever he tells you' *(John 2: 5)* What is Jesus telling you to do?

When we are in heaven God will give us crowns! Paul encourages Timothy that: 'there is in store for me the **crown of righteousness**, which the Lord, the righteous Judge, will award to me on that day - and not only to me, but also to all who have longed for his appearing' *(II Timothy 4:7-8)*. Peter tells us about 'the **crown of glory**' that Jesus will give his faithful followers who have been good shepherds of the flock *(I Peter 5:4)*. James tells us that those who persevere will be rewarded with 'the **crown of life**' *(James 1:12)*. Let us keep loving and following the Lord. This crown is also promised to the Church in Smyrna, if they remain faithful *(Revelation 2:10)*. The Church at Philadelphia was told: 'Hold on to what you have, so that no-one will take your **crown**' *(Revelation 3:11)*. We should keep trusting in difficult times. We will then be rewarded with a crown in heaven. The hymn [448]*The Old Rugged Cross* reminds us that in heaven we will exchange the cross for a crown: *I will cling to the old rugged cross and exchange it someday for a crown.*

In Revelation a vision of heaven shows the elders wearing golden crowns: 'They **lay their crowns** before the throne and say: "You are worthy, our Lord and God, to receive glory and honour and power"' *(Revelation 4: 4, 10-11)*. They are given crowns and then lay them before the throne of God. As in *Love Divine, all loves excelling*[449]:

> *Finish then thy new creation,*
> *pure and spotless let us be; ....*
> *till in heaven we take our place,*
> ***till we cast our crowns before thee,***
> *lost in wonder, love and praise!*

---

[448] Celebration Hymnal for Everyone, McCrimmons, 1994, hymn 573, verse 4 and chorus, George Bennard 1873 -1960

[449] The New English Hymnal, The Canterbury Press, Norwich, 1987, p. 407, hymn 408, verse 3, Charles Wesley 1707-1788

God rewards us with crowns and then our response will be to lay them before God's throne. Billy Graham expressed this: [450] 'In 2001, the Queen bestowed on him an Hon. KBE... In his speech of response, Graham said: 'I look forward to the day when I can see Jesus face to face, and lay at his feet any honour I've ever received, because he deserves it all." Just like the Elders in heaven, redeemed sinners will have the wonderful joy of casting their crowns before the throne' *(Revelation 4:4,10-11).*

The Crowning of Mary [451]'is no mere honorary title…. Mary actually participates in the power of Christ, through her powerful intercession.'

[452] *Queen assumed into Heaven, pray for us.*

---

[450] Church Times, No. 8084, 23rd February 2018, p. 36

[451] The Rosary –Joy. Light. Sorrow. Glory: Pope John Paul 11, 28th March 2003, Sixth Edition 2005, Agora Printing, Averbode, p. 52

[452] Dictionary of Mary 'Behold your Mother', Catholic Book Publishing Co. New Jersey 1997, 1985, p.241

CHAPTER 21

QUEEN OF ANGELS

This chapter is about **Queen of Angels**, the 38[453]th title in the Litany of Loreto. In the previous Chapter we explored how and why Mary is given the title 'Queen'.

What does the Bible tells us about Angels?

Angels are mentioned in 34 of the 66 books in the Bible[454], where the Hebrew word מַלְאָךְ *mal'âk* means 'messenger, agent'. The meaning of ἄγγελος *angelos*, the New Testament Greek word translated as 'angel' is [455]'one sent, a messenger, angel' with the verb 'to tell, to announce'. Hope

[453] Dictionary of Mary 'Behold your Mother', Catholic Book Publishing Co. New Jersey 1997, 1985, p.241

[454] Analytical Concordance to the Holy Bible, Robert Young, United Society for Christian Literature, Lutterworth Press London, 1973, p.37-38

[455] The Analytical Greek Lexicon, London: Samuel Bagster and Sons Ltd, 1973, p. 3

Price tells us that: [456]'Angels are most frequently mentioned, but there are also several references to cherubim. **Archangels** appear only twice and seraphim are described in detail only once.' **Cherubim**, [457]'the second most frequently mentioned category of angelic being in the Bible, are the strong guards used by God to enforce His word.' Cherubim guarded 'the way to the tree of life' *(Genesis 3:24)*, after Adam and Eve were sent away from the Garden of Eden. Statues of Cherubim were made to guard the Ark of the Covenant where God met with Moses and the people worshipped *(Exodus 25:22)*. Solomon's Temple had huge golden cherubim guarding the Ark *(II Chronicles 5:7-8)*. Ezekiel had clear visions of cherubim which he describes in detail *(Ezekiel 1:9,10)*. Isaiah describes **Seraphim** in his vision of heaven and how they worship God *(Isaiah 6:2-4)*.

In the **Old Testament** there are many occasions when God sent angels to give messages to people, announce news or give instructions to them. Angels were sent by God to encourage, protect and help people. God sent an **angel** to Hagar, to announce God's message *(Genesis 16:7-12)*. Later 'the angel of God' spoke to Hagar at Beersheba and God provided a well of water *(Genesis 22:17-20)*. **Angels** helped Lot and his family to escape from Sodom *(Genesis19: 15-21)*. 'The angel of the Lord' spoke to Abraham to help and encourage him *(Genesis 22:11,15)*. Abraham trusted that an angel would help his servant find a wife for Isaac *(Genesis 24:7-58)*. Jacob dreamt about angels at Bethel *(Genesis 28:12-15)*. Later an angel spoke to Jacob in a dream to help him with his work *(Genesis 31:11)*, and angels met him to give encouragement on his journey home *(Genesis 32:1)*. 'The angel of the Lord' appeared to Moses in the burning bush *(Exodus 3:2)*. 'The angel of God' travelled with the Israelites to protect them on their journey from Egypt *(Exodus 14:19; 32:34a)*. The manna sent by God to feed the Israelites was 'the bread of angels' *(Psalm 78:25)*. Balaam's donkey saw the 'angel of the Lord' *(Numbers 22:21-35)*. An angel helped Gideon realise that God had chosen him to lead *(Judges 6:11-22)*. God sent an angel to tell Manoah and his wife that they would have a son and gave instructions about caring for Samson *(Judges 13)*.

---

[456] Angels True stories of how they touch our lives: Hope Price, Pan Books, 1994, p. 54
[457] Ibid., p. 56

Angels are powerful and they were [458]'God's agents in judgement', for example at Sodom and Gomorrah *(Genesis 19:1-29)*, and the angel who destroyed the Assyrian army at the time of Isaiah and King Hezekiah *(II Kings 19:35)*. An angel gave food and drink to Elijah when he was depressed and exhausted *(I Kings 19:5-7)*. Elisha and his servant saw the protecting angels and realised: 'Those who are with us are more than those who are with them' *(II Kings 6:15-17)*. An angel protected Daniel's friends in the fiery furnace *(Daniel 3:19-30)*, and sheltered Daniel in the lions' den *(Daniel 6:22)*. The kings were impressed recognising that the God whom Daniel and his friends worshipped was 'the living God' *(Daniel 3:29, 6:26-27)*. Angel Gabriel explained Daniel's vision *(Daniel 9:21ff)*, and an angel came to Daniel 'to explain to you what will happen to your people in the future' *(Daniel 10:10-12:4)*. Archangel Michael is 'one of the chief princes' *(Daniel 10:13)*, and he has an important role in fighting against evil. Jude tells us that the Archangel Michael 'was disputing with the devil about the body of Moses' *(Jude 9)*. Zechariah had many angelic encounters *(Zechariah 1:9-19, 2:3, 3:1-6, 4:1-5, 5:5-10, 6:4-5)*, when angels announced and explained God's messages, told him prophetic messages to speak and gave him explanations and understanding. The angel assured them of God's love as 'the apple of his eye' *(Zechariah 2: 8)*.

In the **Old Testament** we see that God sent angels to bring messages and to give help, explanations, encouragement and protection. Psalm 91 promises angelic protection for those who keep close to God as 'he will command his angels concerning you to guard you in all your ways; they will lift you up in their hands so that you will not strike your foot against a stone' *(Psalm 91:11-12)*. They were also agents in God's judgement.

In the **New Testament** we read more about angels. In the **Gospels** Angel Gabriel was sent to the temple in Jerusalem to tell Zechariah about the birth of John *(Luke 1:8-20)*. Gabriel went to Nazareth to announce to Mary that God had chosen her to be the mother of his Son *(Luke 1:26-38)*. An angel was sent to reassure Joseph that Mary's expected baby was 'from the Holy Spirit' and will be called Immanuel, meaning 'God with us' *(Mt 1:18-25)*. Angels told good news to the shepherds *(Luke 2:8-14)*. An angel

---

[458] Angels God's secret agents: Billy Graham, Hodder, 1988, Chapter 9: p. 81 - 89

warned Joseph to escape with his family to Egypt *(Matthew 2:18)*, so they would be safe. Later 'an angel of the Lord appeared in a dream to Joseph in Egypt' *(Matthew 2:19-20)*, telling him to take his family back to Israel as those who wanted to take Jesus' life were dead. These angels announced messages, revealed God's purposes and gave protection. After Jesus endured the temptations in the desert 'angels attended him' *(Mark 1:13)*, and an angel strengthened Jesus in the Garden of Gethsemane *(Luke 22:43)*. Jesus tells us that children, 'these little ones' have 'their angels in heaven' *(Matthew 18:11)*, which has led to the idea of people having 'guardian angels'. God sends angels to take believers to heaven, when they die *(Luke 16:22)*.

Easter Sunday morning was a time of great **joy** for the angels! Matthew describes how on Easter Sunday morning 'an angel of the Lord came down from heaven and, going to the tomb, rolled back the stone and sat on it. His appearance was like lightening, and his clothes were white as snow' *(Matthew 28:2-3)*. This glorious angel announced the wonderful news of the resurrection of Jesus. Mark records this, too *(Mark 16:1-7)*, and he told them to tell the disciples the good news. Luke writes about two angels at the tomb who told the women 'He is not here, he has risen' *(Luke 24:6)*. They reminded the women that Jesus had told his followers that he would be crucified and rise on the third day. John tells us that two angels spoke to Mary Magdalene *(John 20:18)*. The angels announced the resurrection of Jesus with joy!

In **Acts** angels are sent by God to further the mission of the Early Church in spreading the good news about Jesus, so more people come to believe and receive salvation. Two angels spoke to the disciples after Jesus' Ascension into heaven, assuring them that Jesus will return *(Acts 1:10-11)*. The disciples followed Jesus' instructions and returned to Jerusalem to wait for God to send the Holy Spirit on the Day of Pentecost; to empower them for their work of mission and evangelism. An angel told Philip to go to the desert road so he met the Ethiopian eunuch *(Acts 8:26)*. An angel appeared to Cornelius *(Acts 10: 3-6)*, with clear directions about how to find Simon Peter so Cornelius and his household came to believe in Jesus. An angel rescued Peter from prison *(Acts 12:6-10)*, so he could continue to spread the good news. In the hardship and danger of the storm on Paul's journey to Rome, God sent an angel to cheer and encourage Paul *(Acts*

27:23-24). We can imagine the 'rejoicing in heaven over one sinner who repents' *(Luke 15:7)*. The spread of the good news at the time of the Early Church and many people coming to know, love and follow Jesus was a time of great joy in heaven when the Angels rejoiced!

Some of the **Epistles** tell us more about angels, as R.A. Torrey explains in his book[459]. Angels are created beings *(Colossians 1:16)*. They are greater than man in power and might *(II Peter 2:11, II Thessalonians 1:7)*. There are ranks and orders of angels which are subject to the Lordship of Jesus *(Jude 9, I Thessalonians 4:16, I Peter 3:22)*. There are innumerable hosts of angels *(Hebrews 12:22)*. Angels worship Jesus *(Hebrews 1:6)*, and we are not to worship them *(Revelation 22:8-9)*. We read: 'Are not all angels ministering spirits sent to serve those who will inherit salvation?' *(Hebrews 1:14)* There is a hierarchy of angels as in heaven Jesus is 'far above all rule and authority, power and dominion, and every title that can be given, not only in the present age but also in the one to come *(Ephesians 1:21)*.

The book **Revelation** records John's vision of heaven with many references to angels. We have glimpses of heavenly worship *(Revelation 4:8)*. Churches have an angel as letters are written 'To the angel of the church in' seven places *(Revelation 2,3)*. Seven angels are given a trumpet and sound them *(Revelation 8-11)*. 'And there was war in heaven. Michael and his angels fought against the dragon' and defeated him *(Revelation 12:7)*. Of three angels, one tells us to worship God and give him glory *(Revelation 14:7)*. Seven angels pour out bowls of wrath in chapter 16. [460]'The angels are executioners of God's wrath toward the wicked as well as his mercy toward the righteous.' Angels in heaven announce what is happening: 'the great supper of God' *(Revelation 19:17)*, and that Babylon has fallen. *(Revelation 18:2)* An angel shows John 'a new heaven and a new earth' with 'the Holy City' *(Revelation 21)*, and the river of life *(Revelation 22)*. Jesus sent his angel to give John these revelations *(Revelation 22:16)*. Some of the events recorded in this Revelation have already taken place and others are yet to happen. This book of the Bible shows the amazingly important role of angels in heaven.

---

[459] What the Bible teaches: R.A.Torrey, London Nisbet & Co Ltd p.499 - 509
[460] Ibid., p. 509

It is special to write this chapter on **Mary Queen of Angels**: at the time of writing, my husband is Vicar of St Michael and All Angels', Maidstone, where I am a Reader, a Licensed Lay Minister and an Anna Chaplain. In that beautiful Church the north aisle stained glass windows have Bible stories with angels from the Old Testament. The south aisle, where the sun shines through, depicts some of the New Testament angelic appearances. This image shows a ceramic Archangel Michael is holding a flaming sword, dressed as a soldier ready to protect, guard and shield. This ceramic hangs in the hall of our Vicarage.

Many **hymns** and **carols** that tell us about the work and ministry of Angels. They help us appreciate angels. In [461] *Angel-voices ever singing* we sing that angels are continually worshipping God in heaven:

Angel-voices ever singing

---

[461] The New English Hymnal, Words Edition, Canterbury Press, Norwich, 1987, number 336, v.1, Francis Pott 1832 - 1909

round thy throne of light;
angel-harps, forever ringing,
Rest not day nor night;
thousands only live to bless thee...

At Christmas we remember the Angel Gabriel's visit to Mary *(Luke 1:26-38)* in [462] ***Gabriel's message***:

The angel Gabriel from heaven came,
his wings as drifted snow,
his eyes as flame.

[463] ***Hark! The Herald Angels Sing*** tells about the shepherds' message *(Luke 2:8-14)* and:

[464] ***Angels from the realms of glory,***
wing your flight o'er all the earth;
ye who sang creation's story,
now proclaim Messiah's birth.

We sing about angelic help *(Hebrews 1:14)* in:

[465] ***Ye holy Angels bright***
who wait at God's right hand,
or through the realms of light
fly at your Lord's command:
assist our song....

---

[462] Carols for Choirs 2: 50 Carols edited and arranged by David Willcocks and John Rutter, Oxford University Press, 1970, number 43, p. 191-192, S. Baring-Gould 1834 - 1924

[463] The New English Hymnal, Words Edition, Canterbury Press, Norwich,1987, p. 27, number 26, Charles Wesley 1707 — 1788

[464] Hymns Ancient and Modern Revised, William Clowes and Sons, Ltd, p. 46, number 64, James Montgomery 1771 - 1854

[465] The New English Hymnal, op. cit., p.472, number 475, v.1, Richard Baxter 1615- 1691

The hymn [466]*Around the throne* describes how angels worship God *(Isaiah 6: 1-3)* and that they are sent to help people *(Hebrews 1:14)*:

Around the throne of God a band
of glorious angels ever stand;
bright things they see, sweet harps they hold,
and on their heads are crowns of gold.
Some wait around him, ready still
to sing his praise and do his will;
and some when he commands them, go
to guard his servants here below.

[467]**Ye watchers and ye holy ones** lists the hierarchy of angels in heaven (Ephesians 1:21).

Ye watchers and ye holy ones,
bright Seraphs, Cherubim and Thrones,
raise the glad strain, alleluia!
Cry out Dominions, Princedoms, Powers,
Virtues, Archangels, Angels' choirs, alleluia!

[468]*It came upon the midnight clear* describes the ministry of angels encouraging us to listen to their song:

It came upon the midnight clear
That glorious song of old
From angels bending near the earth…..

Still through the cloven skies they come……

---

[466] Ibid., p. 475, number 191 v.1 & 2, J. M. Neale 1818 - 1866

[467] Ibid., p. 474, number 478, v.1, Athelstan Riley 1858 - 1945

[468] The New English Hymnal, Words Edition, Canterbury Press, Norwich, 1987, p. 31, number 29 v. 1-3, Edmund Sears 1810-1876

And man, at war with man, hears not
The love-song which they bring;
O hush the noise, ye men of strife,
And hear the angels sing.

How can Mary be addressed as Queen of Angels?

Chapter 20: **Queen Assumed into Heaven** explains from Biblical and Church teaching, why Mary is recognised as Queen of Heaven. The logical step is that she is therefore Queen of the Angels who live in heaven. [469]'Saint Germanus said of Mary "Your honour and dignity surpass all creation: the angels take second place to you in excellence.'

[470]*Hail, holy Queen* addresses Mary as Queen of Angels:

Triumph all ye cherubim,
sing with us, ye seraphim,
heav'n and earth resound the hymn:
Salve, salve, salve Regina.

In [471]**I'll sing a hymn to Mary** we sing of her: "As Queen of all the angels".
Sarah Jane Boss explains: [472]'In the high Middle Ages ... Mary's queenship was firmly establishes and flourishing in Western Christendom. The many visual representations of Mary as queen bear witness to this. Pope Innocent III called her 'Empress of Angels'. The highest honour is given to Mary to conceive and bear God in her very body. So in the traditions of both the Catholic and Eastern Orthodox Churches, the Virgin is said to be higher than the angels, and is crowned and enthroned

---

[469] Dictionary of Mary "Behold your Mother", Catholic Book Publishing Co, New Jersey 1997, 1985, p. 388

[470] The Walsingham Manual, 2016, p. 99, hymn 11, chorus, Hermannus Contractus 1013-1054

[471] Ibid., hymn 20 v. 6, John Wyse 1825-1898

[472] MARY the Complete Resource edited by Sarah Jane Boss, Oxford University Press 2007, p. 159

as Queen of Heaven. It would be hard to overstate the extent of Mary's power and majesty in the culture of Western Europe in the eleventh and twelfth centuries.' Mary is Queen of Angels, because she is the Mother of Jesus and so she is honoured as Queen in Heaven.

Another argument to support Our Lady's having this title **Queen of Angels** is because she is the Mother of Him who created the Angels. Catholic teaching explains more about this: [473] 'Many are the titles, by which Mary is the **Queen of Angels**. She is the Mother of Christ, who created the angels, "for in Him," says St. Paul, "were all things created in heaven and on earth, visible and invisible, whether thrones or dominations, or principalities or powers: all things were created by Him and in Him" *(Colossians 1:6)*. She is, therefore, their Queen.... Mary is assumed into heaven: the angels rejoice.'

The hymn[474] **Ye watchers and ye holy ones** is also significant as we sing of Mary:

> O higher than the Cherubim,
> more glorious than the Seraphim,
> lead their praises, alleluia!
> Thou bearer of the eternal Word,
> most gracious, magnify the Lord, alleluia!
> This supports the argument that Mary is **Queen of Angels**.

The hymn [475]**Hail, Queen of the heavens** has a reference to Mary as Queen of Angels:

> Hail, Mother most pure, hail, Virgin renowned,
> hail, Queen, with the stars as a diadem crowned;

---

[473] http://catholicharboroffaithandmorals.com/Our%20Lady%20Queen%20of%20Angels.html 3rd Nov 2016

[474] The New English Hymnal, Words Edition, Canterbury Press, Norwich, 1987, number 478, v.1-2, Athelstan Riley 1858 - 1945

[475] Universalis App, Universalis publishing, 1996-2019, Birthday of BM, Vespers, Office Hymn, Edward Caswall 1814-1878

> above all the angels in glory untold,
>
> set next to the King in a vesture of gold.

We can understand how Mary can be addressed as **Queen of Angels**, because she is the mother of Jesus and Queen in heaven, so she is Queen of the Angels in Heaven.

What does this mean for us?

We have seen many Biblical examples of people who were helped by angels. Angels were sent by God to announce His messages, to explain, encourage, help and protect. The Book of Hebrews tell us 'Are not all angels ministering spirits sent to serve those who will inherit salvation?' *(Hebrews 1:14)* In recent years many people have received angelic help and some of those experiences are recorded in Hope Price's book[476]. Reading these accounts can make us more aware of God's care and protection for us. How exciting that God may send an angel in disguise to help you!

People in Church history have had visions of angels, which Hope Price includes in her book[477], such as St Cecilia in Rome in the 2nd - 3rd centuries, and St Monica, who was encouraged by an angel to keep praying for her son Augustine. An angel spoke to St Francis of Assisi when he was ill, which lead to his conversion. St Joan of Arc saw Michael the Archangel and other angels in France with messages to encourage the French army. St Teresa of Avila's visions and visits from angels encouraged her faith and inspired her writing.

In the First World War, it is said that angels helped British soldiers. [478]There are accounts written by British officers verifying the help given by angels to protect and help the British soldiers at Mons. 'One man said he saw 'a troop of angels 'between us and the enemy.' In another account, in August 1918, following a National Day of prayer, angelic help was given to British soldiers, with angelic forces fighting for them, riding

---

[476] Angels True stories of how they touch our lives: Hope Price, Pan Books, 1994

[477] Ibid., p.80-88

[478] Ibid., chapter 9, p.92-102

white horses and wearing white uniforms. We can be encouraged that God gives help and protection; sometimes using angels to look after people.

Billy Graham records how angels helped the RAF in the Second World War in the Battle of Britain in 1940. [479]Air Chief Marshal Lord Hugh Dowding said 'he believed angels had actually flown some of the planes whose pilots sat dead in their cockpits.' Graham also reports that an angel helped American soldiers in the Battle of Bastogne. [480] Gilbert Morris records that an angel dressed as a lieutenant told Sergeant William Raines how to stop the German machine gun, so his friends were saved.

Billy Graham calls angels 'God's secret agents', writing:[481] 'Yes, angels are real. They are not the product of our imagination, but were made by God Himself. Think of it! Whether we see them or not, God has created a vast host of angels to help accomplish His work in the world. When we know God personally through faith in His Son, Jesus Christ, we can have confidence that the angels of God will watch over us and assist us.'

Psalm 91 promises angelic protection for those who keep close to God *(Psalm 91:11-12)*. We can pray, asking God to send his angels to protect us. Psalm 34 gives a wonderful picture of the protection of angels *(Psalm 34:7)*. Let us keep trusting and following the Lord, enjoying the protection of angels' encamping around us and keeping us safe from harm and danger. We can be encouraged that God may send angels to help us *(Hebrews 1:14)*. Just as God said to Moses: 'My angel will go ahead of you' *(Exodus 23:23)*, we can trust that God will help and protect us even sending angels.

We can imagine the 'rejoicing in heaven over one sinner who repents' *(Luke 15:7,10)*. The spread of the good news from the time of the Early Church with people coming to know, love and follow Jesus gives great joy in heaven! The book of Hebrews tells us to be hospitable to strangers: 'for by so doing some people have entertained angels without knowing it *(Hebrews 13:2)*. Are you hospitable?

---

[479] Angels God's secret agents: Billy Graham, Hodder, 1988, p. 123

[480] The Angel of Bastogne, Digital Edition based on the Printed Edition, B&H Publishing Group, Nashville, Tennessee, 2005

[481] Graham, op. cit., p. 36-37

We can pray asking for angelic protection at night, using this lovely prayer used as an end of day prayer at a school I taught in; we recommend this to baptism families:

> Lord, keep us safe this night,
> secure from all our fears;
> may angels guard us while we sleep,
> 'till morning light appears. Amen.

We should live preparing for Jesus to come again with His holy angels. Jane Williams suggests that angels invite us to join in their song of praise:[482] 'They long to teach us their song, so that we, with them, can sing a hymn of praise.' We should [483]'Thank God for the ministry of His blessed angels.' Jesus was 'made ... a little lower than the angels; (God) crowned him with glory and honour' *(Hebrews 2:7)*. Jesus is now crowned with glory and honour and so is Mary. The Church will be honoured in heaven as the Bride of Christ *(Revelation 21, I Corinthians 6:3)*.

When preparing Intercessions at our Church of St Michael and All Angels I sometimes include this prayer:

[484]*Father in heaven, the angels sing by day and night around your throne: Holy, holy, holy is the Lord God Almighty. With Michael, prince of the angels, who contends by our side, and with the whole company of heaven, we worship you.*

The Collect for Michaelmas asks for angelic help: [485]*O Everlasting God, who hast ordained and constituted the services of angels and men in a wonderful order: mercifully grant, that as thy holy angels always do thee service in heaven, so by thy appointment they may succour and defend us on earth, through Jesus Christ our Lord.*

[486] Mary, *Queen of Angels, pray for us.*

---

[482] Angels: Jane Williams, A Lion Book an imprint of Lion Hudson plc, 2006, p. 124

[483] Graham, op. cit., p. 131

[484] Common Worship Festivals p.111 Intercessions for Michael and All Angels

[485] The Book of Common Prayer, W.W.M. Collins and Sons Ltd, Glasgow, p.157

[486] The Walsingham Pilgrim Manual 2016, p.13

CHAPTER 22

QUEEN OF PATRIARCHS

In this chapter I will discuss the 39th title **Queen of Patriarchs**[487]. A patriarch is [488] 'the father and ruler of a family tribe… the twelve sons of Jacob, from whom the twelve tribes of Israel were descended; also the fathers of the race, Abraham, Isaac and Jacob and their forefathers.' These were the very early Biblical fathers, from Adam to Noah, the antediluvian patriarchs, and those between the Flood and the birth of Abraham. 'In later Jewish history the president of the Sanhedrin' was called a Patriarch. In the Early Church the title 'Patriarch' was given to 'bishops generally, becoming at length the official title of the bishops of the four patriarchates of Antioch, Alexandria, and Rome, also later of Constantinople, and of Jerusalem.' The title 'patriarch' is also given to 'the father or founder of

---

[487] Dictionary of Mary 'Behold your Mother', Catholic Book Publishing Co. New Jersey 1997, 1985, p.241

[488] The Shorter Oxford English Dictionary on Historical Principles, H.W. Fowler & J. Coulson, Clarendon Press, Oxford, 1973, p.1528

an order', and 'a venerable old man, the oldest man.' Thus some Church leaders have the title Patriarch as well as some men in the Bible.

What does the Bible tells us about Patriarchs?

God called Abram: '"Leave your country, your people and your father's household and go to the land I will show you. I will make you into a great nation and I will bless you. I will make your name great, and you will be a blessing' *(Genesis 12:1-2)*. Following God's instruction, Abram took his extended family to Canaan. The book of Hebrews *(Hebrews 7:1,4)*, refers to an important incident in the life of 'the **patriarch Abraham**', when he met and was blessed by Melchizedek *(Genesis 14:17-20)*. Sarah gave her maidservant Hagar to Abraham and she gave birth to Abram's son Ishmael *(Genesis 16)*. Later, 'When Abram was ninety-nine years old, the Lord appeared to him and said, "I am God Almighty; walk before me and be blameless. I will confirm my covenant between me and you and will greatly increase your numbers.... No longer will you be called Abram; your name will be Abraham, for I have made you a father of many nations... I will establish my covenant as an everlasting covenant between me and you and your descendants after you for the generations to come, to be your God and the God of your descendants after you"' *(Genesis 17:1-7)*. The sign of the Covenant was circumcision for the Jewish males *(Genesis 17:12)*. God told Abraham the amazing news that Sarah would have a son. There was great joy at Isaac's birth *(Genesis 21:1-7)*.

Isaac trusted when God told Abraham to sacrifice him *(Genesis 22)*, and when his father's servant chose Rebekah as his wife *(Genesis 24)*. When Rebecca was pregnant with twins, God told him 'the older will serve the younger' *(Genesis 25:23)*. God established his Covenant with Isaac *(Genesis 26:24)*. God's plan was for Jacob to be next in the line of patriarchs. Jacob received God's blessing, and fled to his Uncle Laban *(Genesis 27)*. On his journey God met Jacob at Bethel in his dream about the ladder to heaven with the angels *(Genesis 28:13-15)*.

Jacob had twelve sons: Reuben, Simeon, Levi, Judah, Zebulon, Issachar, Dan, Gad, Asher, Naphtali, Joseph and Benjamin and a daughter called Dinah *(Genesis 29:31-30:24, 35:16-18)*. God changed Jacob's name to 'Israel'. 'A nation and a community of nations will come from you, and kings will come from your body. The land I gave to Abraham and Isaac I also give to you, and I will give this land to your descendants after you'" *(Genesis 35:9-12)*. The nation, the Jewish people, took the name **Israelites** from this **Patriarch** who fathered the nation. The twelve sons of Jacob who were the heads of the tribes of Israel were **Patriarchs**. As Jacob lay dying, he blessed each son *(Genesis 49)*. Jacob said to Judah: 'The sceptre will not depart from Judah, nor the ruler's staff from between his feet, until he comes to whom it belongs and the obedience of the nations is his' *(Genesis 49:10)*. We can see that this was a prophecy about King David, who was from the tribe of Judah and a great ruler. Jesus was a descendant of David. *(Matthew 1:1-17)*. *Even* today, Jews trace their ancestry back to their tribe of Israel and their **Patriarch**.

'Patriarchs' is the [489]New Testament Greek word *patriarchēs* πάτριαρχης: πατριά which means 'a family' and ἄρχω *arco* that means 'to rule'. So this word means [490]'head of a father's house'. In the Septuagint, which is the very first translation of the original Hebrew Old Testament into Greek (made in the 3rd and 2nd centuries BC), we find this word in some verses in the Old Testament. 'In Jerusalem also, Jehoshaphat appointed some of the Levites, priests and **heads of Israelite families** to administer the law of the Lord and to settle disputes. And they lived in Jerusalem' *(II Chronicles 19:8)*. When Jehoiada made Josiah King the word 'πάτριαρχης' is used: 'He took with him the **commanders** of hundreds, the nobles, **the rulers** of the people and all the people of the land and brought the king down from the temple of the Lord. They went into the palace ... and seated the king on the royal throne' *(II Chronicles 23:20)*. At the time of King Uzziah we read 'πάτριαρχης' again in the Septuagint, meaning 'family leaders'. The total number of **family leaders** over the fighting men was 2,600 *(II Chronicles 26:12)*.

---

[489] An Expository Dictionary of Biblical Words: W.E. Vine, Thomas Nelson, Inc, 1984 P. 463

[490] Analytical Concordance to the Holy Bible, Robert Young, United Society for Christian Literature, Lutterworth Press London, 1973, p. 734

Jesus was descended from the **Patriarch** Judah. Matthew writes: 'A record of the genealogy of Jesus Christ the son of David, the son of Abraham: Abraham was the father of Isaac, Isaac the father of Jacob, Jacob the father of Judah and his brothers.... and Jacob the father of Joseph, the husband of Mary, of whom was born Jesus, who is called Christ. Thus there were fourteen generations in all from Abraham to David, fourteen from David to the exile to Babylon, and fourteen from the exile to the Christ' *(Matthew 1:1-17)*.

Luke traces Jesus' human ancestry back through the **Patriarchs** and the **Antediluvian Patriarchs** telling us that Jesus was: '... the son of Jacob, the son of Isaac, the son of Abraham, the son of Terah, the son of Nahor, the son of Serug, the son of Reu, the son of Peleg, the son of Eber, the son of Shelah, the son of Cainan, the son of Arphaxad, the son of Shem, the son of Noah, the son of Lamech, the son of Methuselah, the son of Enoch, the son of Jared, the son of Mahalalel, the son of Kenan, the son of Enosh, the son of Seth, the son of Adam, the son of God *(Luke 3: 34-38)*. Enoch was the Patriarch who 'walked with God: and he was not; for God took him' *(Genesis 5: 24 AV)*. Enoch's life was very well-pleasing to God so at the time of his death he was taken up into heaven *(Hebrews 11:5)*.

Jesus referred to David calling the Messiah 'LORD' *(Psalm 110:1)* when he asked the Pharisees about whose son was the Christ. They answered 'David' *(Matthew 22: 41-46)*. Jesus said 'If then David calls him 'Lord' how can he be his son?' *(v. 45)* The Pharisees could not answer that question. However we understand that Jesus was descended from David in his human ancestry and Jesus is the Christ because he is the Son of God *(John 1:14)*. This is explored in Chapter 2: **Holy Mother of God and more 'Mother' titles**.

Jesus had an interesting discussion with the Pharisees about the **Patriarch Abraham**. '"Abraham is our father," they answered. "If you were Abraham's children," said Jesus, "then you would do the things Abraham did."... "I tell you the truth," Jesus answered, "before Abraham was born, I am!" At this, they picked up stones to stone him, but Jesus hid himself' *(John 8:39-40,42,53,56-59)*. The Pharisees claimed to be Abraham's descendants, but they were not men of faith, like Abraham. In the phrase 'I am', Jesus was claiming to be the Messiah. Jesus is the

Christ, 'The Word' who was there in the beginning and 'became flesh and made his dwelling among us' *(John 1:1, 14)*. How amazing that before the incarnation Jesus saw and knew Abraham.

Jesus told a story about the rich man and the beggar Lazarus at his gate who was hungry, ill and neglected. Jesus refers to Abraham in heaven *(Luke 16:22-30)*. This teaches us to care for the poor and that Abraham is in heaven.

In his Sermon on the Day of Pentecost: Peter referred to David as 'patriarch', because David was the male head of his family line. Peter was appealing to the Jews' knowledge of their history to show that Jesus' death and resurrection had been prophesied by David. '"Brothers, I can tell you confidently that the **patriarch** David died and was buried, and his tomb is here to this day. But he was a prophet and knew that God had promised him on oath that he would place one of his descendants on his throne. Seeing what was ahead, he spoke of the resurrection of the Christ, that he was not abandoned to the grave, nor did his body see decay' *(Acts 2: 29-31)*.

Stephen reminded the Jewish leaders about some of the Patriarchs, in his speech before the Sanhedrin. 'Then he gave Abraham the covenant of circumcision. And Abraham became the father of Isaac and circumcised him eight days after his birth. Later Isaac became the father of Jacob, and Jacob became the father of the twelve **patriarchs**. Because the **patriarchs** were jealous of Joseph, they sold him as a slave into Egypt. But God was with him' *(Acts 7: 8-9)*.

Paul explained about the Jews: 'Theirs are the **patriarchs**, and from them is traced the human ancestry of Christ, who is God over all, for ever praised! Amen' *(Romans 9:5)*. Paul wrote about Abraham's faith: 'Therefore, the promise comes by faith, so that it may be by grace and may be guaranteed to all Abraham's offspring-not only to those who are of the law but also to those who are of the faith of Abraham... Against all hope, Abraham in hope believed and so became the father of many nations' *(Romans 4: 16-18)*. We are descendants of Abraham if we have faith.

Paul clarified this to the Galatians: 'Consider Abraham: "He believed God, and it was credited to him as righteousness." Understand, then, that those who believe are children of Abraham. The Scripture foresaw that God would justify the Gentiles by faith, and announced the gospel in advance to Abraham: "All nations will be blessed through you." So those who have faith are blessed along with Abraham, the man of faith' *(Galatians 3 6-9)*. How wonderful that because we 'have faith' we receive blessings from the Lord as we 'are blessed along with Abraham'.

How can Mary be addressed as Queen of Patriarchs?

In Chapter 20 **Queen Assumed into Heaven** we explored and reflected on how Mary is Queen in heaven. If we accept that Mary is Queen in heaven; then we can recognise that she is Queen over all the people who are in heaven, which includes the Patriarchs. If we take the logical step and see Mary as **Queen of Patriarchs**; then that does indeed mean that Mary is Queen of Jewish Patriarchs who are her genealogical ancestors! Some British Royal family history can help us understand this. The late Queen Elizabeth the Queen Mother was a queen because she married the future King George VI. Her ancestors might have been surprised to know that one of their descendants was queen! Older and younger members of her family had to bow and curtsy to her. She was not Queen in her own right but because of whom she married; the future King George VI, so when he became King in 1936, as his wife she became Queen Elizabeth. After the King's death in 1952 his widow had the title 'Queen Elizabeth the Queen Mother.' This analogy can help us see how Mary can be addressed as **Queen of Patriarchs** because she is the mother of Jesus.

The **Patriarchs** made mistakes, but God continued to help and bless them. In Egypt *(Genesis 12:10-20)*, and at Gerar *(Genesis 20)*, Abraham said that Sarah was his sister instead of saying she was his wife. Isaac said the same about Rebekah when they visited Abimelech, because he was afraid *(Genesis 26:7-11)*. Jacob cheated his brother Esau to receive God's blessings *(Genesis 27)*. Mary is Queen of Patriarchs and honoured by them because she outshines them in goodness, faith and trusting God.

In the *Magnificat* Mary praises God and associates herself with Abraham as recipients of the Divine promises: 'He has helped his servant Israel, remembering to be merciful to Abraham and his descendants for ever, even as he said to our fathers' *(Luke 1: 54-55)*.

Mary's title [491] '*Queen of Patriarchs* ... glorifies Her as Queen of Her own chosen people, the culmination of that long line of believing men and women who through joy and tribulation, prosperity and failure, held fast to the promise of God. If we have Mary, it is, humanly speaking, because of the Patriarchs. The Patriarchs constituted God's special family, His chosen family, and as such were a type of the Holy Family which could trace its lineage back to Patriarchal days. The great ancestor was Abraham. Mary was proud of him. She was Jewish, glorying in the loyalty of Her people to God, and knowing that the Incarnation was come because the blood that coursed through Her veins had come in a clear, unpolluted stream from the father Abraham.'

Abraham was told by God to sacrifice his son Isaac and he was willing to obey God. He had the knife in his hand ready, when an angel of the Lord stopped him saying: 'now I know that you fear God, because you have not withheld from me your son, your only son' *(Genesis 22:12)*. God provided a ram *(Genesis 22:13)*. When Jesus was crucified, Mary who knew the Scriptures well, may have thought of Abraham's trust in God and his willingness to sacrifice his son at God's command. On the Cross, Mary's only Son was not spared. Jesus is 'the Lamb of God who takes away the sin of the world' *(John 1:29)*. Abraham and Mary both believed, trusted and obeyed God.

Looking at Art work shows how artists imagined Mary as **Queen of Patriarchs**. This visual representation can be helpful for us to imagine

[491] http://www.salvemariaregina.info/SalveMariaRegina/SMR-175/QueenPatriarchs. htm 7th April 2017

Mary in heaven as **Queen of Patriarchs**. This painting [492] shows Mary being crowned by the Patriarchs. We can imagine Mary being welcomed into heaven at her Assumption and being greeted by the Patriarchs as their most special descendant daughter as **Queen of Patriarchs**. She is also Queen of those Church leaders who have the title Patriarch.

What does this mean for us?

Studying the **Patriarch**s in the Bible and tracing Jesus' human ancestry is interesting and reminds us of our long line of genealogical ancestors. It can be fascinating to discover more about the past generations of your own family. A useful website to do that is ancestry.co.uk. We can give thanks to God for the former generations of our family and may discover a certain trade or profession that continues on in the family, and ancestors with faith.

We can learn from the lives of the Biblical **Patriarchs**. Abraham was a man of faith. He heard from God, trusted the Lord and left his home to go to the land the Lord showed him. This can inspire us to listen to the Lord and be open for God's direction and guidance. Abraham grew in a relationship with God and we all need to grow into a closer living relationship with Jesus. What is the Lord calling you to do?

We can be inspired by the words of the **Covenant** that God made with the **Patriarchs**. This covenant was God's promise of blessing. 'I will make you into a great nation and I will bless you; I will make your name great, and you will be a blessing... and all peoples on earth will be blessed through you' *(Genesis 12:1-3)*. We are included in those who receive God's blessings! How have you been blessed recently?

We can be encouraged that the **Patriarchs** made mistakes, but God continued to help and bless them. We can be glad that when we confess our sins and mistakes then God forgives us and gives us a fresh start *(I John 1:7,9)*.

---

[492] https://uk.images.search.yahoo.com/search/images;_ylt=AwrJ7B1npdpd0YMA0jxNBQx.?p=Mary+Queen+of+Patriarchs&imgl=fPeter_Paul_Rubens_079.jpg&action=click 24th November 2019

God spoke to Patriarch Jacob in a dream *(Genesis 28:12-17)*. Let us be ready for God to speak to us in our dreams!

We give thanks for the New Covenant that Jesus made by His death on the Cross enabling all who believe to come to experience God's mercy, love and help. At the Last Supper, Jesus 'took the cup, gave thanks and offered it to them, saying, "Drink from it, all of you. This is my blood of the **covenant**, which is poured out for many for the forgiveness of sins' *(Matthew 26:26-28)*. This is the new covenant where all who believe and receive Jesus can obtain forgiveness. We remember this at every service of Holy Communion. John explains: 'Yet to all who received him, to those who believed in his name, he gave the right to become children of God' *(John 1:12)*.

Through Jesus all peoples can receive God's blessings, whether they are Jews or Gentiles. The new covenant enables us to receive forgiveness and to <u>know</u> the Lord. '"The time is coming, declares the Lord, when I will make a **new covenant** with the house of Israel and with the house of Judah. This is the covenant I will make with the house of Israel after that time, declares the Lord. I will put my laws in their minds and write them on their hearts. I will be their God, and they will be my people...they will all know me, from the least of them to the greatest. For I will forgive their wickedness and will remember their sins no more"' *(Hebrews 8:8,10-12)*. How wonderful that God puts his laws in our minds and on our hearts; so that we can be led by the Holy Spirit and 'let the peace of Christ rule in your hearts' *(Colossians 3: 15)*. We should respond to the promptings of the Holy Spirit, being ready to do 'good works, which God prepared in advance for us to do' *(Ephesians 2:10)*. What are you prompted to do?

We need regularly to receive Communion so we are spiritually refreshed in receiving the Blessed Sacrament. Jesus said: 'Whoever eats my flesh and drinks my blood remains in me, and I in him' *(John 6:56)*. The *Prayer of Humble Access* beautifully expresses our longing to be closer to Jesus by receiving Holy Communion. We pray:

[493]*We do not presume to come to this your table, merciful Lord, trusting in our own righteousness, but in your manifold and great mercies… Grant us therefore, gracious Lord, so to eat the flesh of your dear Son Jesus Christ and to drink his blood, that our sinful bodies may be made clean by his body and our souls washed through his most precious blood, and that we may evermore dwell in him, and he in us. Amen.*

Patriarch David wrote many Psalms that help and inspire us. Like David we need to grow into a closer relationship with God, knowing that the Lord is 'my Shepherd' *(Psalm 23:1-6)*. How wonderful that the Lord leads us to 'green pastures' by 'quiet waters'. We can know that the Lord is with us in times of sorrow and joy.

[494]Mary, *Queen of Patriarchs, pray for us.*

---

[493] Common Worship Services and Prayers for the Church of England, Church House Publishing, 2000, p. 181

[494] The Walsingham Pilgrim Manual 2016, p.13

CHAPTER 23

QUEEN OF PROPHETS

In this chapter I will discuss the 40th title of Our Lady in the [495]Litany of Loreto.

What does the Bible tells us about Prophets?

The Old Testament is the story of God's wanting His chosen people to be close to Him; while so often they sinned and separated themselves from his loving help and presence. God sent prophets to turn the people back to him. The **prophets** had a two-fold task: the reception and transmission of the revelation. After being called by God, the mind and heart of the prophet was receptive to the divine word, as the prophet understood God's purposes. The true prophets only preached the word of God. Peake's

[495] Dictionary of Mary 'Behold your Mother', Catholic Book Publishing Co. New Jersey 1997, 1985, p.241

Commentary explains the work of the prophet as [496] 'neither a mere foreteller of isolated events nor a mere moral preacher; he was inspired by a vision of the coming Kingdom of God.' The prophets were deeply aware of the moral code of their religion. They saw God controlling history; that God is the creator and will help his people. God controlled other nations and was bringing doom and disaster to the people who were not following his commands. The people had hope of a perfect time in the future with a Messianic King. Prophecy and history are related because God's spoken message through the prophet was relevant at the time of utterance. The Old Testament prophet was God's representative, the link between God and man. The prophets realised that faith and obedience to God were important, and they could rebuke earthly kings. Many prophets performed symbolic acts, to make an idea clear to the people: they showed God's word in action.

Moses prepared the people to listen to God's prophets and taught them how to recognise a true prophet from God: '...The Lord your God will raise up for you a prophet like me from among your own brothers. You must listen to him. The Lord said to me...: If anyone does not listen to my words that the prophet speaks in my name, I myself will call him to account. But a prophet who presumes to speak in my name anything I have not commanded him to say, or a prophet who speaks in the name of other gods, must be put to death." You may say to yourselves, "How can we know when a message has not been spoken by the Lord?" If what a prophet proclaims in the name of the Lord does not take place or come true, that is a message the Lord has not spoken. That prophet has spoken presumptuously. Do not be afraid of him' *(Deuteronomy 18: 14-22)*. The true prophets listened to God and only preached the word of God.

Alec Motyer writes about **The Prophets**. [497]'The people of Israel had become a nation... But they were constantly falling down on their calling and their promises. With idol-worship, civil war, immorality, complacency,

---

[496] Peake's Commentary on the Bible, Edited by Arthur S. Peake, London, T.C. & E.C. Jack Ltd, 1931, p. 427

[497] The Lion Handbook to the Bible, David and Pat Alexander, Lion Publishing, 1973, p. 370

the nation needed to be recalled again and again to the whole point of their existence. The prophets were men raised up by God to do just this – to call the people back to God and his way... Their intention is to recall the people from false priorities; to insist on God's primary requirement that his people should obey his commands and live out his standards.' The prophets spoke God's word and messages to the people.

We read about the **early prophets** in the books of Samuel and Kings. Samuel was called by God when he was a young boy. He said 'Speak for your servant is listening' *(I Samuel 3:10)*. Samuel heard God speak and told God's message to Eli. When David was king in Israel, God sent Nathan the prophet to rebuke him after his relationship with Bathsheba *(II Samuel 12)*. Later Nathan told David that he was not to build the Temple, but his son would build the Temple *(I Chronicles 17)*. Elijah was a prophet in Israel at the time of King Ahab. The contest on Mount Carmel showed 'The Lord – he is God!' *(I Kings 18)* At the time of Elijah and Elisha there were large numbers of prophets who lived in groups or guilds. We read about 'the company of the prophets' at Bethel *(II Kings 2:2)*, and at Jericho *(II Kings 2:5)*, who told Elisha that 'the Lord is going to take your master today' *(II Kings 2:3)*. That is just what happened: 'they were walking along and talking together, suddenly a chariot of fire and horses of fire appeared and separated.... them. Elijah went up to heaven in a whirlwind' *(II Kings 2:11)*.

God called prophets. Amos was an 8th century prophet 'taken from being a shepherd' *(Amos 7:14)*. God spoke to Amos using a basket of ripe fruit. 'Then the Lord said to me, "The time is ripe for my people Israel; I will spare them no longer"' *(Amos 8:1-2)*. Hosea saw God's word reflected in the life of his family: he was told to marry an adulterous wife 'because the land is guilty of the vilest adultery in departing from the Lord' *(Hosea 1:2)*. Isaiah had a vision of heaven and he answered God's call, saying 'Here am I, send me' *(Isaiah 6:8)*. Jonah ran away from God's call but eventually went to Nineveh where the people heard him and repented *(Jonah 1-4)*. Jeremiah was another reluctant prophet *(Jeremiah 1:4-10)*. Ezekiel did many dramatic actions to tell forth God's word *(Ezekiel 4:5,12)*.

In the Bible the '**Minor Prophets**' with their own books are: Daniel, Hosea, Amos, Obadiah, Jonah, Micah, Nahum, Habakkuk, Zephaniah, Haggai, Zechariah and Malachi. The '**Major Prophets**' are Isaiah,

Jeremiah and Ezekiel. Amos and Hosea were 8ᵗʰ Century prophets in Israel, warning the people to turn back to the Lord. As the people did not repent; at the time of King Hoshea, Samaria fell to the Assyrians and the people were deported to Assyria in 722 BC. Later Isaiah, Micah, Nahum, Habakkuk, Zephaniah and Jeremiah prophesied in Judah to tell the people to walk in God's ways. Isaiah said 'Woe to the wicked, disaster is upon them' *(Isaiah 3:11a)*. However, the people did not turn to the Lord, so there were three times when people were taken to Babylon. In 605 BC Daniel went in the first wave of deportation and he was a prophet in Babylon. Ezekiel prophesied in Judah, then in 597 he was deported to Babylon and he prophesied there. In 586 Jerusalem fell to the Babylonians and the Temple was destroyed *(Jeremiah 52)*.

'The Lord, the God of their fathers, sent word to them through his messengers again and again, because he had pity on his people and on his dwelling-place. But they mocked God's messengers, despised his words and scoffed at his **prophets** until the wrath of the Lord was aroused against his people and there was no remedy. He brought up against them the king of the Babylonians... He carried to Babylon all the articles from the temple of God...They set fire to God's temple and broke down the wall of Jerusalem; they burned all the palaces and destroyed everything of value there' *(II Chronicles 36:15-19)*. How sad that more people were taken to Babylon; leaving only 'the poorest people of the land' *(Jeremiah 52:16)*.

After 70 years Cyrus ordered the Temple in Jerusalem to be re-built, 'in order to fulfil the word of the Lord spoken by Jeremiah, the Lord moved the heart of Cyrus king of Persia to make a proclamation throughout his realm and to put it in writing. This is what Cyrus king of Persia says, "The Lord, the God of heaven ... has appointed me to build a temple for him at Jerusalem in Judah. Anyone of his people among you – may the Lord his God be with him, and let him go up"' *(II Chronicles 36:22-23)*. Ezra and Nehemiah were among the many who returned to re-build Jerusalem; with the encouragements of the **Prophets** Haggai, Zechariah and Malachi. In 516 the Temple was rebuilt.

The **prophets** spoke powerful words frequently introduced with the phrase 'Hear the word of the LORD' *(Jeremiah 7:2)*. The prophet received a message from God and then presented the revelation in various ways.

Isaiah sometimes sang God's message, as in Isaiah's Song of the Vineyard *(Isaiah 5)*. Amos spoke a lament to call people to repentance *(Amos 5:1-17)*. Ezekiel used an allegory to communicate a message *(Chapter 16)*, parables *(Chapters 23, 31)*, vision *(Chapter 37)*, and dramatic actions *(Chapters 4,5,12)*. The prophets spoke to exhort the people to turn back to the Lord. Habakkuk asked a question *(1:1-4)*, and prayed *(Chapter 3)*, to communicate his message. [498] Brother Ramon explains 'the role of a prophet is to stand before the people on behalf of God. The prophet was the bearer of the word of God. The Prophets spoke and communicated the message that God wanted the people to hear.'

There were many prophecies about the **Messiah**; Jesus fulfilled over 300 Old Testament prophecies[499]. His birth in Bethlehem was foretold by the prophet Micah *(Micah 5:2)*. Brother Ramon writes about Jesus' fulfilling prophecy as [500]'his ministry was the fulfilment of the whole prophetic tradition'. Jesus said '"Do not think that I have come to abolish the Law or the Prophets; I have not come to abolish them but to fulfil them"' *(Matthew 5:17)*. [501]Brother Ramon explains that: 'The pre-incarnate Christ was present in the old prophets imparting spiritual discernment concerning himself *(I Peter 1:10-11)*; he was the great prophet of fulfilment during his earthly ministry.' Isaiah prophesied about the Messiah: 'The Spirit of the Lord will rest on him – the Spirit of wisdom and of understanding, the Spirit of counsel and of power, the Spirit of knowledge and of the fear of the Lord... with righteousness he will judge the needy, with justice he will give decisions for the poor of the earth' *(Isaiah 11:2-4a)*. Jesus' life helped needy people. Jesus' death on the Cross to take our sins was prophesied by Isaiah: 'He was despised and rejected by men, a man of sorrows, and familiar with suffering... Surely he took up our infirmities and carried our sorrows, yet we considered him stricken by God, smitten by him, and afflicted. But he was pierced for our transgressions, he was crushed for our iniquities; the punishment that brought us peace was upon him, and by

---

[498] The Way of Love, Br Ramon, Marshall Pickering, 1994, p. 170

[499] The Alpha Course, Session 1, Who is Jesus?

[500] Ramon, op. cit., p. 171

[501] The Way of Love, Br Ramon, Marshall Pickering, 1994, p. 171-172

his wounds we are healed. We all, like sheep, have gone astray, each of us has turned to his own way; and the Lord has laid on him the iniquity of us all' *(Isaiah 53:3-6)*.

On Good Friday, [502]Jesus fulfilled 29 Old Testament prophecies in one day. Peter told the people in Jerusalem: 'But this is how God fulfilled what he had foretold through all the prophets, saying that his Christ would suffer.' *(Acts 3:18)* Peter tells us 'Concerning this salvation, the **prophets**, who spoke of the grace that was to come to you, searched intently and with the greatest care, trying to find out the time and circumstances to which the Spirit of Christ in them was pointing when he predicted the sufferings of Christ and the glories that would follow. It was revealed to them that they were not serving themselves but you, when they spoke of the things that have now been told you by those who have preached the gospel to you by the Holy Spirit sent from heaven' *(I Peter 1:10-12)*. Jesus' death for our salvation was prophesied in the Old Testament.

Jesus is a Prophet. Moses told the people that 'The Lord your God will raise up for you **a prophet** like me from among your own brothers. You must listen to him' *(Deuteronomy 18:15)*. Jesus is this Prophet. Later Peter applied this verse to Jesus *(Acts 3:22)*. The crowds recognised Jesus as a prophet. At Caesarea Philippi, Jesus asked who people said he was. 'They replied, "Some say John the Baptist; others say Elijah; and still others, Jeremiah or one of the **prophets**"' *(Matthew 16:14)*. The man born blind told the Pharisees about Jesus that 'he is a prophet' *(John 9:17)*. Jesus prophesied about the fall of Jerusalem, which happened in the year 70 AD, saying: "the time will come when not one stone will be left on another; every one of them will be thrown down" *(Luke 21:6)*. Jesus prophesied to the women of Jerusalem *(Luke 23:28-30)*. We read: 'In the past God spoke to our forefathers through the **prophets** at many times and in various ways, but in these last days he has spoken to us by his Son, whom he appointed heir of all things, and through whom he made the universe' *(Hebrews 1: 1-2)*. God speaks through Jesus whom we can recognise as a Prophet, communicating God's message of repentance, forgiveness and love.

---

[502] The Alpha Course, Session 1, Who is Jesus?

Jesus honoured John the Baptist as 'more than a prophet' *(Matthew 11: 7-11)*. John the Baptist prepared the way for the coming of Jesus, by calling people to repentance *(Matthew 3:1-12 and Luke 3:1-18)*. John's preaching in the desert was prophesied by Isaiah *(Isaiah 40:3, Mark 1:2-3)*. John recognised that Jesus is the Messiah, 'who takes away the sin of the world' *(John 1:29)*. John was preaching and baptising. One day he baptised Jesus *(Mark 1:4-11)*. 'Then John gave this testimony: "I saw the Spirit come down from heaven as a dove and remain on him. I would not have known him, except that the one who sent me to baptise with water told me, 'The man on whom you see the Spirit come down and remain is he who will baptise with the Holy Spirit.' I have seen and I testify that this is the Son of God"' *(John 1:29-34)*.

The Holy Spirit gives the gift of prophecy to the Church. 'Now to each one the manifestation of the Spirit is given for the common good. To one there is given through the Spirit the message of wisdom, to another the message of knowledge by means of the same Spirit, to another faith by the same Spirit, to another gifts of healing by that one Spirit, to another miraculous powers, to another **prophecy**, to another distinguishing between spirits, to another speaking in different kinds of tongues, and to still another the interpretation of tongues' *(I Corinthians 12:7-10)*. St Paul told the Corinthian Church: 'Follow the way of love and eagerly desire spiritual gifts, especially the gift of **prophecy**... But everyone who prophesies speaks to men for their strengthening, encouragement and comfort... For you can all **prophesy** in turn so that everyone may be instructed and encouraged. The spirits of prophets are subject to the control of prophets. For God is not a God of disorder but of peace' *(I Corinthians 14:1-5,29-33)*. Some charismatic Churches in these days have the gift of **prophecy** as part of their worship. That is a way that people can hear the Lord speak to them. Words of prophecy are inspired by the Holy Spirit so that people receive 'strengthening, encouragement and comfort'.

How can Mary be addressed as Queen of Prophets?

Mary was a 'Prophet' when she sang the *Magnificat*, because it is a prophetic utterance, telling forth God's word and the Lord's desire to reach out to the poor, lowly and hungry. The *Magnificat* is said or sung every evening at Evensong. It is easy to become over-familiar with these words, so the radical social impact is not recognised. 'Mary said: "He has scattered those who are proud in their inmost thoughts. He has brought down rulers from their thrones but has lifted up the humble. He has filled the hungry with good things but has sent the rich away empty. He has helped his servant Israel, remembering to be merciful to Abraham and his descendants for ever, even as he said to our fathers"' *(Luke 1: 46-55).*

T. Hancock writes: [503]'the *Magnificat* has as its motive the scattering, disappointment, and depression by God's Son of those classes in every nation... whom Mary calls 'the proud', 'the mighty,' and 'the rich'... When the Church, evening after evening, in all her parishes, is saying this hymn, she is unconsciously foretelling... that greatest of all revolutions, which the Blessed Virgin saw to be involved in the birth and work of Him whom she carried in her womb. To Mary ... was revealed the stupendous social and political reversal which the birth of the Son of God as the Son of Man, as the son of the poor carpenter's wife was bound sooner or later to produce in all the world.... He is exalting the humble and meek; that He is filling the hungry with good things and that He is sending the rich empty away .... Her so-called hymn is nothing less than a disguised socialist war-song.'

The *Magnificat* is a **prophetic** utterance, when Mary was telling forth in song what God will do. There are close links with Jesus' manifesto at Nazareth at the beginning of his public ministry: Jesus read verses from Isaiah 61: "'The Spirit of the Lord is on me, because he has anointed me to preach good news to the poor. He has sent me to proclaim freedom for the prisoners and recovery of sight for the blind, to release the oppressed, to proclaim the year of the Lord's favour." Then he rolled up the scroll,

---

[503] Religion in Victorian Britain, Volume 111 Sources, James R. Moore, Manchester University Press, 1998, p. 98-100

gave it back to the attendant and sat down. The eyes of everyone in the synagogue were fastened on him, and he began by saying to them, "Today this scripture is fulfilled in your hearing"' *(Luke 4:18-21).* Jesus said he will bring good news to the poor, freedom to the oppressed and healing to the blind. Jesus announced that he would help the poor and lowly; just as His Mother sang in her *Magnificat.* Jesus did and does all these works!

We have seen that the *Magnificat* was considered subversive in the nineteenth century. The idea of 'lifting up the lowly' was certainly counter-cultural then; as it is today. Even in the nineteenth century the attitude of many to poverty was: [504]'Poverty was morally tolerable'. We can see Mary as **Queen of Prophets** because she spoke words of prophecy in the *Magnificat*; expressing God's love and concern for the poor.

Fr Canice writes about the *Magnificat*: [505]'the sacred words of Mary's canticle are akin to prophecy: they have their origin in the revelations which were made to her by Gabriel and which were developed interiorly in her by the light of the Holy Spirit. Considered in that manner the *Magnificat* merits a distinguished place amongst prophetic utterances in the broad sense and, though we may not assert that Mary was a prophetess, she remains worthy of the glorious name of '**Queen of Prophets**' which the Church has bestowed upon her.'

There are seven recorded words [506] of Mary described as 'childlike wonder' *(Luke 1:34)*; obedient servant *(Luke 1:38)*; Scriptural knowledge *(Luke 1:38)*; joyful praise *(Luke 1:46-55)*; gentle authority *(Luke 2:48)*; tender charity *(John 2:3)*; and deep faith *(John 2:5)*. The wonder and questioning reminds us of Jeremiah's surprise at God's call *(Jeremiah 1:6)*. The faith, obedience and charity of Mary are a wonderful example to us all; because Mary is speaking in line with God's plan. Indeed 'Do whatever he tells you' *(John 2:5)*, is what the Old Testament prophets said; to do

---

[504] Religion in Victorian Britain, Volume 11 Controversies, Gerald Parsons, Manchester University Press, 1997, p. 43

[505] Mary: A Study of the Mother of God, Fr Canice O.F.M.Cap, M.H.Gill and Sons Ltd, Dublin, 1950, p. 117-118

[506] Dictionary of Mary 'Behold your Mother', Catholic Book Publishing Co, New Jersey 1997, 1985, p. 498-501

whatever God tells you, following His commandments. This phrase is a concise and precise summary of all the teachings of the Old Testament prophets and John the Baptist who prepared the way for Jesus. This, and other spoken words of Mary, helps us to see her indeed as **Queen of Prophets**, because she spoke words of prophecy, expressing God's will for the people.

Hilda Graef [507] recognises Mary as **Queen of Prophets** because she fulfils prophecy from the Old Testament. She comments on this verse about Eve: 'And I will put enmity between you and the woman, and between your offspring and hers; he will crush your head, and you will strike his heel' *(Genesis 3:15)*. Graef writes that this verse is: 'according to tradition the first mention in the Bible of Christ and his Mother, the Woman and her seed.' As Eve did not crush the head of the serpent so 'it seems obvious that 'the woman' must be another than Eve, indeed it must be Mary herself, as the 'second Eve', who through her obedience repaired the damage done by the first.' Mary is seen to fulfil God's word spoken in the Garden of Eden.

Br Ramon explains that [508] Mary 'is the obedient servant of the Lord through whom the Christ would come into the world. As the Fathers of the Church said, Eva became Ave (Hail), as Mary reversed the disobedience of Eve, so Christ might reverse the fall of Adam.' Br Ramon recognises that Mary enables the reversal of the sin of Eve, because she gave birth to Jesus who died so all who believe in Him can be forgiven. *(John 3:16-17)*.

Mary fulfilled this prophecy in Isaiah: 'The virgin will be with child and will give birth to a son, and will call him Immanuel' *(Isaiah 7:14)*. Hilda Graef comments that [509] 'the whole tenor of the passage appears to indicate an extraordinary event, indeed, 'a sign'. Coppens[510], after a careful

---

[507] Mary: A History of Doctrine and Devotion: Hilda Graef, Christian Classics, Westminster, 1987, The Liturgical Press Collegeville, Minnesota, p. 1

[508] When they Crucified my Lord: Brother Ramon, BRF, 1999, p. 104

[509] Mary: A History of Doctrine and Devotion: Hilda Graef, Christian Classics, Westminster, 1987, The Liturgical Press Collegeville, Minnesota, p. 3

[510] La Prophetie de la Almah, J. Coppens, in ETL (1952) pp. 668ff

analysis of other possibilities, concludes that 'the text is a prophecy of the Messiah and his mother in the strict, literal sense.'

Jesus's birth fulfilled this prophecy. The Angel told Joseph about the virginal conception of Jesus; and Matthew explains that this is the fulfilment of Isaiah's prophecy: 'what is conceived in her is from the Holy Spirit... All this took place to fulfil what the Lord had said through the prophet: "The virgin will be with child and will give birth to a son, and they will call him Immanuel"-which means, "God with us"' *(Matthew 1:20-23).*

Hilda Graef[511] refers to G.R. Driver[512] who wrote about the significance of an expected virginal birth. He wrote 'the idea was current among the Canaanites... and other nations of the Middle East that the extraordinary, even virginal birth of a child was to introduce a new era of happiness' *(Matthew 1:20-23).* Jesus' birth indeed introduced 'a new era of happiness', with people coming to realise God's love and receive forgiveness, peace and help in their lives as Jesus came to bring abundant life *(John 10:10).*

Rev Eamon R. Carroll writes [513]'"Queen of prophets" is one of the titles of our Lady in the Litany of Loreto. For many Catholics calling Mary "queen of prophets" is a reminder that the prophets of the Old Testament looked ahead to the Mother of the Messiah as well as the Messiah himself. In early Christian understanding, however, our Lady was herself also regarded as a prophet. There had been no prophets in Israel for some centuries before Christ, and the revival of prophecy was expected as a sign of the coming of messianic times. The gift of prophecy was given to Mary of Nazareth in her role of preparing for the Messiah; that she is a prophet is part of the Gospel portrait of the Virgin Mother of Jesus.' We gave seen this above *(Luke 1:46-55, John 2:5).*

We should take notice of messages that Mary has given in visions and apparitions, when she continues to speak prophetically. When Mary has

---

[511] Mary: A History of Doctrine and Devotion: Hilda Graef, Christian Classics, Westminster, 1987, The Liturgical Press Collegeville, Minnesota, p. 4

[512] Canaanite Myths, G.R. Driver, 1925, p.125

[513] https://catholicus.wordpress.com/2006/09/20/mary-queen-of-prophets/ 3rd November 2016

appeared in apparitions to people she has spoken prophetic words from God: at Lourdes to Bernadette; at Fátima to Lucia, Francisco and Jacinta; and at Medjugorje[514] where she continues to give messages, speaking as **Queen of Prophets**.

Mary is **Queen of Prophets** because she fulfilled prophecy, including the woman in heaven *(Revelation 12:1-2)*. She was a prophet by speaking forth God's prophetic messages. In Chapter 20 **Queen Assumed into Heaven**, we explored how Mary is Queen in heaven. If we accept that Mary is Queen in heaven; then we can recognise that she is Queen over all the people who are in heaven. This includes the prophets of the Lord from the Old Testament days, John the Baptist and all those in the Christian Church who have been used in the gift of prophecy. This means that we can recognise Mary as the Queen of Prophets in heaven.

What does this mean for us?

Mary said 'Do whatever he tells you' *(John 2:5)*. This phrase is a concise and precise summary of all the teachings of the Old Testament prophets and John the Baptist who prepared the way for Jesus. What is Jesus telling you to do?

The *Magnificat* shows God's care and concern for the poor and the lowly. How do you show God's love and care for the poor? Do you give food to a food bank? Do you give money to charities that help the poor?

How wonderful that 'All Scripture is God-breathed and is useful for teaching, rebuking, correcting and training in righteousness' *(II Timothy 3:16-17)*. The **prophetic books** were written with God's message for the people at that certain time in history; and yet God still speaks through those words today. We need to be ready for the Lord to speak when we read the Bible. What has the Lord shown you recently through the Bible?

One of my favourite Bible verses is: 'So do not fear, for I am with you; do not be dismayed, for I am your God. I will strengthen you and help you; I will uphold you with my righteous right hand' *(Isaiah 41:10)*.

---

[514] http://www.medjugorje.ws/en/messages/ 7th February 2018

This verse has often given me encouragement and assurance that the Lord will be with me and help me, when I am facing difficult and challenging situations. Which verses in prophetic books are special to you?

Jesus' birth indeed introduced 'a new era of happiness', with people coming to realise God's love and receive forgiveness, peace and help in their lives as Jesus came to bring abundant life, saying: 'I am come that they may have life, and have it to the full' *(John 10:10)*. This is such good news to share about the love of Jesus and the 'abundant life' we can enjoy. Whom can you share this good news with?

A Collect reminds us about the importance of prophets in the foundation of the Church:

[515]*O Almighty God, who hast built thy Church upon the foundation of the apostles and **prophets**, Jesus Christ himself being the head cornerstone: grant us so to be joined together in unity of spirit by their doctrine, that we may be made a holy temple acceptable unto thee.'*

[516] The *Te Deum Laudamus* at Morning Prayer describes the wonderful heavenly worship:

*We praise thee, O God; we acknowledge thee to be the Lord. All the earth doth worship thee, the Father everlasting. To thee all angels cry aloud, the heavens and all the powers therein... The **goodly fellowship of the prophets** praise thee....*

[517]Mary, Queen of Prophets, pray for us.

---

[515] Common Worship Services and Prayers for the Church of England, Church House Publishing, 2000, p. 515, Collect for Simon and Jude

[516] Ibid., p. 67

[517] The Walsingham Pilgrim Manual 2016, p.13

CHAPTER 24

QUEEN OF MARTYRS AND
QUEEN OF CONFESSORS

In this chapter I will discuss two of the '**Queen**' titles: the 42nd title **Queen of Martyrs** and the 43rd title is **Queen of Confessors** in the [518]Litany of Loreto.

What does the Bible tell us about Martyrs and Confessors?

Martyr means 'witness'. Μαρτυριον *(marturion)* is [519]'testimony or witness borne, a declaration of facts' as μαρτυρια (marturia) means [520]'**testimony, bearing witness**'. John the Baptist 'came as a witness to testify concerning

---

[518] Dictionary of Mary 'Behold your Mother', Catholic Book Publishing Co. New Jersey 1997, 1985, p.241

[519] An Expository Dictionary of Biblical Words: W.E. Vine, Thomas Nelson, Inc, 1984, p. 680

[520] Ibid., p. 681

that light' who is Jesus *(John 1:7)*. John's testimony was that he was preparing the way for the Lord *(John 1:20,23)*. He gave testimony about what happened at Jesus' baptism, and said 'I have seen and I testify that this is the Son of God' *(John 1:32-34)*. The New Testament Greek word is μαρτυς *(martus)* means [521]a witness who gives evidence and testifies. Jesus said to Nicodemus about Himself that 'He testifies to what he has seen and heard, but no one accepts his testimony' *(John 3:32-33)*. This word μαρτυς is used at Jesus' trial when the chief priests wanted to find evidence and testimony against Jesus: 'Many testified falsely against him, but their statements did not agree *(Mark 14:55-56)*.

This word is used for '**witnesses**' when Jesus talked to the apostles before His Ascension, saying: 'But you will receive power when the Holy Spirit comes on you; and you will be my witnesses in Jerusalem, and in all Judea and Samaria, and to the ends of the earth" *(Acts 1:8)*. Jesus told the apostles to go and be witnesses; giving evidence testifying to the love, death and resurrection of Jesus' helping more people come to follow Him.

The New Testament Greek word μαρτυς *(martus)* can also mean [522]'one who bears 'witness' by his death'. 'Martyr' is defined as [523]'Literally, 'one who is put to death because of his or her faith in Jesus Christ.' **Stephen** was the first **Martyr** in the Church. He testified to the truth about Jesus and as a result he was stoned to death *(Acts 6:8-8:1,7:55-59)*. Stephen had a vision of heaven as he died and he was given the grace to forgive those who stoned him. Paul was later filled with remorse that 'when the blood of your martyr Stephen was shed, I stood there giving my approval and guarding the clothes of those who were killing him' *(Acts 22:20)*. Stephen's martyrdom was followed by a time of persecution for the Church, for **confessors**; those who confessed the faith in Jesus. 'On that day a great persecution broke out against the church at Jerusalem' *(Acts 8:1b)*. Later **James** suffered martyrdom *(Acts 12:1-2)*.

We are encouraged that the Old Testament people of faith *(Hebrews 11)* are watching us and cheering us on: 'we are surrounded by such a great

---

[521] The Analytical Greek Lexicon, London: Samuel Bagster and Sons Ltd, 1973, p.268

[522] Vine, op. cit., p. 680

[523] Catholicism: Richard P. McBrien, HarperCollins, 1994, p. 1244

cloud of **witnesses**' *(Hebrews 12:1)*. Those who have witnessed and given testimony about their faith in Jesus, and martyrs who have died for their faith in Jesus, are honoured in heaven. 'After this I looked and there before me was a great multitude that no-one could count, from every nation, tribe, people and language, standing before the throne and in front of the Lamb. They were wearing white robes and were holding palm branches in their hands. And they cried out in a loud voice: "Salvation belongs to our God, who sits on the throne, and to the Lamb."….. These are they who have come out of the great tribulation; they have washed their robes and made them white in the blood of the Lamb.' *(Revelation 7:9-17)*.

Through the history of the Christian Church from the times recorded in the Acts of the Apostles, many saints and confessors of the faith have suffered persecution, torture and martyrdom. [524] 'The 2nd-century Church Father Tertullian wrote that "the blood of martyrs is the seed of the Church," implying that the martyrs' willing sacrifice of their lives leads to the conversion of others. Relics of the saints are still revered in the Catholic and Orthodox Churches. The lives of the martyrs became a source of inspiration for some Christians, and their relics were honoured.' How wonderful that all those martyrs are in heaven wearing white where 'God will wipe away every tear from their eyes' *(Revelation 7:17)*.

Other martyrs whose names we recognise from the New Testament are: [525]'The holy **Apostle Philip**, bound with his head to a pillar, and **stoned**, at Hierapolis, in Phrygia, A.D. 54. **James**, the son of Alpheus, or brother of the Lord, cast down from the temple, stoned, and **beaten to death** with a club, A.D. 63. **Barnabas**, a companion of the Apostle Paul, dragged out of the city and burned, at Salamina in Cyprus, A.D. 64. **Mark**, the holy Evangelist, dragged to the stake at Alexandria, died on the way, A.D. 64. **Simon Peter**, the holy Apostle, **crucified** with his head downward, under Emperor Nero, A.D. 69. **Paul**, the Apostle of Christ, sorely persecuted, and finally **beheaded,** at Rome, under the emperor

---

[524] https://en.wikipedia.org/w/index.php?title=Christian_martyrs&action=edit&section=4 27th April 2017

[525] http://www.gospelfuel.com/a-list-of-new-testament-martyrs/ outlined in the book, Martyrs Mirror 27th April 2017

Nero, A.D. 69. **Aristarchus**, a traveling companion of Paul, **slain** at Rome, under Nero, about A.D. 70. **Epaphras**, a fellow prisoner of Paul, **slain** under Nero, about A.D. 70. Four fellow labourers and relatives of Paul, namely, **Priscilla, Aquila, Andronicus**, and **Junia, martyred** at Rome, under Nero, about A.D. 70. **Silas**, or Silvanus, scourged at Philippi, in Macedonia, and **died a martyr**, about A.D. 70. **Onesiphorus**, a friend of Paul, and **Porphyrius**, his companion, tied to wild horses, and dragged, or **torn to death**, at Hellespontus, through the edict of Nero, about A.D. 70. **Andrew**, the holy Apostle, **crucified** at Patras, in Achaia, about A.D. 70. **Bartholomew**, the holy Apostle of Christ, first greatly tortured, then **flayed alive,** and finally **beheaded**, in Armenia, by King Astyages, about A.D. 70. **Thomas**, the holy Apostle of Christ, tormented with red-hot plates, **cast into a furnace**, and his side pierced with spears by the savages at Calamina, about A.D. 70. **Matthew**, the holy Evangelist, nailed to the ground, and **beheaded** at Nad-davar, under King Hytacus, about A.D. 70. **Simon Zelotes** and his brother **Judas Thaddeus**, both slain for the truth of Christ – the one **crucified**, and the other **beaten to death** with sticks, about A.D. 70. **Matthias**, the holy Apostle of Christ, tied on a cross upon a rock, stoned, and then **beheaded**, A.D. 70. **Luke**, the holy Evangelist, **hanged** on a green olive tree, in Greece, A.D. 93. **Antipas**, the faithful witness of Jesus Christ, **burned** at Pergamos in a red-hot brazen ox, A.D. 95. **Timothy**, the spiritual son of the Apostle Paul, **stoned** to death by the heathen idolaters at Ephesus, about A.D. 98. The world's worst tortures could not make these believers deny the Lord Jesus. The more they were persecuted, the more their numbers grew.'

The dictionary tells us that a **confessor** is: [526]'one who avows and adheres to his faith under persecution and torture, but does not suffer martyrdom.' **John**, was a **confessor** of the faith, [527]'**banished** to the Isle of Patmos, by Emperor Domitian, A.D. 97.' Christian Confessors were persecuted and were prepared to be martyred for their faith in Jesus. The

[526] The Shorter Oxford English Dictionary on Historical Principles, H.W. Fowler & J. Coulson, Clarendon Press, Oxford, 1973, p.395

[527] http://www.gospelfuel.com/a-list-of-new-testament-martyrs/ outlined in the book, Martyrs Mirror 27th April

early Christians refused to worship the Roman gods or pay homage to the Emperor.

The **Bible** tells us about the Christian faith that **confessors** confess. The Christian faith is written in *The Creeds* as they are statements of Christian faith based on the Bible. [528] These affirmations of faith express the faith that **confessors** confessed about Jesus, and some Christians were and are **martyred** for believing. These are Biblical and clearly express the Christian faith about Jesus:

Though he was divine, he did not cling to equality with God, but made himself nothing. Taking the form of a slave, he was born in human likeness. He humbled himself and was obedient to death, even the death of the cross. Therefore God has raised him on high, and given him the name above every name: that at the name of Jesus every knee should bow, and every voice proclaim that Jesus Christ is Lord, to the glory of God the Father. (Philippians 2.6-11) Amen.

Let us declare our faith in the resurrection of our Lord Jesus Christ: *Christ died for our sins in accordance with the Scriptures; he was buried; he was raised to life on the third day in accordance with the Scriptures; afterwards he appeared to his followers, and to all the apostles: this we have received, and this we believe. (I Corinthians 15:3-7) Amen.*

[529]The *Apostles' Creed* was the statement of faith to be believed and confessed by those being baptised and is said at Baptism and Confirmation Services and at Morning and Evening Prayer:

I believe in God, the Father Almighty, creator of heaven and earth.

I believe in Jesus Christ, his only Son, our Lord, who was conceived by the Holy Spirit, born of the Virgin Mary, suffered under Pontius Pilate, was crucified, died, and was buried; he descended to the dead. On the third day he rose again; he ascended into heaven, he is seated at the right hand of the Father, and he will come to judge the living and the dead.

---

[528] Common Worship Services and Prayers for the Church of England, Church House Publishing, 2000, p.147

[529] Ibid., p. 43

*I believe in the Holy Spirit, the holy catholic Church, the communion
of saints, the forgiveness of sins, the resurrection of the body, and the life
everlasting. Amen.*

[530]The *Nicene Creed* is said at Mass, stating the faith of the Church:

*We believe in one God, the Father, the Almighty, maker of heaven and
earth, of all that is, seen and unseen...*

*We believe in one Lord, Jesus Christ, the only Son of God, eternally
begotten of the Father, God from God, Light from Light, true God from true
God, begotten, not made, of one Being with the Father. Through him all
things were made. For us and for our salvation he came down from heaven,
was incarnate from the Holy Spirit and the Virgin Mary, and was made man.
For our sake he was crucified under Pontius Pilate; he suffered death and was
buried. On the third day he rose again in accordance with the Scriptures; he
ascended into heaven and is seated at the right hand of the Father. He will
come again in glory to judge the living and the dead, and his kingdom will
have no end.*

*We believe in the Holy Spirit, the Lord, the giver of life, who proceeds
from the Father and the Son. With the Father and the Son he is worshipped
and glorified. He has spoken through the prophets. We believe in one holy,
catholic and apostolic Church. We acknowledge one baptism for the forgiveness
of sins. We look for the resurrection of the dead, and the life of the world to
come. Amen.*

A well-known confessor of the Christian faith is given the title
'**Confessor**'. The Anglo-Saxon King Edward was known as Edward the
Confessor because of his deep faith and [531] 'sanctity'.

The hymn *God, whose city's sure foundation* [532] honours confessors and
martyrs who followed Jesus, living and dying to serve the Lord in England:

Here in England through the ages,
while the Christian years went by

---

[530] Ibid., p. 173

[531] Exciting Holiness, Canterbury Press, Norwich, 2007, p. 438-439

[532] The New English Hymnal, The Canterbury Press, Norwich, 1987, p. 217, hymn 199,
verse 2, G. A. Alington 1872-1955

> *Saints, **confessors**, **martyrs**, sages,*
> *strong to live and strong to die,*
> *wrote their names upon the pages*
> *of God's blessed company.*

How can Mary be addressed as Queen Martyrs and Queen of Confessors?

Saint Alphonsus Liguori recognised Mary as **Queen of Martys** because she suffered so terribly seeing her beloved Son die on the Cross. Although Mary's body was not wounded, her heart was pierced with such terrible grief that St Bernard says she was wounded [533] 'not by the sword of the executioner but by bitter sorrow of heart.' Saint Alphonsus Liguori asks us to reflect on Mary's great suffering and then 'consider the Greatness of the **Sufferings**, by which Mary became the Queen of Martyrs; for the Sufferings of her Great Martrydom, exceeded those of all the Martyrs; being in the first place, the Longest, in Point of Duration; and in the Second Place, the Greatest, in Point of Intensity.' We can imagine **Mary, Queen of Martyrs** crowned as a Queen with her suffering and pierced heart, reminding us of Simeon's words 'a sword will pierce your own soul too' *(Luke 2:35b)*.

Mary is given the title Queen of Confessors because the Bible records her confession of faith. At the Annunciation Mary believed and trusted in God's plan for her life saying: 'I am the Lord's servant. **May it be to me as you have said**' *(Luke 1:38)*. In the *Magnificat* Mary praises the Lord and **'rejoices in God my Saviour'** *(Luke 1:47)*, confessing her faith. At the Temple in Jerusalem Simeon's words were a warning of future suffering endured by Confessors of the faith, that 'a sword will pierce your own soul too' *(Luke 2:35)*. Mary's response after the visit to Jerusalem when Jesus was twelve years old was to pray and reflect and 'treasure all these things in her heart' *(Luke 2:5)*. At Cana, Mary had deep faith in trusting that Jesus would turn the water into wine. Her words; 'Do whatever he tells

---

[533] http://copiosa.org/liguori/liguori_dolors.htm 27th April 2017

you' *(John 2:5)* are a confession of her faith. At the Cross Mary stayed with Jesus, while most of his friends stayed away. 'Near the **cross of Jesus stood his mother'** *(John 19: 25).* Mary's standing and staying at the Cross was a powerful confession of her faith in God and love for Jesus. By remaining there even if that meant arrest and persecution shows Mary as a Confessor of the faith.

This reflection helps us understand why Mary is addressed as **Queen of Confessors**. Mary had strong faith and trust in God and confessed her faith in Jesus. In Chapter 20 **Queen Assumed into Heaven** we explored and reflected on how Mary is Queen in heaven, over all the people in Heaven, which includes the **Martyrs and Confessors**. We can see why Mary is given these titles, **Queen of Martyrs** and **Queen of Confessors**.

What does this mean for us?

There are **martyrs** in the Church today. We should be faithful in praying for **confessors** of the faith who are being persecuted, tortured, imprisoned and face martyrdom because of their faith in Jesus.

To **confess** our faith, we need to understand and explain our faith to others. When we say an affirmation of faith in a Church service; think about what you are saying. If you do not understand some of the phrases then ask your priest or minister to explain. Then you will be better equipped to share and confess your faith to others.

Grow in faith through courses, pilgrimages, talks, study days and reading books that teach you more about the Christian faith so you keep growing into a closer relationship with Jesus and growing in knowledge and understanding about the Christian faith.

When Jesus talked to the apostles before His Ascension, he used the word '**martyr**' Μαρτυς *(Acts 1:8).* Jesus told the apostles to go and testify to His life, love, death and resurrection to help more people come to believe. We are called to **be witnesses**; living in such a way that people who do not yet know Jesus are drawn through us to know Jesus and follow him. Peter wrote: 'Always be prepared to give an answer to everyone who asks you to give the reason for the hope that you have' *(I Peter 3:15).* Whom does the Lord want you to witnesses to now? People in your family? People at work? How can you witness about Jesus to your friends? Our Christian testimony can include how we first came to know Jesus, but it is also good to **witness** to the ongoing help and love of Jesus that we experience; so we have a recent testimony to share. What is your Christian testimony?

When you go to Mass on a Saint's Day if that saint was a **martyr** the priest will wear red vestments to remind us about the blood of the martyrs. If the saint was not martyred then the priest will wear white vestments to represent the purity of the saints, the **confessors** of the faith who have been given the title 'Saint'.

[534] In the *Te Deum Laudamus* at Morning Prayer we imagine heavenly worship:

> *We praise thee, O God; we acknowledge thee to be the Lord.*
> *All the earth doth worship thee, the Father everlasting.*
> *To thee all angels cry aloud, the heavens and all the powers therein.....*
> **The noble army of martyrs praise thee...**

Christians are told 'do not be surprised' when they experience times of suffering, like the martyrs and confessors suffered. Peter tells us: 'rejoice that you participate in the sufferings of Christ... if you suffer as a Christian, do not be ashamed, but praise God that you bear that name' *(I Peter 4:12-16)*. Paul realised that to 'know Christ' would mean 'sharing in his sufferings' *(Philippians 3:10-11)*. Suffering was the experience of Christians in the past. When we go through times of difficulty we should pray and ask the Lord to help us. Those times can be a time of growing to 'know Christ' in a deeper way.

[535] *Queen of Martyrs and Queen of Confessors, pray for us.*

---

[534] Common Worship Services and Prayers for the Church of England, Church House Publishing, 2000, p. 67
[535] The Walsingham Pilgrim Manual 2016, p.13

CHAPTER 25

QUEEN OF APOSTLES AND QUEEN OF ALL SAINTS

In this chapter I will explore two more of the 'Queen' titles in the [536]Litany of Loreto the 41st title **Queen of Apostles** and 45th the title is **Queen of All Saints**.

What does the Bible tells us about Apostles and All Saints?

Apostle is the New Testament Greek word ἀπόστολος *apostolos* meaning [537]"one sent forth' as ἀπό means 'from' and στέλλω *stello* means 'to send'. The word is used of the Lord Jesus to describe His relationship to God the Father. Jesus prayed to the Father 'Jesus Christ whom you have

---

[536] Dictionary of Mary 'Behold your Mother', Catholic Book Publishing Co. New Jersey 1997, 1985, p.241

[537] An Expository Dictionary of Biblical Words: W.E. Vine, Thomas Nelson, Inc, 1984, p. 30 -31

sent' *(John 17:3)*. We are told to 'fix your thoughts on Jesus, the apostle and high priest whom we confess' *(Hebrews 3:1)*.

The twelve disciples chosen by the Lord for special training were called **Apostles**. The New Testament Greek word ἀπόστολος *apostolos* means [538]'one sent as a messenger or agent, the bearer of a commission, messenger'. We read that word in Jesus' commission to twelve disciples whom he called 'Apostles'. 'He called his twelve disciples to him and gave them authority to drive out evil spirits and to heal every disease and sickness. These are the names of the twelve apostles: first, Simon (who is called Peter) and his brother Andrew; James son of Zebedee, and his brother John; Philip and Bartholomew; Thomas and Matthew the tax collector; James son of Alphaeus, and Thaddaeus; Simon the Zealot and Judas Iscariot, who betrayed him...' *(Matthew 10: 1-8)*. The Apostles were sent out as messengers of the good news of God's love, with a commission to preach and to bring the healing love of Jesus to the needy.

Peter defined an apostle as a man who had been with them all through Jesus' ministry. Thus, when they voted to replace Judas, Peter said 'it is necessary to choose one of the men who have been with us the whole time the Lord Jesus went in and out among us.... For one of these must become a witness with us of his resurrection" *(Acts 1:21-22)*. Barsabbas and Matthias were candidates for this position. 'Then they prayed, "Show us which of these two you have chosen to take over this **apostolic** ministry", ... the lot fell to Matthias; so he was added to the eleven apostles' *(Acts 1: 24-26)*.

In heaven 'the wall of the city had twelve foundations and on them were the names of the twelve apostles of the Lamb'. *(Revelation 21: 14)*. Those twelve apostles, including Matthias, are especially honoured in heaven. The **Apostles of the Lamb** were the foundation of the Early Church and are given an exalted place in heaven.

'Apostle' is defined by McBrien as [539]'Literally, 'one who is sent'. A missionary of the Church in the New Testament period.' We will see that this title was given to those who were sent to preach the Gospel, which included the twelve apostles but also others whom God called to travel and

---

[538] The Analytical Greek Lexicon, London: Samuel Bagster and Sons Ltd, 1973, p. 47

[539] Catholicism: Richard P. McBrien, HarperCollins, 1994, p 1234

proclaim the good news. In those exciting early days of the Church, after the coming of the Holy Spirit at Pentecost, when three thousand believed and were baptised *(Acts 2:1-13,41)*, the apostles were teaching, leading worship and praying for the sick. The new believers: 'devoted themselves to the apostles' teaching and to the fellowship, to the breaking of bread and to prayer. Everyone was filled with awe, and many wonders and miraculous signs were done by the apostles' *(Acts 2:42-43)*.

Apostles were the main leaders of the Early Church as Paul explains: 'And in the church God has appointed first of all apostles, second prophets, third teachers, then workers of miracles, also those having gifts of healing, those able to help others, those with gifts of administration, and those speaking in different kinds of tongues' *(I Corinthians 12:28)*.

The Church is 'built on the foundation of the apostles and prophets, with Christ Jesus himself as the chief cornerstone' *(Ephesians 2:20)*. The Apostles travelled to pray with people to be filled with the Holy Spirit. Peter and John were sent to Samaria. 'Peter and John placed their hands on them, and they received the Holy Spirit' *(Acts 8:15-17)*.

Later in the Early Church the title 'Apostle' was given to believers who had not been with Jesus in his earthly ministry. [540]Paul, although he had seen the Lord Jesus, in a vision on the Damascus Road *(Acts 9:3-6)*, had not 'companied with' the Twelve 'all the time' of His earthly ministry.' So according to Peter's definition of an Apostle, Paul did not qualify for this title. However, God called Paul directly to take the Gospel to the Gentiles, telling Ananias 'This man is my chosen instrument to carry my name before the Gentiles and their kings and before the people of Israel' *(Acts 9: 15)*. God sent Paul with a commission to take the good news of Jesus to the Gentiles. Paul told the Romans about his calling from the Lord Jesus: 'Through him and for his name's sake, we received grace and **apostleship** to call people from among all the Gentiles to the obedience that comes from faith' *(Romans 1:5)*. Paul explained to the Galatians about his apostleship and the commission he had received from God. 'For God, who was at work in the ministry of Peter as an apostle to the Jews, was also

---

[540] An Expository Dictionary of Biblical Words: W.E. Vine, Thomas Nelson, Inc, 1984, p. 30 -31

at work in my ministry as an apostle to the Gentiles' *(Galatians 2:8)*. Paul felt he should be called an Apostle: 'Am I not free? Am I not an apostle? Have I not seen Jesus our Lord? Are you not the result of my work in the Lord?' *(I Corinthians 9:1)*. Paul wrote later with a humble attitude: 'For I am the least of the apostles and do not even deserve to be called an apostle, because I persecuted the church of God' *(I Corinthians 15:9)*.

Other later apostles mentioned in Acts are Barnabas, who was with Paul as an apostle in Iconium *(Acts 14:4,14)*. Paul writes to tell the Romans that Andronicus and Junias 'are outstanding among the apostles' *(Romans 16:7)*. Paul, Silas and Timothy are described as apostles *(I Thessalonians 2:7)*. They were sent out by God with a commission to bring the good news of the love of Jesus to those who do not yet know Him. The original twelve Apostles were saints and some others; having their own saints' days on the Calendar of Saints. Many of these Apostles were also martyred for their faith.

In the Church today, Bishops continue the apostolic ministry of the disciples. The Collect at the Service of the Consecration of a Bishop makes this clear:

[541] *'ALMIGHTY God, who by thy Son Jesus Christ didst give to thy holy **Apostles** many excellent gifts, and didst charge them to feed thy flock: Give grace, we beseech thee, to all Bishops, the Pastors of thy Church, that they may diligently preach thy Word, and duly administer the godly discipline thereof....'* The new Bishop is told by the Archbishop: [542] *'Receive the Holy Ghost for the office and work of a Bishop in the Church of God, now committed unto thee by the imposition of our hands...'* Bishops today continue the same apostolic ministry as the early apostles by travelling to the Parishes in their Diocese to pray for people to be filled with the Holy Spirit at Confirmation Services. This follows the pattern of Peter and John in Samaria *(Acts 8:14-17)*, and Paul at Ephesus *(Acts 19:1-7)*.

---

[541] Common Worship Ordination Services Study Edition, Church House Publishing, London, 2007, p.101

[542] Ibid., p.108

Saints is the New Testament Greek word for ἅγιος hagios meaning 'holy'; Vine tells us that this word is [543]'used of believers, it designates all such and is not applied merely to persons of exceptional holiness, or to those who, having died, were characterized by exceptional acts of 'saintliness'. 'His saints' are also described as 'them that believed'. They are called 'holy ones' in Jude 14.' When people believe in Jesus and choose to follow Him they are 'set apart to God' and 'God's work of grace in making each believer holy begins.'[544] 'All members of the Church of God already are sanctified in Christ Jesus.' The letter to the Hebrews tells us about Jesus' death on the cross that 'by one sacrifice he has made perfect for ever those who are being made holy' *(Hebrews 10:14)*. Therefore, all believers and followers of Jesus are saints! That includes us and all Christian believers. So '**All Saints**' includes us if we believe and follow Jesus. Saints wear white in heaven *(Revelation 19:7-8)*. White is a symbol of purity and holiness.

Paul writes that we are all 'called to be saints' *(Romans 1:7, I Corinthians 1:2 AV)*. God is calling all believers to be holy, following and serving Jesus. A Lent Course explored this where the aim of the first session was [545]'to widen our understanding of the meaning of 'saint'. Paul [546]lists the blessings that all Christians, all **saints** have in Christ: we are 'inheritors of all God's promises', we have 'access to the truth about God's love' and 'growing spiritual discernment through growth in the knowledge of God' *(Ephesians 1:18-20)*. Paul commends their faith and 'love towards all the **saints**' *(Ephesians 1:15)*. Saints share the **love** of Jesus. Paul prays that 'with the eyes of your heart enlightened, you may know what is the hope to which he has called you, what are the riches of his glorious inheritance among the **saints**' *(Ephesians 1:18)*. Paul teaches them about the armour of God *(Ephesians 6:10-18)*, and asks them to: 'keep on praying for all the saints' *(Ephesians 6:18)*.

---

[543] *An Expository Dictionary of Biblical Words*: W.E. Vine, Thomas Nelson Publishers, 1985 p.544

[544] *What the Bible Teaches*: R.A. Torrey Nisbet & Co p.347

[545] Called to be Saints, Lent 2002, Churches Together in Britain and Ireland, Church House Publishing, 2001, p. 1

[546] The Ministry of the Word Handbook for Preachers BRF 2000 p.363

Saints follow the teachings of Jesus and his commandment to 'love one another'; as Jesus said at the Last Supper: "A new command I give you: Love one another. As I have loved you, so you must love one another. By this all men will know that you are my disciples, if you love one another" *(John 13:34-35)*. Jesus also said 'do to others as you would have them do to you' *(Luke 6:31)*. The Beatitudes *(Matthew 5:3-12, Luke 6:20-23)*, are challenging teaching from Jesus about our attitude and behaviour to those who have harmed us. Jesus also said 'Love your enemies, do good to those who hate you' *(Luke 6:27)*. The writers of the Pilgrim Course say: [547]'believe that the Beatitudes, and trying to live them out, is one of the best ways of loving God with all your heart and understanding the Christian vision for the world.'[548] 'They reassure us that in times of realising our need of God; and when suffering rejection and sorrow; that Jesus will be with us and help us.'

Saints are **joyful**! 'O sing unto the LORD a new song: let the congregation of saints praise him' *(Psalm 149:1)*. 'Let the **saints** be joyful with glory: let them rejoice in their beds'! *(Psalm 149:5)*. The Saints were cheerful and gave thanks to the Lord even in difficult situations. St Paul's letter to the Philippians, sent from his time in prison in Rome, tells us to '**Rejoice** in the Lord always' *(Philippians 4:4)*. Saints rejoice in Heaven at the fall of Babylon *(Revelation 18:20)*.

The Church has given the title '**Saint**'; to particularly holy people. A definition of 'saint' in the book *Catholicism* is not the Biblical definition whereby all believers are called to be saints and are addressed as saints. Saints are: [549]'Those who have been transformed fully by the grace of Christ and are with God in the heavenly kingdom.' We can learn from the lives of these saints and be inspired by them. We can also commemorate those saints who, though largely unknown, have faithfully played inspired others. Saints are remembered by the Church on their Saint's Day, which

---

[547] *Pilgrim Course for the Christian Journey The Beatitudes* Church House Publishing 2015 p.9

[548] *Ibid.* p. 11

[549] Catholicism: Richard P. McBrien, HarperCollins, 1994, p 1250

is the anniversary of their death. The [550]*Common Worship Lectionary* lists 'Holy Days' which including Saints with Collects and Bible readings, who are commemorated in the Church of England. [551]*Exciting Holiness* gives information about Saints with Collects and Bible readings for the 'Festivals and Lesser Festivals of the Calendars of The Church of England, The Church of Ireland, The Scottish Episcopal Church and the Church in Wales'.

There are many hundreds of Saints in the **Roman Catholic** Church's list of Saints. [552] 'One list says there are 810 canonized Roman Catholic saints... Among the Eastern **Orthodox** and Oriental Orthodox Communions, the numbers may be even higher.'

Some hymns tell us about the Saints. On All Saints' Day we sing:

> [553]*For All the Saints who from their labours rest,*
> *who thee by faith before the world confest.*

This pictures heaven in the last verse:

> *From earth's wide bounds, from ocean's farthest coast,*
> *through gates of pearl streams in the countless host,*
> *singing to Father, Son and Holy Ghost. Alleluya!*

In the hymn [554]*Ye watchers and ye holy ones* we have another picture of heaven:

> *All Saints triumphant, raise the song Alleluya, Alleluya, Alleluya.*

We think about the saints in heaven in:

---

[550] The Common Worship Lectionary, New Revised Standard Version, Anglicized Edition, Oxford University Press, 1999, p. 1100 -1211

[551] Exciting Holiness, Canterbury Press, Norwich, 2007

[552] https://en.wikipedia.org/wiki/List_of_saints 23rd April 2017

[553] The New English Hymnal, The Canterbury Press, Norwich, Words Edition, 1987, p. 215, hymn number 197, W. Walsham How 1823-1897

[554] Ibid., p. 474, hymn number 478, v. 1, 3, Athelstan Riley 1858-1945

> [555] *Give us the wings of faith to rise*
> *within the veil, and see*
> *the saints above, how great their joys,*
> *how bright their glories be.*

These hymns express in song the glorious celebration in heaven where the saints worship God after living lives of faith and service. Our All Saints' hymns also remind us that saints experience times of suffering. The 2nd verse of *Give us the wings of faith* paints a picture of saints' enduring hard times:

> *Once they were mourning here below,*
> *their couch was wet with tears;*
> *they wrestled hard, as we do now,*
> *with sins and doubts and fears.*

This can be an encouragement to us when we go through difficulties to know that if we turn to God for help, the Lord will help us, as he helped those saints of long ago. The hymn [556] *For all the saints* refers to '*darkness drear*' '*when the strife is fierce, the warfare long*' and then encourages us that, in those dark times, Jesus is '*their one true Light*' and they hear '*the distant triumph-song and hearts are brave again*'.

The hymn *God, whose city's sure foundation* [557] honours the saints who followed Jesus, living and dying to serve the Lord in England. We give thanks for English **saints:**

> *Here in England through the ages,*
> *While the Christian years went by*
> ***Saints**, confessors, martyrs, sages,*
> *Strong to live and strong to die,*

---

[555] *Hymns Old & New*, Anglican Edition, Kevin Mayhew Ltd, Bury St Edmunds, Suffolk, 1996, hymn 156, verses 1 and 2, Isaac Watts 1674-1748

[556] The New English Hymnal, The Canterbury Press, Norwich, Words Edition, 1987, p. 215, hymn number 197, W. Walsham How 1823-1897

[557] Ibid., p. 217, hymn 199, verse 2, C.A. Alington 1872-1955

Wrote their names upon the pages
Of God's blessed company.

[558] In the *Te Deum Laudamus* at Morning Prayer, we imagine the amazing worship in heaven when: **The glorious company of the apostles praise thee.**

How can Mary be addressed as Queen of Apostles and Queen of All Saints?

Jacques Bur [559] tells us that Pope Pius XII wrote in *Lumen Gentium, 66* that: 'Mary has by grace been exalted above all angels and men to a place second only to her Son, as the most holy mother of God who was involved in the mysteries of Christ: she is rightly honoured by a special cult in the Church.' Jacques Bur explains: [560]'The other saints developed something of the holiness of Jesus by imitating one or other of his virtues more specifically. St Francis specially imitated Christ in his poverty. St Dominic above all followed his love of truth... The holiness of Christ is of such richness that it takes a multitude of saints to reflect the diversity of its many aspects.... But Mary is distinct from all the other saints because she imitated the holiness of her son in the most absolute and the simplest way... a synthesis of the three theological virtues of faith, hope and love... She went unseen... Distance was required to see in the life of Mary all the grace and glory of God that she received.'

Saint Augustine describes how Mary is **Queen of All Saints**. In reflecting on the devotion due to the saints, St Augustine taught that Mary [561]'is not to be offered the worship that is owed to God alone, but her

[558] Common Worship Services and Prayers for the Church of England, Church House · Publishing, 2000, p. 67

[559] How to understand the Virgin Mary: Jacques Bur, SCM Press Ltd, Translation 1994 John Bowden and Margaret Lydamore, p. 52

[560] Ibid. p. 54

[561] MARY the Complete Resource edited by Sarah Jane Boss, Oxford University Press 2007, p. 156

unique status as Mother of God means that she is marked out above other holy men and women. *Latreia* is the worship and adoration due only to God. *Hyperdoulia* for Mary is a type of devotion that is somewhat greater than that due to the other saints. *Doulia* is a Greek word meaning 'service' to honour all the saints.'

Sarah Jane Boss recognises Mary's position as **Queen of All Saints** as she writes: [562]'Mary's regal status can be read as a sign of her super-eminent position among the saints of the Church – a position of such central importance that she can be portrayed as holding the office of highest authority after that of Christ.'

This all shows us how Mary is seen to be so highly exalted, so Mary must indeed be **Queen of Apostles** and **Queen of All Saints**, expressed in the hymn [563]*I'll sing a hymn to Mary*:

> *The saints are high in glory,*
> *with golden crowns so bright;*
> *but brighter far is Mary*
> *upon her throne of light.*

In the Chapter 20: **Queen Assumed into Heaven** we explored how Mary is Queen in heaven. If we accept that Mary is Queen in heaven; then we can recognise that she is Queen over all the people who are in heaven, including the **Apostles** and **All Saints**. We can see why Mary is given these titles, **Queen of Apostles** and **Queen of All Saints.**

What does this mean for us?

Apostles were sent out by God with a commission to bring the good news of the love of Jesus to those who do not yet know Him. Is the Lord sending you to take His message to people you know who do not yet know Jesus?

---

[562] MARY the Complete Resource edited by Sarah Jane Boss, Oxford University Press 2007, p. 159

[563] The Walsingham Pilgrim Manual, 2016, p. 109, hymn number 20, verse 5, John Wyse 1825-1898

Do you have family and friends who do not yet know Jesus? We should try to live our lives in such a way that people who do not know Jesus are drawn through us to know Jesus and follow him. We should be good witnesses for Jesus by our conversations, actions and attitudes *(I Peter 3:15)*. Whom does the Lord want you to witnesses to now?

We are encouraged to be <u>active</u> in sharing our faith; and also encouraged that this will lead us to discover more of the blessings and good things that we have in Christ. 'I pray that you may be active in sharing your faith, so that you will have a full understanding of every good thing we have in Christ' *(Philemon 6)*.

How should we live as '**saints**'? Believers are called to be 'holy'[564] and by God's grace the work of sanctification continues in our lives. We should confess our sins and receive absolution *(I John 1:7)*. The Holy Spirit helps, convicts and challenges us so that we are changed to be more like Jesus *(I Corinthians 3:18)*.

The Holy Spirit helps us to **pray** *(Romans 8:26-27)*. We should pray for other Christians, for those in our Church and the Church in this and other lands, being open for the Holy Spirit to guide our prayers. The prayers of the saints rise like incense in heaven *(Revelation 5:8)*.

Saints experience times of **suffering**. All the stories of the saints who lived in the past show they had times of suffering in their lives. Indeed, all of us go through times of suffering. The Beatitudes *(Matthew 5:3-10, Luke 6:20-23)*, encourage us that in troubled times of rejection, poverty, sorrow, emptiness, criticism, distress and even physical suffering which persecuted Christians in other countries endure today; that Jesus will be close to us and help us.

'Do you not know that the **saints** will <u>judge</u> the world?' *(I Corinthians 6:2)* Believers, then, should settle disputes without needing to go to 'the ungodly for judgement' *(I Corinthians 6:1-8)*. We should seek to settle disagreements amicably.

Let us remember that the Saints were **joyful**, cheerful, and gave thanks to the Lord even in difficult situations. St Paul's letter to the Philippians,

---

[564] *An Expository Dictionary of Biblical Words*: W.E. Vine, Thomas Nelson Publishers, 1985 p. 307

sent from his time in prison in Rome, tells us to 'Rejoice in the Lord always' *(Philippians 4:4)*. How easy it is to complain and be critical; yet if we are following the example of the saints we should be cheerful people showing joy by our positive, thankful conversations and our smiles!

Saints are called to share the love of Jesus with others. St Paul commended the Ephesian Christians on 'their love' *(Ephesians 1:15)*, and we know Jesus' new commandment: 'Love one another' *(John 13:34)*. Let us follow the teachings of Jesus *(Luke 6:31)*, and be active in sharing, love, care and kindness.

Saint Teresa of Ávila challenges us to show **love** and care saying: [565] *"Christ has no body now but yours. No hands, no feet on earth but yours. Yours are the eyes through which he looks compassion on this world. Yours are the feet with which he walks to do good. Yours are the hands through which he blesses all the world. Yours are the hands, yours are the feet, yours are the eyes, you are his body. Christ has no body now on earth but yours."* How can you 'do good' and share the love and compassion of Jesus with others? How can you use your feet, hands and eyes to be active in showing Jesus' love?

A little girl once said, [566] '**saints** are what the light shines through'. Let us receive afresh the light and love of Jesus so we can live as saints, sharing the love and light of Jesus with people we meet; being people through whom 'the light shines through'!

Let us read about the saints, learn from the example of their lives and be inspired in a closer walk with Jesus by reading and reflecting on the lives of the well-known saints and the [567]'countless less well-known people' who 'have served God faithfully, and some of them have triggered faith and action in others.' It can be inspirational and challenging to read about the saints.

---

[565] https://www.goodreads.com/quotes/66880-christ-has-no-body-now-but-yours-no-hands-no 20th February 2018

[566] The Ministry of the Word Handbook for Preachers BRF 2000 p.364

[567] Called to be Saints, Lent 2002, Churches Together in Britain and Ireland, Church House Publishing, 2001, p.27

We are called to follow the example of the Saints, as we pray in the Collect for All Saints' Day: [568]*'Almighty God, grant us grace so to follow your blessed saints in all virtuous and godly living that we may come to those inexpressible joys that you have prepared for those who truly love you'.*

I love the Collect for the **Saints** and Martyrs of England, where we pray to God: [569]*We praise you for the **saints** of our own land and for the many lamps their holiness has lit; and we pray that we also may be numbered at the last with those who have done your will and declared your righteousness.* Their holiness has lit many lamps and that is a challenge and encouragement to us to live holy lives and lead others to the light of Christ so they help yet more people come to know the light and love of Jesus.

A Collect reminds us about the foundation of the Church: [570]*O Almighty God, who hast built thy Church upon the foundation of the **apostles** and prophets, Jesus Christ himself being the head cornerstone....*

[571] *Queen of Apostles and Queen of All Saints, pray for us.*

---

[568] The Common Worship Lectionary, New Revised Standard Version, Anglicized Edition, Oxford University Press, 1999, p. 342

[569] Ibid., p. 1201

[570] Common Worship Services and Prayers for the Church of England, Church House Publishing, 2000, p.515, Collect for Simon and Jude

[571] The Walsingham Pilgrim Manual 2016, p.13

CHAPTER 26

QUEEN CONCEIVED
WITHOUT ORIGINAL SIN

Queen conceived without original sin is the 46th title of Mary in the [572]Litany of Loreto. In the [573]Walsingham Manual this title is: **Queen conceived without stain.**

What does the Bible tells us about the original sin?

Paul writes that no one is righteous 'for all have sinned' *(Romans 3:23).* Earlier he argued: 'There is no-one righteous, not even one; there is no-one who understands, no-one who seeks God. All have turned away, they have together become worthless; there is no-one who does good, not even one' *(Romans 3:9-18).* Here Paul is quoting from Psalms *(Psalm 14:1-3*

---

[572] Dictionary of Mary 'Behold your Mother', Catholic Book Publishing Co. New Jersey 1997, 1985, p.241

[573] The Walsingham Pilgrim Manual 2016, p.13

& Psalm 53:1-3). This clarifies that everyone has sinned and needs the forgiveness freely offered to us through faith in Jesus. How wonderful that through trusting that Jesus took our sins when he died on the Cross we can receive God's forgiveness. Paul explains: 'all have sinned and fall short of the glory of God and are justified freely by his grace through the redemption that came by Christ Jesus. God presented him as a sacrifice of atonement, through faith in his blood. He did this to demonstrate his justice ... so as to be just and the one who justifies those who have faith in Jesus' *(Romans 3: 23-26)*.

John writes in his Epistle that everyone has sinned. He writes: 'If we claim to be without sin, we deceive ourselves and the truth is not in us. If we confess our sins, he is faithful and just and will forgive us our sins and purify us from all unrighteousness. If we claim we have not sinned, we make him out to be a liar and his word has no place in our lives' *(I John 1:8-10)*. These verses tell us clearly that 'all have sinned' *(Romans 3:23)*, and that anyone claiming to have not sinned is not telling the truth.

The Bible tells us only Jesus was without sin. '..... For we do not have a high priest who is unable to sympathize with our weaknesses, but we have one who has been tempted in every way, just as we are - **yet was without sin...**' *(Hebrews 4:15)*. How wonderful that Jesus understands our weaknesses, but he did not sin, so he was able to take our sin when he died on the Cross. As we sing: [574]*There was no other good enough to pay the price of sin; He only could unlock the gate of heaven and let us in.* Only Jesus could 'pay the price of sin', because only Jesus was without sin. Article 15 of the Thirty-Nine Articles of the Church of England states that Christ alone was without sin: [575]'Christ in the truth of our nature was made like unto us in all things (sin only except), from which he was clearly void, both in his flesh and in his spirit. He came to be the Lamb without spot, who, by the sacrifice of himself once made, should take away the sins of the world.'

---

[574] The New English Hymnal, Melody, The Canterbury Press, Norwich, 16th Impression, 2004, p. 155, number 92, verse 4, Mrs C. F. Alexander 1818- 1895

[575] A Theological Introduction to The Thirty-Nine Articles: E.J. Bicknell, 3rd Edition revised by H.J. Carpenter, Longmans, 1959, p.172

The Bible shows us that 'original sin' goes back to the Fall of Adam and Eve in the Garden. Adam and Eve disobeyed God's instructions and ate the fruit from the tree in the middle of the Garden of Eden. God had said: 'but you must not eat from the tree of the knowledge of good and evil, for when you eat of it you will surely die' *(Genesis 2:17)*. Eve tempted Adam as: "The woman saw that the tree was good to eat, and fair to the eyes, and delightful to behold; and she took of the fruit thereof, and did eat, and gave to her husband, and he did eat" *(Genesis 2:6)*. Paul explained to Timothy that sin came from Eve who was deceived in the Garden of Eden: 'For Adam was formed first, then Eve. And Adam was not the one deceived; it was the woman who was deceived and became a sinner' *(I Timothy 2:13-14)*. Eve's sin led to the Fall with Adam and Eve's having to leave the Garden of Eden, no longer knowing God's closeness and friendship. [576]'This first sin led to men and women being estranged from God, from one another and from the earth with which they struggle for food, clothing and shelter.' We begin life with a sinful nature. When Noah and his family came out of the Ark, God said: 'Never again will I curse the ground because of man, even though every inclination of his heart is evil from childhood' *(Genesis 8:21)*. God knows that from childhood the inclination of people's hearts is to do wrong.

Paul explains to the Romans that, owing to the fall of Adam, everyone is tainted with sin: 'Therefore, just as sin entered the world through one man, and death through sin, and in this way death came to all men, because all sinned – for before the law was given, sin was in the world.... Again, the gift of God is not like the result of the one man's sin: The judgment followed one sin and brought condemnation, but the gift followed many trespasses and brought justification. For if, by the trespass of the one man, death reigned through that one man, how much more will those who receive God's abundant provision of grace and of the gift of righteousness reign in life through the one man, Jesus Christ. Consequently, just as the result of one trespass was condemnation for all men, so also the result of one act of righteousness was justification that brings life for all men' *(Romans*

---

[576] Mary: The Complete Resource, edited by Sarah Jane Boss, Oxford University Press, 2007, p. 50

5: 12-17). Jesus is seen here as the 'second Adam' who has repaired the damage done by the first Adam, by his death on the Cross. A commentary explains: [577]'A contrast between Adam and Christ. Adam introduced sin and death into the world; Christ brought righteousness and life... We do not start life with even the possibility of living it sinlessly; we begin it with a sinful nature.' We start life tainted with original sin.

St Anselm, 1033-1109, Archbishop of Canterbury, believed that [578]'although the potential for original sin is present in everyone from conception, it does not take effect until a child has reached the age at which it should have the possibility of exercising free will.' This can be when a child is very young. David acknowledged after his adultery with Bathsheba: 'Surely I was sinful at birth, sinful from the time my mother conceived me' *(Psalm 51:5).* This supports the belief in original sin, as does: 'Even from birth the wicked go astray; from the womb they are wayward and speak lies' *(Psalm 58:3).* St Paul writes about original sin to the Ephesians: 'All of us also lived among them at one time, gratifying the cravings of our sinful nature and following its desires and thoughts. Like the rest, we were by nature objects of wrath' *(Ephesians 2:3).*

The doctrine of 'original sin' is clear in the Thirty-Nine Articles of the Church of England. Article 9 states: [579]'Original sin standeth not in the following of Adam; but it is the fault and corruption of the nature of every man, that naturally is engendered of the off-spring of Adam; whereby man is very far gone from original righteousness, and of his own nature inclined to evil, so that the flesh lusteth always contrary to the Spirit; and therefore in every person born into this world, it deserveth God's wrath and damnation.' Article 10 tells us [580]'The condition of man after the fall of Adam is such that he cannot turn and prepare himself, by his own natural strength and good works, to faith and calling upon God:

---

[577] Glo Computer Commentary for this passage

[578] Boss, op. cit., p. 209

[579] A Theological Introduction to The Thirty-Nine Articles: E.J. Bicknell, 3rd Edition revised by H.J. Carpenter, Longmans, 1959, p.171

[580] A Theological Introduction to The Thirty-Nine Articles: E.J. Bicknell, 3rd Edition revised by H.J. Carpenter, Longmans, 1959, p.172

Wherefore we have no power to do good works, pleasant and acceptable to God, without the grace of God by grace'. Carpenter comments on this that even if: [581]'we no longer believe in the historical existence of Adam, but such phrases sound strange to our ears. But the truth of original sin is not in the least affected by any view that we may hold about the historical value of Genesis. The whole religious experience of Israel bore witness to the sinfulness of the human heart, and this fact of universal conviction of sin shaped the story of Genesis.' We can recognise the truth of original sin, even if we choose to question the story of Adam and Eve.

In the *Catechism* in the *Book of Common Prayer* this belief is taught to those preparing for Confirmation; saying my names were given 'In my Baptism, wherein I was made a member of Christ and a child of God.' [582]'This implies that prior to Baptism the child was not entitled to these privileges. By nature we are 'born in sin and children of wrath;' in Baptism we are made 'children of grace.' St Augustine of Hippo, 354-430, taught this doctrine; that [583]'original sin is the wickedness to which all humanity has been subject since Adam's and Eve's fall from grace... but it is washed away by the waters of baptism, since baptism accomplishes remission of all sins.'

The Immaculate Conception is not found in the Bible. [584]Fr Nicholas Turner says that the Immaculate Conception is 'a philosophical rationalisation as it is not in Scripture.' Many theologians today do not believe in the immaculate conception of Mary; using as their arguments the Bible verses quoted above and the Church's teaching about original sin.

---

[581] Ibid., p.178

[582] The Prayer Book Its History, Language and Contents: Evan Daniel, Gardner. Darton & Co, London, 1892, p. 361

[583] Mary: The Complete Resource, edited by Sarah Jane Boss, Oxford University Press, 2007, p. 209

[584] Conversation following Fr Turner's lecture at Walsingham Bible Week on *Our Lady in the Old Testament*, 10:15 am, 24th October 2017

How can Mary be described as Queen conceived without original sin and stain?

It is important to be clear about the Church's teaching and understanding from the Bible about the sinful state of everyone, before we consider the claims made for Mary about her conception without sin and how she is without stain. However [585]'The doctrine of Mary's immaculate conception teaches that she was conceived without original sin... without the stain of original sin... From the early centuries of Christianity it was widely believed that Mary never committed any actual sins during her life and this became the Church's universal teaching.'

Holstein describes the background explaining: [586]'The Mystery of the Incarnation gave rise, from earliest times, to the Church's conviction of Mary's holiness. Chosen by the Father to be the Mother of His Son, and accepting this mission by characterising herself as the *'servant of the Lord'*, Mary could never have consented to an offence against God. According to an expression favoured by Eastern Christians, she is the 'all-holy', *panagia*. The proclamation in the 5th century (Council of Ephesus, 431) of her title 'Mother of God', reinforced this persuasion of her exceptional holiness.... All holy, Mary obviously was exempt from sin... Mary was never away from God. Like the servant of Psalm 123, she kept her eyes on her Lord to do his will at the least sign of it.' He presents the argument that because of Mary's holiness and obedience to God, she must have been conceived without sin. St Augustine believed that Mary was conceived without original sin. Holstein explains: 'Latin theology was firm on two things: every human being is infected with original sin and bears its consequences; this hereditary sin is remitted through the merits of Christ, the Redeemer of the entire human race.'

[585] Boss, op. cit., pp 208f

[586] Dictionary of Mary 'Behold Your Mother', Catholic Book Publishing Co., New Jersey, 1985, p. 190-192

Some theologians including St Thomas Aquinas and St Bonaventure believed [587]'Mary inherited the legacy of Adam and contracted original sin. But she was sanctified in her mother's womb.' In the 13th century Duns Scotus argued: [588]'In making to His Mother an anticipated application of His merits to preserve her from the taint of original sin, which as a daughter of Adam she had naturally to incur, Jesus Christ became more fully her Redeemer.' It is significant that Hugh Latimer (1485-1555) [589]'seems to accept Mary's sinlessness' as he wrote to Morice about Mary: [590]'If she were a sinner, then she was redeemed or delivered from sin by Christ, as others sinners be: if she were no sinner, then she was preserved from sin by Christ; so that Christ saved her, and was necessary Saviour, whether she sinned or no'.

This is shown in *The Magnificat* when Mary 'rejoices in God my Saviour' *(Luke 1:47)*. Mary acknowledges her need of God's being her Saviour. It is important that the Anglican writers at the time of the English Reformation are [591]'unanimous in asserting Mary's need of a Saviour... They are also unanimous in affirming Mary's virginity both before and after the birth of Christ.' [592]'The assertion by the Council of Trent that in speaking of original sin, it did not intend to include 'the blessed and immaculate virgin Mary, who gave birth to God' increased the pressure on Anglican theologians to distance themselves from teaching which they saw as going beyond the witness of Scripture... The rejection of the immaculate conception by some Anglican writers was supported by the critical reading of the text of the Vulgate.'

---

[587] Dictionary of Mary 'Behold Your Mother', Catholic Book Publishing Co., New Jersey, 1985, p. 192

[588] Ibid., p. 192

[589] Mary: The Complete Resource, edited by Sarah Jane Boss, Oxford University Press, 2007, p. 247

[590] Ibid.

[591] Ibid., pp 249f

[592] Ibid., p. 246

In 1854 the Immaculate Conception was defined as dogma by The Roman Catholic Church. [593]'In the Apostolic Constitution *Ineffabilis Deus*, Pope Pius IX wrote, "We declare, pronounce, and define that the doctrine which holds that the most Blessed Virgin Mary, in the first instance of her conception, by a singular grace and privilege granted by Almighty God, in view of the merits of Jesus Christ, the Saviour of the human race, was preserved free from all stain of original sin, is a doctrine revealed by God and therefore to be believed firmly and constantly by all the faithful." So the Roman Catholic Church and many Anglican Anglo-Catholics believe. [594] 'The **Immaculate Conception**, according to the teaching of the Catholic Church, was the conception of the Blessed Virgin Mary in the womb of her mother, Saint Anne, free from original sin by virtue of the foreseen merits of her son Jesus Christ. The Catholic Church teaches that Mary was conceived by normal biological means, but God acted upon her soul (keeping her "immaculate") at the time of her conception.' This is the doctrine of prevenient grace. She was **conceived without stain**, and so in heaven now Mary is seen as **Queen conceived without original sin**.

Vollert describes Mary's holiness. [595]'Mary was called to be the physical mother of God the Saviour. She was called to share actively in the events of Christ's life, to cooperate in the mysteries of the incarnation... To carry out this mission, the most important ever confided to a human being, she was invested with objective holiness; God consecrated her with a consecration that corresponds to her vocation. She also has subjective holiness; impelled by her intense personal love of God, itself the fruit of grace, she freely accepted the divine gift.' Mary's love and devotion to God was: 'As the eyes of slaves look to the hand of their master, as the eyes of a maid look to the hand of her mistress, so our eyes look to the Lord our God, till he shows us his mercy' *(Psalm 123:2)*.

---

[593] http://catholicism.about.com/od/beliefsteachings/f/Imm_Concept_FAQ.htm 26th Nov 2016

[594] https://en.wikipedia.org/wiki/Immaculate_Conception 26th Nov 2016

[595] A Theology of Mary: Cyril Vollert S.J., Herder and Herder New York, 1965, p. 197-198

Cardinal Newman explains by connecting Eve and Mary: [596]'It was fitting then in God's mercy that, as the woman began the *destruction* of the world, so woman should also begin its *recovery*, and that, as Eve opened the way for the fatal deed of the first Adam, so Mary should open the way for the great achievement of the second Adam, even our Lord Jesus Christ, who came to save the world by dying on the cross for it. Hence Mary is called by the holy Fathers a second and a better Eve, as having taken that first step in the salvation of mankind which Eve took in its ruin.' Mary is putting right the damage done by Eve; by enabling the birth of Jesus, who is the second Adam; who died on the Cross so we can be forgiven and be reconciled to God, experiencing God's love.

The story of St Bernadette who had visions of Our Lady at Lourdes, gives support to the idea of Mary's Immaculate Conception. The Virgin Mary appeared to [597]'the peasant girl Bernadette Soubirous, a poverty-stricken, pure-hearted adolescent, who saw a vision of a 'Beautiful Lady' near her home town of Lourdes in 1858.' The first apparition was on 11th February 1858 and the validity of the 'Lady' being Mary 'was established on 25th March 1858, when she announced herself as the '**Immaculate Conception**'.' Here Mary called herself by this title, which had been proclaimed by the Pope four years earlier in 1854. The healing water at Lourdes is a place many pilgrims have visited and continue to visit to receive healing. The amazing miracles and healings that people have received from Jesus through Mary's intercession and the waters at Lourdes can be seen as evidence that Mary should be addressed with the titles **Queen conceived without original sin and Queen conceived without stain**.

Br Ramon SSF explains that [598] Mary 'is the obedient servant of the Lord through whom the Christ would come into the world. As the Fathers of the Church said, Eva became Ave (Hail), as Mary reversed the disobedience of Eve, so Christ might reverse the fall of Adam.' Br Ramon along with Cardinal Newman recognises that Mary enables the reversal

---

[596] http://www.cardinaljohnhenrynewman.com/mary-gate-of-heaven-cardinal-newman/ 4th July 2017

[597] Writing on the case of the Video 'The Song of Bernadette'

[598] When they Crucified my Lord: Brother Ramon, BRF, 1999, p. 104

of the sin of Eve, because she gave birth to Jesus who died on the Cross so all who believe in Him can be cleansed and forgiven. 'For God so loved the world that he gave his one and only Son, that whoever believes in him shall not perish but have eternal life. For God did not send his Son into the world to condemn the world, but to save the world through him' *(John 3:16-17)*.

Hilda Graef explains that Genesis 3:15 is [599]'according to tradition the first mention in the Bible of Christ and his Mother, the Woman and her seed. As Eve did not crush the head of the serpent so it seems obvious that 'the woman' must be another than Eve, indeed it must be Mary herself, the 'second Eve', who through her obedience repaired the damage done by the first.' Through Mary's obedience Jesus was born and died on the Cross to set us free from sin. Thus we can see Mary in this verse, when God said to the serpent: 'And I will put enmity between you and the woman, and between your offspring and hers; he will crush your head, and you will strike his heel' *(Genesis 3:15)*. How wonderful that the sin of Eve has been reversed!

Fr Rodney Marshall [600] writes: 'St Ireneus, writing in 2nd Century says this: 'the knot of Eve's disobedience was loosed by the obedience of Mary. For what the Virgin Eve had bound fast by unbelief, this did the Virgin Mary set free through faith.' The 'knot' of sin, mistakes, guilt and condemnation resulting from Eve's disobedience is 'undone' through Mary's obedience. Through Mary's reversing of the sin of Eve she gave birth to Jesus, who died on the cross to set us free. Jesus said 'if the Son sets you free, then you will be free indeed' *(John 8:36)*. St Paul rejoices that 'you have been set free from sin and have become slaves to righteousness' *(Romans 6: 18)*.

Hilda Graef writes about the Virgin birth, quoting G.R. Driver's writing: [601] 'the idea was current among the Canaanites and other nations

---

[599] Mary A History of Doctrine and Devotion, Hilda Graef, Christian Classics, Westminster, 1987, The Liturgical Press Collegeville Minnesota, p.1

[600] Sermon by Fr Rodney Marshall given in Sheffield in October 2016 and printed in AVE The Magazine of The Society of Mary, Annunciationtide, 2017, p.12

[601] Graef, op. cit., p.4 quoting Canaanite Myths: G.R. Drive, 1925, p. 125

of the Middle East that the extraordinary, even virginal birth of a child was to introduce a new era of happiness.' The birth of Jesus brought much joy to people and introduced 'a new era of happiness.' The sorrow that came into the world through the sin of Eve is reversed by the joy resulting from Jesus' birth. Cally Hammond writes that [602] the Immaculate Conception 'is the name given to a belief made binding on all Roman Catholics in 1854. This teaches that Mary was conceived 'without spot of sin' (the word 'immaculate' in Latin means 'without spot').' [603]Alphonsus Liguori wrote in *The Glories of Mary* in 1750: 'the principal reason for the immaculate conception was that Mary was predestined to be the Mother of God.' This was the reason why she was conceived without the stain of original sin.

One Church of England lectionary [604] tells us 'The Immaculate Conception was a feast (and a doctrine) first developed in the West in the Anglo-Saxon England of the early eleventh century on an older and rather different Byzantine basis. (Gregory Dix) ... As a result of our study, the Commission offers the following agreements, which we believe significantly advance our consensus regarding Mary. We affirm together... that in view of her vocation to be the Mother of the Holy One, Christ's redeeming work reached 'back' in Mary to the depths of her being and to her earliest beginnings... In the night of the Advent expectation, Mary began to shine like a true Stella Matutina. For just as the Morning Star, together with the Dawn, precedes the rising of the Sun, so Mary from the time of her Immaculate Conception preceded the coming of the Saviour, the Sun of Righteousness.' I write about **Morning Star** in Chapter 15.

The explanation that 'Christ's redeeming work reached back in Mary to the depths of her being and to her earliest beginnings', is a helpful clarification of the belief in Mary's Immaculate Conception. It is all because God's grace was working in Mary to prepare her to be the Mother of his Son. Indeed, in the *Magnificat* Mary 'rejoices in God my Saviour'

---

[602] Joyful Christianity: Cally Hammond, SPCK, 2009, p.12-13

[603] Mary: The Complete Resource, edited by Sarah Jane Boss, Oxford University Press, 2007, p. 230

[604] Order for the Eucharist and for Morning and Evening Prayer in the Church of England 2017, Tufton Books, p. xxxiv

(Luke 1:47). Mary acknowledges here that God is her Saviour. Mary, like everyone else needed Jesus to cleanse and save her.

In the nineteenth century [605]'Catholic devotion to the **Immaculate Virgin** expressed itself in many ways. A growing number of congregations were dedicated to her.'

Some hymns remind us that Mary is **Queen conceived without original sin**. Mary is the purest creature created by God, so we sing [606]*O Purest of creatures, sweet Mother, sweet maid.*

> [607]***Hail, Queen of the heavens**, hail Mistress of earth;*
> *hail, Virgin most pure of **immaculate birth**....*
> *thee God in the depth of eternity chose,*
> *and formed thee **all fair** as his glorious spouse.*

We [608]*Sing of Mary, **pure** and lowly Virgin Mother **undefiled**.* This hymn describes Mary as pure and immaculate, **Queen conceived without original sin and stain:**

> [609]*In **splendour arrayed**, in **vesture of gold**...*
> *a Mother **all-pure**,*
> *th' **immaculate** one.*

The[610] Sibylline Oracles tell us about the Annunciation and Mary's being immaculate: Thus spoke the archangel to the maiden: "Receive, O

---

[605] Mary A History of Doctrine and Devotion, Hilda Graef, Christian Classics, Westminster, 1987, The Liturgical Press Collegeville Minnesota, p.126

[606] The Walsingham Pilgrim Manual 2016, hymn 26, p.117, F. W. Faber 1814 -1863

[607] Universalis App, Universalis publishing, 1996-2019, Birthday of BM, Vespers, Office Hymn, Edward Caswall 1814-1878

[608] The Walsingham Pilgrim Manual, 2016, p. 121, hymn number 33, v. 1, Roland Palmer 1891- 1985

[609] Ibid., pp 109f, hymn number 21, vv 1, 4, St John Henry Newman 1801- 1890

[610] In Praise of Mary, Hymns from the first millennium of the Eastern and Western Churches, St Paul Publications, May 1981, p.14, Sibylline oracles

Virgin, The Lord in your **immaculate** womb.'" [611]The Akathistos Hymn explains that:

> *The Creator of heaven and of earth*
> *made you thus **immaculate**,*
> *to dwell within your womb.*

What does this mean for us?

It is important to remember that Mary is a 'type' of the Church. Boulet explains the significance of this after we have been reflecting on Mary's holiness. [612]'Mary, it should be noted, is the archetype of the Church. This means that something of Mary's holiness is spread abroad in the church by the Holy Spirit and is diffused, through the medium of the Church and Church members, into our hearts so that we might live according to the Gospel and build up the Body of Christ.' We should seek to be holy and live holy lives that are pleasing to God. I explored the word 'Holy' in Chapter 2 about Mary's title **Holy Mary**. The New Testament Greek word for '**holy**' is [613]hagios (ἁγος) and it is translated 'separate from common condition and use, dedicated', when used to describe things and of people 'holy' and 'saints'. Believers are called to be 'holy'[614] and by God's grace the work of sanctification, of becoming more holy, continues in our lives.

This means that we should regularly confess our sins and receive God's forgiveness, so we keep walking in the light *(I John 1:7-9)*. We should try to live our lives following the promptings of the Holy Spirit *(Romans 8:5-16);* so we 'live a life worthy of the calling you have received' *(Ephesians 4:1b-3)*. Then we will: 'Be imitators of God, therefore, as dearly loved children and live a life of love, just as Christ loved us and gave himself up

---

[611] Ibid., p.39, Akathistos Hymn

[612] Dictionary of Mary 'Behold Your Mother', Catholic Book Publishing Co., New Jersey, 1985, p. 189

[613] Analytical Greek Lexicon, Samuel Bagster & Sons Ltd, London, 1973, p.3

[614] *An Expository Dictionary of Biblical Words*: W.E. Vine, Thomas Nelson Publishers, 1985 p. 307

for us as a fragrant offering and sacrifice to God' *(Ephesians 5:1-2)*. What is the Holy Spirit prompting you to do? How can you imitate God today and 'live a life of love'?

[615] *Hail holy Queen, mother of mercy, our life, our sweetness and our hope, all hail! To thee do we cry, poor banished children of Eve.*

[616] *Queen conceived without original sin, pray for us.*

---

[615] Walsingham Pilgrim Manual 2016, p. 15

[616] Dictionary of Mary 'Behold your Mother', Catholic Book Publishing Co. New Jersey 1997, 1985, p.241

CHAPTER 27

QUEEN OF THE MOST
HOLY ROSARY

Queen of the most holy Rosary is the 48th title of Mary in the Litany of Our Lady, the [617]Litany of Loreto, [618]added by Pope Leo XIII in 1883.

What does the Bible tells us about the Rosary?

The Bible does not mention the Rosary, because it is a form of prayer developed from the 13th Century. There were originally fifteen 'Mysteries of the Rosary': five Joyful, five Sorrowful and five Glorious Mysteries. Thirteen of these are Biblical events. In October 2002 the five Luminous Mysteries were added by Pope John Paul II and they are events in the life

---

[617] Dictionary of Mary 'Behold your Mother', Catholic Book Publishing Co. New Jersey 1997, 1985, p.241

[618] http://www.salvemariaregina.info/SalveMariaRegina/SMR-169/Star.htm 24th June 2017

of Jesus from the Bible: reading and reflecting on the Bible is important when praying the Rosary.

There are many leaflets, booklets and books giving instructions about praying the Rosary. My husband, Fr Neil Bryson, clearly explains for people who are new to the Rosary that: [619]'The rosary is a form of devotional prayer, and can be used for meditation as well as for intercession. It concentrates on twenty different events or mysteries in the life of Our Lord, divided into joyful, luminous, sorrowful and glorious. Each major grouping of beads has a large bead and ten small beads, which is called a decade. Using beads helps us use our body in prayer as well as our mind, spirit and tongue. We know we're at the end of a decade when we reach the chain. We pray *Our Father* on the big bead, *Hail Mary* on each of the small beads, and *Glory be to the Father* on the chain.... I invite you to make the sign of the cross with the crucifix as we say together, *In the name of the Father and of the Son and the Holy Spirit. Amen.* We make an act of faith together in the words of the *Apostles' Creed.* I now invite you to think of something you can thank God for, and then we'll pray the opening prayers. After the crucifix there is a big bead then three small ones. As we make our thanksgiving, we say *Our Father* on the big bead and *Hail Mary* on each of the small ones, ending with *Glory be to the Father* on the chain.' The Joyful Mysteries of the Rosary followed, with the reading of a Bible passage before each Mystery. At the end, the group prayed the Concluding Prayers that are at the end of this Chapter.

Fr Neil explains: [620]'The Rosary is traditionally credited to St Dominic who received it in a vision in 1208. However we can trace the idea of using beads in prayer further back. For example, in c. 1075, Lady Godiva bequeathed a circle of precious stones threaded on cord to a monastery; the Countess had used them in prayer. What St Dominic contributed was a set of meditations on the life of Our Lord accompanied by familiar prayers: these are known as mysteries. There are twenty mysteries in four sets of five. They can be used for meditation, intercession and thanksgiving. Each

---

[619] Rosary leaflet for the Parish of All Saints Boyne Hill; Fr Neil Bryson, 6th October 2012

[620] Rosary leaflet for the Parish of All Saints Boyne Hill; Fr Neil Bryson, 31st July, 2013

mystery has a large bead and ten small beads, which is called a decade.... The prayer is divided into two parts: either the leader or the congregation starts each prayer.' The Rosary can also be prayed by a person on their own.

[621] 'Pope John Paul II, in his apostolic letter *Rosarium Virginis Mariae* in October 2002, recommended an additional set called the *Luminous Mysteries* (or the "Mysteries of Light"). The original *Mysteries of Light* were written by George Preca, the only Maltese official Catholic Saint; (they were) later reformed by the Pope.'

Ten Bible verses can be read before the *Hail Mary* for each of the Mysteries of the Rosary, giving opportunity for Bible reading and reflection when praying the Rosary, as Edward Sri provides in his book.[622] He divides each Mystery into ten sections to be read before each decade of the Rosary. In this way, although the Rosary is not in the Bible; this form of prayer does involve reading and meditation on Bible verses and passages.

The Five **Joyful Mysteries** are: [623]The Annunciation *(Luke 1:28)*, The Visitation *(Luke 1:42)*, The Nativity *(Luke 2:7)*, The Presentation *(Luke 2:28)*, and the Finding in the temple *(Luke 2:46)*.

The Five **Sorrowful Mysteries** are: [624] the Agony in the Garden *(Mark 14:35)*, the Scourging at the Pillar *(Mark 15:15)*, the Crowning with Thorns *(Mark 15:17)*, Carrying the Cross *(John 19:17)*, and The Crucifixion *(Luke 23:33)*. Edward Sri's suggested ten Bible readings for the Crucifixion include readings from three of the Gospels, with Jesus' seven words from the Cross, to focus on the love of Jesus in dying on the Cross so we can be forgiven and be reconciled to God. [625]These verses are 'Father forgive them; for they know not what they do' *(Luke 23:33-34)*. Then the criminal and the penitent thief speaking to Jesus and Jesus's reply *(Luke 23:39-43)*. The

[621] https://en.wikipedia.org/wiki/Rosary#Mysteries_of_the_Rosary 1st November 2017

[622] The New Rosary In Scripture: Edward Sri, Charis Servant Books, Cincinnati, Ohio, 2003, p. 155-174

[623] Dictionary of Mary 'Behold Your Mother', Catholic Book Publishing Co., New Jersey, 1985, p. 407

[624] Ibid., p. 408

[625] The New Rosary In Scripture: Edward Sri, Charis Servant Books, Cincinnati, Ohio, 2003, p. 169

next reading is from John's Gospel when Jesus spoke to his Mother and the beloved disciple *(John 19:26-27)*. Then Jesus' last four words from the Cross, 'My God, my God, why hast thou forsaken me?' *(Matthew 27:46)* Jesus said 'I thirst' *(John 19:28)*. Jesus said 'It is finished' *(John 19:29-30)*, and 'Father into thy hands I commit my spirit!' *(Luke 23:46)*.

The Five **Glorious Mysteries** are: [626]The Resurrection *(Mark 16:6)*, The Ascension *(Mark 16:19)*, the Descent of the Holy Spirit *(Acts 2:4)*, the Assumption of Mary and the Crowning of Mary *(Revelation 12:1)*. The first two Glorious Mysteries are about Jesus, the third is the coming of the Holy Spirit and the last two are about Mary. Cally Hammond explains the Glorious Mysteries are: [627]'a traditional prayer which provides five fragments from Scripture for meditation.'

The **Mysteries of Light** focus on Jesus as we rejoice with Mary that her Son is the light of the world who illumines the darkness of our hearts and lives. The five Mysteries of Light are: The Baptism of the Lord *(Matthew 3:1-17)*, The Wedding at Cana *(John 2:1-12)*, Jesus' Proclamation of the Kingdom of God *(Mark 1:15)*, The Transfiguration *(Luke 9: 28-36)*, and the Institution of the Eucharist *(John 13:1-11, Matthew 26:26-29)*. We see that the Rosary points to Jesus and by using the Scriptures in Rosary booklets, this form of prayer involves Bible reading and reflection.

How can Mary be described as Queen of the most holy Rosary?

The Rosary is '**most holy**' because it is a form of prayer that helps us to learn more about the life of Jesus and the Lord's love for us. The New Testament Greek word for '**holy**' is [628] *hagios* (ἁγιος), translated 'separate from common condition and use, dedicated', when used to describe things. The Rosary is a special set of beads that is set apart to be used for prayer, Bible reading and reflection.

---

[626] Dictionary of Mary op. cit., p. 409

[627] Glorious Christianity, Walking by faith in the life to come, Cally Hammond, SPCK, 2012, p. xiv

[628] Analytical Greek Lexicon, Samuel Bagster & Sons Ltd, London, 1973, p.3

Mary can be regarded as '**Queen**' of the holy Rosary because Saint Dominic was given the Rosary from Mary in a vision. We discover that: [629] 'Tradition holds that Our Lady gave the Rosary to Saint Dominic Guzman in 1206 as a form of gospel-preaching and popular prayer. For more than seven centuries, the Rosary devotion has been one of the most popular devotional practices in the church. Its combination of vocal and mental prayer have made it a prime tool for contemplation... Our Lady's Rosary is the key to open the treasury of grace to us. Although prayer beads had been popular before Dominic's time, he and his friars quickly adopted the Rosary as an excellent way to teach the mysteries of Christianity to a largely illiterate European population. In 1470, Blessed Alan of Rupe founded the first Rosary Confraternity, and thereby launched the Dominican Order as the foremost missionaries of the Rosary. Through the efforts of Blessed Alan and the early Dominicans, this prayer form spread rapidly throughout Western Christendom.'

Praying the Rosary includes praying the *Hail Mary* ten times in each decade, asking Mary to pray for us. Mary is **Queen** and can be seen as **Queen of the Holy Rosary** because in the Rosary we learn more about Jesus as Mary always points to Jesus *(John 2:5)*.

Laurenceau[630] describes the Rosary as 'treasure and prayer of its own.' He sees the Rosary 'is loved by the common folk', it 'fosters faith', 'is a humble prayer of petition', and 'has missionary power' as it is 'an education in the Faith and one of the surest and most effective ways to conversion'. The Rosary also 'highlights Mary's maternal role'; encouraging us 'to talk with Mary as we talk with our mother'. By praying the Rosary, we 'get close to Jesus and ultimately to the Father.'

7th October is the Feast Day of Mary **Queen of the most holy Rosary** because a victory in the Battle of Lepanto on 7th October 1571 was achieved, because people prayed the Rosary asking for Mary's intercession. [631] 'The

---

[629] http://holyspiritinteractive.net/features/somethingaboutmary/queenofrosary.asp 7th September 2017

[630] Dictionary of Mary 'Behold Your Mother', Catholic Book Publishing Co., New Jersey, 1985, p. 410

[631] https://en.wikipedia.org/wiki/Our_Lady_of_the_Rosary 7th September 2017

Feast of Our Lady of the Rosary, formerly known as the **Feast of Our Lady of Victory** and **Feast of the Holy Rosary**, is a feast day of the Roman Catholic Church, celebrated on 7 October, the anniversary of the decisive victory of the combined fleet of the Holy League of 1571 over the Ottoman navy at the Battle of Lepanto…. In 1960 Pope John XXIII changed the title to "Feast of Our Lady of the Rosary". **Our Lady of the Rosary** is the patron saint of several places around the world and Churches are dedicated to Our Lady of the Rosary.

Mary encouraged the praying of the Rosary, when she appeared in visions and apparitions. [632]At Lourdes in 1858 Our Lady told St. Bernadette to pray many rosaries. When Bernadette saw the beautiful lady, she instinctively took her Rosary in her hands and knelt down. The lady made a sign of approval with her head, and took into her hands a Rosary which hung on her right arm. As Bernadette prayed, Our Lady passed the beads of her Rosary through her fingers, but said nothing except the Gloria at the end of each decade. In 1917 [633] at Fátima, Mary told the children to pray the Rosary often. Our Lady told Blessed Bartolo Longo to propagate the Rosary, and promised that those who would encourage this devotion would be saved. [634]Through the years, Our Lady has re-affirmed her approval of this devotion, and her pleasure in the title "Queen of the Rosary." To Blessed Alan, she made fifteen promises to those who devoutly recite her beads. She told him: "Immense volumes would have to be written if all the miracles of my Holy Rosary were to be recorded." Our Lady's promises include: Those who shall have served me constantly by reciting the Rosary shall receive some special grace. I promise my special protection and great graces to all who devoutly recite my Psalter.' This is encouragement from Mary herself, for us to pray the Rosary.

[635]'Popes throughout history have loved the Rosary… Pius XI dedicated the entire month of October to the Rosary. Pope St. Pius X said, "Of all the prayers, the Rosary is the most beautiful and the richest in graces; of all it

---

[632] Video *The Song of Bernadette*

[633] http://www.salvemariaregina.info/SalveMariaRegina/SMR-169/Star.htm 24th June 2017

[634] http://www.salvemariaregina.info/SalveMariaRegina/SMR-169/Star.htm 24th June 2017

[635] http://www.salvemariaregina.info/SalveMariaRegina/SMR-169/Star.htm 24th June 2017

is the one most pleasing to Mary, the Virgin Most Holy." Pope Leo XIII repeatedly recommended the Rosary as a most powerful means whereby to move God to aid us in meeting the needs of the present age. In 1883, he inserted the invocation, "Queen of the Most Holy Rosary, pray for us!" into the Litany for the Universal Church… Pope John Paul II tells us to "… love the simple, fruitful prayer of the Rosary."… Founders of most religious orders have either commanded or recommended the daily recitation of the Rosary. The Benedictines speedily adapted this devotion in their ancient cloisters. The Carmelites were happy to receive the Rosary as well as their rule from the Dominicans. The Franciscans made their rosaries out of wood, and preached this devotion as well as poverty…. Inspired by the example of their founder, the Jesuits invariably propagated the devotion.'

[636] 'When it was a felony to teach the Catholic Catechism, and death for a priest to say Mass, the Irish mothers used their rosaries to tell their little ones the story of Jesus and Mary, and thus kept the Faith green in the hearts of their children. Saint John Vianney, the Curé d'Ars, declared emphatically that in the nineteenth century it was the Rosary which restored religion in France. Likewise, in the dark days of persecution in Mexico, in our own century, the sturdy Mexican Catholics clung faithfully to their rosaries.'

Hilda Graef tells us that: [637]'The Shrine of Walsingham, which had been destroyed in 1538, was restored in the early twentieth century, and is now a place of pilgrimage for Anglicans as well as for Catholics, the Rosary being recited there by both.' At the Anglican Shrine of Our Lady of Walsingham there are daily Shrine Prayers. [638]'Each week-night the mysteries incorporate intercessions for the sick, those in spiritual or temporal need, the departed, as well as for members of the Walsingham 'family'.

---

[636] http://www.salvemariaregina.info/SalveMariaRegina/SMR-169/Star.htm 24th June 2017

[637] Mary A History of Doctrine and Devotion, Hilda Graef, Christian Classics, Westminster, 1987, The Liturgical Press Collegeville Minnesota, p.134

[638] Walsingham Pilgrim Manual, 2016, p. 52

What does this mean for us?

Praying the Rosary may help you listen to the Lord and know his presence with you. The [639]'repetition of a prayer over and over again is a technique for lulling the mind into a meditative state in which – to put things in Christian terms – it may become attentive to the movement of the Holy Spirit. The more it is used, the easier it becomes to slip into a meditative state... It makes the reassurance of God's presence close at hand: the trust that the meditator is grounded in the divine may be summoned by the movement of a hand or the silent recitation of simple words.' However: [640]'even among devout Catholics with a great devotion to the Virgin Mary, there are those for whom bead meditation has little to offer. Having said this, one should not ignore the fact that, for most people, to become at all expert in the technique of rosary meditation demands a good deal of practice. It is like learning a new language or cultivating a new friendship: you really have to devote time and effort to it.'

This encourages us to try praying the Rosary and keep practising, to see if it is a helpful way for us to pray. Cally Hammond encourages us to pray the Joyful Mysteries of the Rosary so we become more confident and joyful in our Christian faith. [641]'If joyful Christianity means anything it means living a faith that is brimming with *confidence*. To show how we can find this kind of confidence in faith, we shall explore the 'joyful mysteries', through which Christians have long reflected on key moments in the life of Jesus, and use them to see how God is at work in our everyday lives... The prayer called the joyful mysteries sheds light on what the incarnation means.' Cally recommends the Sorrowful Mysteries of the Rosary so that we grow into a deeper relationship with Jesus. [642]'When we really focus our attention on these key moments in the Passion, we move into

---

[639] Mary: The Complete Resource, edited by Sarah Jane Boss, Oxford University Press, 2007, p. 386

[640] Mary: The Complete Resource, edited by Sarah Jane Boss, Oxford University Press, 2007, p. 393

[641] Joyful Christianity, Finding Jesus in the world, Cally Hammond, SPCK, 2009, p. xv- xvi

[642] Passionate Christianity, A journey to the Cross, Cally Hammond, SPCK, 2007, p. viii-ix

a new realm of encounter; for the Passion is not only a historical event we can read about, but something we can experience, and in which we participate. These five events in Jesus' life encourage us to think deeply, both emotionally and intellectually, about the meaning of faith.' She suggests we 'see them from the inside, imaginatively', so we picture the scenes as well as 'consider them from the outside, dispassionately.' In the Rosary we grow to know and love Jesus more.

Praying the Rosary is encouraged because with Mary we focus on Jesus. [643]'Its recitation, if done in a relaxed and recollective manner, takes the nature of a contemplative prayer, a meditation on the Mysteries of the Lord's life as seen through the eyes of her who was closest to the Lord. To pray the Rosary is to contemplate with Mary the Lord made flesh, crucified and raised for our salvation.'

Would you like to pray the Rosary? This may be a helpful way for you to pray, using a Rosary booklet or at Shrine Prayers at Walsingham on Pilgrimage.

[644]*O God, whose only-begotten Son, by his life, death and resurrection has purchased for us the rewards of eternal salvation: grant that we, meditating on these mysteries in **the most holy rosary of the blessèd Virgin Mary**, may both imitate what they contain and obtain what they promise; through the same Jesus Christ our Lord. **Amen.***

[645] *Queen of the most holy Rosary, pray for us.*

---

[643] Dictionary of Mary 'Behold your Mother', Catholic Book Publishing Co., New Jersey, 1997, 1985, p. 406

[644] Rosary leaflet with Concluding Prayers for Rosary Services: Fr Neil Bryson, 6th October 2012

[645] The Walsingham Pilgrim Manual 2016, p.14

CHAPTER 28

QUEEN OF FAMILIES

In this chapter we consider the 49th title in the [646]Litany of Loreto, Queen of families.

What does the Bible tells us about families?

The **Old Testament** is the story of the Jewish **family** chosen and loved by God. The New Testament Greek word *patria* πατριά means [647]'an ancestry, lineage... a family or tribe'. God told Abram: "I will make you into a great nation and I will bless you; I will make your name great, and you will be a blessing...." *(Genesis 12:2-3)*. At the first Passover in Egypt, Moses said, 'each man is to take a lamb for his **family**, one for each household' *(Exodus 12:3)*. Later in the twelve tribes of Israel there were '**family** heads of the

---

[646] Dictionary of Mary 'Behold your Mother', Catholic Book Publishing Co. New Jersey 1997, 1985, p.241

[647] An Expository Dictionary of Biblical Words: W.E. Vine, Thomas Nelson, Inc, 1984, p. 225

Israelite tribes' *(Numbers 32:28)*. The Hebrew word for family is *mishpachah* מִשְׁפָּחָה. The first eight chapters of I Chronicles list the names of the descendants of the Jewish family from Abraham, tracing the line back to Adam. The Jews greatly value the importance of tracing and knowing their family ancestry.

Paul longs for the Jews to recognise that Jesus is the Messiah: 'Theirs is the adoption as sons; theirs the covenants, the receiving of the law, the temple worship and the promises. Theirs are the patriarchs' *(Romans 9:4-5)*. He writes: 'my heart's desire and prayer to God for the Israelites is that they may be saved…..' *(Romans 10:1-4)*.

The Bible tells us about the **Holy Family** of Mary, Joseph and Jesus. St Luke's Gospel *(chapters 1-2)*, tells us about Jesus' birth at Bethlehem *(Luke 2:1-7)*, the visit of the Shepherds *(Luke 2:8-20)*, Jesus' circumcision *(Luke 2:21)*, and the Presentation at Jerusalem *(Luke 2:21-38)*. Matthew tells us about an angel's visit to Joseph *(Matthew 1:18-24)*; the visit of the Wise Men *(Matthew 2:1-12)*; and the subsequent escape to Egypt because God spoke to Joseph in a dream *(Matthew 2:13-14)*. Later the family returned to Nazareth in Galilee *(Matthew 2:19-23, Luke 2:39-40)*. Jesus visited Jerusalem on a pilgrimage holiday with family and friends from Nazareth *(Luke 2:41-52)*. We honour Joseph as a caring and protective step-father, who provided for his family by working as a carpenter *(Mark 6:2-3)*.

Jesus said his **family** were the people who followed him. When Jesus was told that his mother and brothers were outside, Jesus said: "…whoever does the will of my Father in heaven is my brother and sister and mother" *(Matthew 12:48-50)*. How wonderful that we are members of God's **family** if we seek hear and to do the will of our Father in heaven. Jesus says that following Him may cause divisions in families *(Luke 12:52-53)*. Here [648]'Luke includes a passage that points to the need for disciples to respond to the urgency of the times even at the expense of causing divisions within their own families…'

---

[648] The Oxford Bible Commentary, edited by John Barton and John Muddiman, Oxford University Press, 2001, p. 945

The Bible describes the **Church** as God's family [649] using the New Testament Greek word *oikos* οἶκος, which means 'a household or family'. This word is used to encourage people to care for widows in their family, rather than leaving others in the Church to provide financial help. 'But if a widow has children or grandchildren, these should learn first of all to put their religion into practice by caring for their own **family** and so repaying their parents and grandparents, for this is pleasing to God' *(I Timothy 5:4)*.

Church leaders need to set a good example to the Church. 'Now the overseer must be above reproach, the husband of but one wife, temperate, self-controlled, respectable, hospitable, able to teach, not given to drunkenness, not violent but gentle, not quarrelsome, not a lover of money. He must manage his own **family** well and see that his children obey him with proper respect. (If anyone does not know how to manage his own family, how can he take care of God's church?)' *(I Timothy 3:2-3,5)*. The family of a Church leader should be an illustration and inspiration for others in the Church to follow so that Church families demonstrate respect, love, care and order.

St Paul prays for the Church, that he sees as God's family: 'For this reason I kneel before the Father, from whom his whole **family** in heaven and on earth derives its name. I pray that … Christ may dwell in your hearts through faith. And I pray that you, being rooted and established in love, may have power, together with all the saints, to grasp how wide and long and high and deep is the love of Christ' *(Ephesians 3:14-18)*. Vine explains that here 'the reference being to all those who are spiritually related to God the Father, He being the Author of their spiritual relationship to Him as His children, they being united to one another in a "family" fellowship.' The Church is described as a family where all grow to experience more of the love of Jesus.

How amazing that when we come to believe in Jesus; receiving forgiveness through Jesus' death on the Cross, then we become a member of his **family**. 'If by the Spirit you put to death the misdeeds of the body, you will live, because those who are led by the Spirit of God are sons of God. For you did not receive a spirit that makes you a slave again to fear,

---

[649] Vine, op. cit., p. 225

but you received the Spirit of sonship. And by him we cry, "Abba, Father." The Spirit himself testifies with our spirit that we are **God's children....'** *(Romans 8:11-17).* We 'are God's children' and can call God 'Abba', which is the informal word 'Daddy'. We have been adopted into God's family. [650] 'Christians are adopted sons by grace; Christ, however, is God's Son by nature. 'Abba, Father' is expressive of an especially close relationship to God.' Jesus taught us to pray to God as 'Our Father' telling us: "This, then, is how you should pray: Our Father in heaven, hallowed be your name...." *(Matthew 6:9).* The Sacrament of Baptism welcomes new members of Jesus's family.

God promises to bless **families** who are obedient to Him with the gift of children *(Deuteronomy 28:4,11)*: 'Sons are a heritage from the Lord, children a reward from him' *(Psalm 127:3)*. How wonderful that the Lord 'settles the barren woman in her home as a happy mother of children' *(Psalm 113:9)*. Sarah *(Genesis 21:1-2)*; Rebecca *(Genesis 25:21)*; Rachel *(Genesis 30:22-24)*; Hannah *(I Samuel 1:10-20)*, and Elizabeth *(Luke 1:13-14,57-60)*, are examples of barren women who prayed; the Lord heard and answered their prayers with the gift of a baby. This is encouragement to pray for couples who long to conceive a baby. 'God sets the lonely in families' *(Psalm 68:6)*. We are told that: 'A wife of noble character, provides food for her family' *(Proverbs 31:10,15)*.

God wants us 'to be conformed to the image of his Son, in order that he might be the firstborn within a large family' *(Romans 8:29)*. God's family is a **growing** family and we all need to be active in helping Jesus' family to grow.

How can Mary be addressed as Queen of families?

Reverend Matthew R. Mauriello explains about this title's addition to the Litany of Loreto. [651] 'Our Holy Father, Pope John Paul II has inserted a

---

[650] Glo Computer Commentary for these verses

[651] https://www.udayton.edu/imri/mary/q/queen-of-families.php 3rd Nov 2016 This article appeared in the *Fairfield County Catholic* January 1996. Reprinted with permission of the author and publisher.

new invocation, "Queen of Families," in the Litany of the Blessed Virgin. On December 31, 1995, the Sacred Congregation for Divine Worship sent a letter to the Episcopal conferences of the world informing of the Holy Father's addition to the litany. This new title is to be inserted in the litany after "Queen of the Most Holy Rosary" and before "Queen of Peace."' Queen of families is, then, the 49th title in the Litany. The invocation "Queen of Families" is a relatively new title and flows naturally from the fact that Mary is Mother of the Church. The family is considered the 'domestic church', since it is there that the seed of faith which is planted in the Sacrament of Baptism is nourished and flourishes by the teaching and good example of the parents and members of the home.

'The family is the smallest cell of the church which builds up the Mystical Body of Christ. It is in the family that we find the first school of prayer and the moral and social virtues that form the basis for society. The family is the place which builds up the world by guarding and transmitting virtues and values from parent to child by what is taught and lived.

'In 1964, during the proceedings of the Second Vatican Council, four hundred bishops petitioned the Holy See for the inclusion of this title in the litany. During the recent International Year of the Family, many bishops and lay organizations as well requested that an invocation be proposed which would speak of Mary's relation to the Holy Family of Nazareth. Mary called herself the 'Handmaid of the Lord' *(Luke 1:38)*, and through her obedience to the Will of God she accepted her vocation as wife and mother in the family of Nazareth. She put herself in God's service and thereby put herself in the service of others. In the Apostolic Exhortation, *Familiaris Consortio*, promulgated by the late Pope John Paul II on November 22, 1981, the Holy Father wrote, "May the Virgin Mary, Mother of the Church, be also mother of the 'family church'. Through her maternal help, may every Christian family be a 'little church' in which the mystery of Christ is relived." We ask **Mary, Queen of Families** to bless, guide and protect each of our families.' This is why Mary has been given this title.

We can learn more from these reflections about **Mary, Queen of families**. It is interesting that [652] 'This is a relatively new Marian Title, flowing quite naturally from the fact that Mary is **Mother of the Church**. She is also Mother of the Domestic church – that is, the Christian family… This is because of the role of Mary seen and portrayed in the Holy family of Nazareth. Mary called herself the "Handmaid of the Lord" *(Luke 1:38)*, and through obedience to the word of God she accepted her lofty, yet not easy vocation as wife and mother putting herself at God's service and at the service of others: a service of love…The family as we know is the nucleus of the society and also of the church.'

The title Mary, Mother of the Church helps our understanding of Mary as **Queen of families**. On the Cross, 'When Jesus saw his mother there, and the disciple whom he loved standing nearby, he said to his mother, "Dear woman, here is your son," and to the disciple, "Here is your mother." From that time on, this disciple took her into his home' *(John 19:26-27)*. Mary became John's 'mother' and took on a motherly role for the Early Church. She was there in the upper room on the day of Pentecost *(Acts 1:14)*. I explore Mary's other 'Mother' titles in Chapters 2 and 3. *Queen of Families* was added in 1995.

In Chapter 20 **Queen Assumed into Heaven** we reflected how Mary is Queen in heaven. If we accept that Mary is Queen in Heaven; then we can recognise that she is Queen over all the people who are in Heaven, which includes **families**. Scott Hahn appreciates Mary's motherly role, writing [653]'Mary then is a mother to the **family** of God'. We can picture the Holy Family with Mary, Joseph and baby Jesus and with other children, who are being included into the Holy Family; imagining Mary presenting Jesus to the children and looking at them with

---

[652] http://www.antiessays.com/free-essays/Mary-Queen-Of-Families-720588.html 14th July 2017

[653] Hail, Holy Queen: Scott Hahn, Darton, Longman and Todd Ltd, London 2010 p.142

What does this mean for us?

Have you become a member of God's **family** by believing in Jesus and receiving his forgiveness? Have you invited Jesus into your life and have the assurance that you a beloved child in God's family? Have you opened the door and asked Jesus to come into your life? *(Revelation 3:20)* Do you have the assurance of being one of God's **children**?

The family of a Church leader should be an illustration and inspiration for others in the Church to follow so Church families demonstrate respect, love, care and order. Is your family a good example for others to follow? *(I Timothy 3:2-3,5)*

How wonderful that the Lord 'settles the barren woman in her home as a happy mother of children' *(Psalm 113:9)*. Do you know of a couple who long to conceive a baby? Then pray for them as the Lord still hears and answers prayers for a baby.

Do you help to make your Church community like a loving family? How could you help your Church to be more like a caring family? Do you care for the elderly and needy in your own family? *(I Timothy 3: 4)*

The Jews value the importance of tracing and knowing their family ancestry. A Jewish friend told me in the 1980s that she was descended from Levi and Asher, which was of great significance to her. Have you discovered about your ancestors? A useful website to do that is www.ancestry.co.uk. We give thanks to God for the former generations of our family and may discover that they had great faith. Some may have worked in a certain trade or profession that continues in the family to the present day.

God's family is a **growing** family and we all need to be active in helping Jesus' family to grow *(Romans 8:29)*. How can you help God's family to grow? We can pray for people who do not know Jesus and be ready to talk to them and share our faith. 'Always be prepared to give an answer to everyone who asks you to give the reason for the hope that you have. But do this with gentleness and respect' *(I Peter 3:15)*. We do not know when we may be asked about our faith, so we need to be ready to talk about how knowing Jesus helps us in our lives and encourage people to come to Church and meet with Jesus. It is very powerful to talk about how Jesus has helped you in a difficult time.

Mary understands families because she is a mother. We can think of Mary as **Mother of the Church** as well as **Queen of families**. Some Christians like to ask Mary to pray especially about concerns in their families and to pray for families to be loving and caring like the Holy Family.

[654] *Queen of families, pray for us.*

---

[654] The Walsingham Pilgrim Manual 2016, p.14

CHAPTER 29

QUEEN OF PEACE

In the [655]Litany of Loreto Queen of Peace is the last title in the list of 50 titles. [656]Peace is defined as: '**freedom from war** or **hostilities, freedom from disturbance and quarrels, absence of noise, stillness, quiet and silence** and is used in expressions of salutation.'

What does the Bible tells us about peace?

Peace is the Hebrew word *shalom* meaning [657]'completeness, peace'. Isaac made a peace treaty with the men from Gerar *(Genesis 26:31)*. Moses instructed the people, 'When you march up to attack a city, make its people

---

[655] Dictionary of Mary 'Behold your Mother', Catholic Book Publishing Co. New Jersey 1997, 1985, p.241

[656] The Shorter Oxford English Dictionary on Historical Principles, H.W. Fowler & J. Coulson, Clarendon Press, Oxford, 1973, p.1533

[657] Analytical Concordance to the Holy Bible, Robert Young, United Society for Christian Literature, Lutterworth Press London, 1973, p. 736

an offer of peace' *(Deuteronomy 20:10)*. After the Gibeonite deception 'Joshua made a treaty of peace with them' *(Joshua 9:15)*. Eli said to Hannah, "Go in **peace**, and may the God of Israel grant you what you have asked of him'" *(I Samuel 1:17)*. Samuel was born in answer to Hannah's prayer. When he was prophesying the death of King Ahab, Micaiah answered, 'the Lord said, "These people have no master". Let each one go home in peace' *(I Kings 22:17)*. The Lord told David that his son Solomon would be a: 'a man of peace and rest, and I will give him rest from all his enemies on every side. His name will be Solomon, and I will grant Israel peace and quiet during his reign' *(I Chronicles 22: 9)*. How wonderful that 'The Lord blesses his people with **peace**' *(Psalm 29:11)*. The Messiah is 'The Prince of Peace' *(Isaiah 9:6)*. Isaiah proclaims the good news of peace, 'You will go out in joy and be led forth in peace' *(Isaiah 55:12)*. We see that peace, *shalom*, is a gift from God to His people. Jeremiah writes to the exiles in Babylon, 'Also, seek the **peace** and prosperity of the city to which I have carried you into exile… Pray to the Lord for it, because if it prospers, you too will prosper' *(Jeremiah 29:7)*. After the prophecy about the dry bones the Lord says: 'I will make a covenant of peace with them…' *(Ezekiel 37:26)*. The new Temple will be a place of peace: 'in this place I will grant peace,' declares the Lord Almighty *(Haggai 2:9)*. The Psalmist rejoices that God protects them as 'He grants peace to your borders' *(Psalm 147:14)*.

Peace is also used in the Old Testament in the Authorised Version of the Bible to mean 'to keep silent' or 'to be silent'. This is the Hebrew word [658]*chârash* חָרַשׁ when Job says 'Hold your peace' *(Job 13:13 AV)*, or 'keep silent' *(Ibid. NIV)*. In New Testament Greek the word is *sigaō* σιγάω and it is used when Jesus answered the question about paying taxes and those sent were unable to trap him 'held their peace' *(Luke 20:26 AV)*, or 'became silent' *(Ibid. NIV)*. Silence can help us feel at peace. Silence in worship and prayer is special and a time to hear from the Lord and let His peace guide and direct us. Peaceful times of silent reflection are significant times of knowing the Lord's presence with us.

---

[658] Ibid.

The Hebrew word [659]*shâlam* שָׁלַם means 'to cause or make peace'. This is used when the 'vassals of Hadadezer' realised they had been defeated by the Israelites they 'made peace with Israel' *(II Samuel 10:19)*. The 'peace offering' *shelem* שָׁלֶם *(Leviticus 3)*, was one of the sacrificial offerings required under the Old Covenant to enable forgiveness and peace with God. '**The Lord bless you** and keep you; the Lord make his face shine upon you and be gracious to you; the Lord turn his face towards you **and give you peace**' *(Numbers 6:24-26)*.

Perfect **peace** *shâlôm* שָׁלוֹם is promised in Isaiah: 'You will keep in perfect peace him whose mind is steadfast, because he trusts in you' *(Isaiah 26:3)*. The peace that God gives is 'perfect' and we are encouraged here to keep trusting God so we are kept in calm, tranquillity and perfect peace. Isaiah uses *shâlôm* to prophesy that: 'My people will live in peaceful dwelling-places' *(Isaiah 32:18)*. *Shâlôm* is the word used as a greeting. *Shabbat shalom* is the traditional greeting to wish someone a peaceful Sabbath. Jesus used this traditional greeting '**peace be with you**', when He appeared to the disciples on the evening of Easter Day and again when he appeared when Thomas was with them a week later *(John 20:19,21,26)*. Jesus wanted peace to replace the doubt, fear and guilt that the disciples were feeling on Easter Sunday evening. Most Epistles begin with the greeting of **peace** for the readers *(Ephesians 1:2, Philippians 1:2, I Peter 1:2; see also Revelation 1:4)*.

The Messiah will be called '**Prince of Peace**' and 'of the increase of his government and peace there will be no end' *(Isaiah 9:6-7)*. Isaiah prophesied about the coming of Jesus with a message of peace. The Psalmist writes: 'Great peace have they who love your law' *(Psalm 119:65)*. If Jesus rules in our lives then we will experience increasing peace. Paul tells us: 'Let the peace of Christ rule in your hearts, since as members of one body you were called to peace. And be thankful' *(Colossians 3:15)*. On the night of Jesus' birth the angel announced the good news to the shepherds and angels sang: "Glory to God in the highest, and on earth **peace** to men on whom his favour rests" *(Luke 2:14)*.

---

[659] Ibid., p. 737

'**Peace**' *eirēnē* εἰρήνη is the New Testament Greek word meaning [660]'peace, unity, concord'; and 'peaceable' is the New Testament Greek word *eirēnikos* εἰρηνικός and this means [661] 'peace, tranquillity, concord, a salutation expressive of good wishes, a blessing, to be at peace, to cultivate peace, peaceable, disposed to peace and concord.' Jesus healed the woman on the way to Jairus' house saying: "Go in peace and be freed from your suffering" *(Luke 8:48)*. Jesus spoke kindly to the woman who expressed her love by anointing his feet: "Your faith has saved you; go in peace" *(Luke 7:50)*. When Jesus sent out the seventy-two we read the word 'peace' εἰρήνη as he told them: "When you enter a house, first say, 'Peace to this house'" *(Luke 10:5-6)*.

Peace is Jesus' gift to us as Jesus said: '**Peace** I leave with you; my peace I give you. I do not give to you as the world gives. Do not let your hearts be troubled and do not be afraid' *(John 14:27)*. Jesus wants us to know and live in His peace *(John 16:33)*. Jesus calmed the storm when he said to the waves, "Quiet! Be still!" *(Mark 4:39)*

God's wisdom is 'peace- loving' *(James 3:17)*. We show wisdom if we are 'peace-loving' or peaceable. Jesus said: 'Blessed are the **peacemakers**, for they will be called sons of God' *(Matthew 5:9)*. St Paul tells us 'as far as it depends on you, live at peace with everyone' *(Romans 12:18)*. Jesus teaches us "…be at peace with each other" *(Mark 9:50b)*. P aul writes: 'live in peace. And the God of love and **peace** will be with you' *(II Corinthians 13:11)*, and 'live in peace with each other' *(I Thessalonians 5:13b)*. The third quality of the fruit of the Spirit is 'peace' *(Galatians 5:22)*. Paul advises Timothy: 'pursue righteousness, faith, love and peace' *(II Timothy 2:22)*. We should pray about our worries and receive 'the **peace** of God, which transcends all understanding' *(Philippians 4:6-7)*.

We have peace with God because we believe that Jesus died on the cross so we can be forgiven *(Romans 5:1-2)*. We are thankful that 'the punishment that brought us **peace** was upon him, and by his wounds we are healed' *(Isaiah 53:5)*; 'making peace through his blood, shed on the cross' *(Colossians 1:20)*. 'God has called us to **live in peace**' *(I Corinthians 7:15b)*. God wants

---

[660] Analytical Concordance to the Holy Bible, Robert Young, United Society for Christian Literature, Lutterworth Press London, 1973, p. 736
[661] Analytical Greek Lexicon, Samuel Bagster & Sons Ltd, London, 1973, p. 119

there to be peace in our worship and Churches *(I Corinthians 14:33)*. God's discipline 'produces a harvest of righteousness and **peace**' *(Hebrews 12:10-11)*. How wonderful that Jesus is our peace and that Gentiles as well as Jews are invited to know Jesus and live in His peace *(Ephesians 2:13-14, John 3:16)*. We should 'seek peace and pursue it' *(I Peter 3:11)*.

However, Jesus also said: "Do not suppose that I have come to bring peace to the earth. I did not come to bring peace, but a sword" *(Matthew 10:34)*. This seems to contradict the verses about peace that we have read above. [662]'At first glance this saying sounds like a contradiction of "Prince of Peace" *(Isaiah 9:6)*, "on earth peace to men" *(Luke 2:14)*, and "Peace I leave with you" *(John 14:27)*. It is true that Christ came to bring peace—peace between the believer and God, and peace among humans. Yet the inevitable result of Christ's coming is conflict—between Christ and the antichrist, between light and darkness, between Christ's children and the devil's children. This conflict can occur even between members of the same family' *(Matthew 10:35-36, Mark 10:29-30)*. Paul warns of a time of distress: 'While people are saying, "Peace and safety", destruction will come on them suddenly' *(I Thessalonians 5:3-5)*. John reveals a time when the rider of the red horse 'was given power to take peace from the earth and make men slay one another' *(Revelation 6:4)*. Wars are such times, when people long for peace again.

How can Mary be addressed as Queen of Peace?

This 50th title was added to the Litany of Loreto in the First World War, at a time of much prayer for peace. [663]'The invocation 'Queen of Peace' was inserted in the Litany of the Blessed Virgin by Pope Benedict XV in 1917 when the world was being torn apart by war. The Pope specifically related this act to the long hoped-for peace in that day. He said 'May this pious and ardent invocation rise to Mary… May her loving and most merciful solicitude be moved to obtain for this convulsed world the peace so greatly desired!' Thus, the title 'Queen of Peace' is a logical outgrowth

---

[662] Glo Computer Bible Commentary for Matthew 10:34

[663] Dictionary of Mary 'Behold your Mother', Catholic Book Publishing Co., New Jersey, 1997, 1985, p. 299

of the title 'Help of Christians.' By helping Christians, Mary enables them to overcome their adversaries and bring about peace.' I investigate **Help of Christians** in Chapter 18.

Mary is the **Queen of Peace** because she is the Mother of Jesus, the Messiah, who is 'The Prince of Peace' *(Isaiah 9:6)*.

In her apparitions at Medjugorje, Mary referred to herself as **Queen of Peace**. [664] 'On July 25th 1990 Mary said: 'I have come here as the **Queen of Peace** and I desire to enrich you with my motherly peace.'... Since 1981, in a small village called Medjugorje, in Bosnia-Herzegovina, the Blessed Virgin Mary has been appearing and giving messages to the world... In Her own words She tells us, *"I have come to tell the world that God exists. He is the fullness of life, and to enjoy this fullness and peace, you must return to God"*. Since the apparitions began in 1981, over 40 million people of all faiths, from all over the world, have visited Medjugorje and have left spiritually strengthened and renewed. Countless unbelievers and physically or mentally afflicted, have been converted and healed. Our Lady's Messages are Messages of Peace and Love, and are meant to guide each one of us to a closer relationship with God.'

Churches dedicated to Mary as Queen of Peace, include [665]'The Foujita Chapel in Reims, France, is dedicated to Our Lady, Queen of Peace as a reaction to the horror and devastation caused by the 1945 Bombing of Hiroshima and Bombing of Nagasaki... A notable example is the Queen of Peace Church in Bray, Co. Wicklow, Ireland.'

Mary points people to Jesus who gives peace *(John 2:5,14:27)*. St Ignatius reflects: [666]'The virginity of Mary and her giving birth were hidden from the ruler of this age, as was also the death of the Lord – three mysteries to be loudly proclaimed, yet which were accomplished in the silence of God.' Mary's virginity and the birth of Jesus are mysteries of **peace** and silence. Mary is:

[667]*Lady of silences* **Calm** *and distressed.*

---

[664] https://www.medjugorje.org/olmpage.htm 6th May 2017

[665] https://en.wikipedia.org/wiki/Our_Lady_of_Peace 3rd November 2016

[666] *Silence, A Christian History:* Diarmaid MacCulloch, Penguin, 2014, p.50

[667] Selected Poems, T.S. Eliot, Faber and Faber, London, 1972, Ash Wednesday, p. 85-86

T.S. Eliot calls her 'Lady of Silences' and we see in the Bible that the recorded words of Mary are few and special; as we noted in our reflections in Chapter 1. [668]'Mary's words hold special meaning for us. Meditation on her words and on her life will inevitably open up ways in which we too can grow in our servanthood.'

Mary is addressed as **Queen of Peace** because people have come to know the **peace** of Jesus through her intercessions and messages. Mary knew God's peace, calm and tranquillity in her life. In the Chapter 20 **Queen Assumed into Heaven** we explored and reflected on how Mary is Queen in heaven. As **Queen** in Heaven she enjoys peace in heaven now and so we see how she can be addressed with the title **Queen of Peace**.

What does this mean for us?

We are encouraged to keep trusting God so we are kept in calm, tranquillity and perfect peace *(Isaiah 26:3)*. We need to follow the teachings of the Lord as: 'Great peace have they who love your law' *(Psalm 119:65)*. Letting Jesus rule in our lives will increase peace *(Colossians 3:15)*. We should let the peace of Christ rule in our hearts and guide us to do, say and think those things that please the Lord.

Silence in worship and prayer provides a special time to hear from the Lord and let His peace guide and direct us. Peaceful times of silent reflection are often significant times of knowing the Lord's presence. Take time soon for silent prayer and reflection so you meet with Jesus and know the Lord's peace directing you along paths of peace.

We show wisdom if we are 'peace-loving' or peaceable *(Matthew 5:9)*. Jesus commends peacemakers with a special blessing of being called God's children. We need to live as peace-makers by making peace in the different situations we meet; by seeing good in others and not joining in gossip and criticism *(Romans 12:18)*. How can you be a peacemaker at home? How can you be a peacemaker at work?

---

[668] Dictionary of Mary 'Behold your Mother', Catholic Book Publishing Co, New Jersey 1997, 1985, p. 498

We should pray about all our worries and anxieties and then trust that the Lord will help in all those situations. We can receive peace in physical and emotional storms *(Mark 4:39)*. Peace will replace fear and anxiety as we trust that the Lord in His love and mercy will help in all those situations in the best ways *(Philippians 4:6-7)*. We should 'pursue righteousness, faith, love and peace' *(II Timothy 2:22)*.

Through Jesus' death on the Cross we can receive peace *(Isaiah 53:5, Colossians 1:20)*. We should confess our sins to God and repent so we can receive forgiveness and peace.

We should remember to pray much for peace in our towns, villages and in our country and also to pray for peace to come to those countries around the world where there is conflict *(Jeremiah 29:7)*.

The words of the hymn attributed to St Francis of Assisi [669] *Make me a channel of your peace* teach us more about living in peace. We should bring love where there is hatred; pardon where there is injury; hope in despair; forgiveness and pardon instead of holding onto resentments. Other hymns teach us about peace. Our lives should radiate the peace of Jesus and this should flow through us to others, as we sing: [670] *Peace is flowing like a river, flowing out through you and me, spreading out into the desert, setting all the captives free.* Perfect peace is Jesus' gift to us *(John 14:27)*. If we live in peace then others will recognize that we know Jesus and hopefully they will want to meet Jesus too! [671] *Peace, **perfect peace**, is the gift of Christ our Lord, Thus, says the Lord, will the world know my friends.* In [672] *Sweet Sacrament divine* we sing about **peace** because when we receive Holy Communion we sacramentally receive Jesus and can be filled afresh with peace:

> Sweet **Sacrament of peace**,
> dear home of every heart,

---

[669] Celebration Hymnal for Everyone, McCrimmons, 1994, hymn 478, v. 1-4, Sebastian Temple 1928-1997

[670] Ibid., hymn 595, v.1, Anonymous

[671] Ibid., hymn 597, v.1, Kevin Mayhew 1942-2021

[672] The New English Hymnal, The Canterbury Press, Norwich, 1987, p. 316, hymn 307, v. 2, Francis Stanfield 1835-1914

where restless yearnings cease,
and sorrows all depart.

We can pray the Morning Prayer Collect asking for peace: [673]O God, who art the author of **peace** and lover of concord, in knowledge of whom standeth our eternal life, whose service is perfect freedom: Defend us, thy humble servants, in all assaults of our enemies; that we, surely trusting in thy defence, may not fear the power of any adversaries; through the might of Jesus Christ our Lord. Amen.

Evensong has a lovely Collect for peace too: [674]O God, from whom all holy desires, all good counsels, and all just works do proceed: Give unto thy servants that **peace** which the world cannot give: that both our hearts may be set to obey thy commandments, and also that by thee we being defended from the fear of our enemies may pass our time in rest and quietness; through the merits of Jesus Christ our Saviour. Amen

The Service of Compline has a lovely hymn when we pray for a peaceful night's sleep: [675]

Before the ending of the day,
Creator of the world, we pray,
that with thy wonted favour thou
wouldst be our guard and keeper now.

From all ill dreams defend our eyes,
from nightly fears and fantasies;
tread under foot our ghostly foe,
that no pollution we may know.

[676] *Queen of peace, pray for us.*

---

[673] Common Worship Services and Prayers for the Church of England, Church House Publishing, London, 200, p. 71

[674] Common Prayer. Hymns A&M, WM Collins & Sons, Glasgow, pre 1953, p. 56

[675] Common Worship Services and Prayers for the Church of England, Church House Publishing, London, 2000 p. 90

[676] The Walsingham Pilgrim Manual 2016, p.14

CHAPTER 30

OUR LADY OF WALSINGHAM

The [677]Litany of Loreto lists 50 titles given to Mary. In the [678]Walsingham Manual, **Our Lady of Walsingham** is listed at the end. Walsingham is a village in Norfolk, England.

What does the Bible tell us about Our Lady of Walsingham?

The Bible does not mention Walsingham, but as the house at Nazareth is important at Walsingham; we will discover what the Bible says about that **house** and other houses. Water is significant at Walsingham, so we explore some Biblical references to **water**.

When the Angel Gabriel visited Mary with the Annunciation, she was living in the **home** of her parents, Anna and Joachim in Nazareth *(Luke*

---

677 Dictionary of Mary 'Behold your Mother', Catholic Book Publishing Co. New Jersey 1997, 1985, p.241
678 The Walsingham Pilgrim Manual 2016, p.13

1:26-38). This is the **house** that Lady Richeldis saw in a vision. [679]'In 1061 according to tradition' the Virgin Mary appeared in a vision to Lady Richeldis de Faverche at Walsingham asking her 'to build a replica of Mary's **house** in Nazareth, the house where Gabriel appeared to Mary.'

After the birth of Jesus in Bethlehem *(Luke 2:1-8)*, and the flight to Egypt *(Matthew 1:13-23)*, the Holy Family returned to Nazareth and lived in Joseph's **house** with the carpenter's shop: 'So was fulfilled what was said through the prophets: "He will be called a Nazarene" *(Matthew 1:23)*. 'They returned to Galilee to their own town of Nazareth. And the child grew and became strong; he was filled with wisdom, and the grace of God was upon him *(Luke 2:39-40)*. They returned here after the visit to Jerusalem for Passover when Jesus was twelve years old *(Luke 2:51-52)*.

In the Old Testament the Hebrew word *bayith* בַּיִת meaning 'house and household' is often used, filling three pages of my Analytical Concordance. [680] This word is used for the houses of the Israelites in Egypt when they celebrated Passover *(Exodus 12:7)*. Moses said: 'These commandments that I give you today are to be upon your hearts. Impress them on your children. Talk about them when you sit at **home** and when you walk along the road… Write them on the door-frames of your **houses** and on your gates' *(Deuteronomy 6:6-7,9)*. The home was to be a place of learning following the commandments. *Bayith* is also used for 'the house of the LORD' *(I Samuel 1:7, I Samuel 1:24-28)*. David wrote 'Let us go to the house of the LORD' *(Psalm 122:1)*. The house of the LORD, the Temple, was built by David's son Solomon *(I Kings 5-8)*, explored in Chapter 12 **House of Gold**.

The New Testament Greek word for house and household, is *oikos* οἶκος or *oikia* οἰκία which means [681]'house, home, dwelling, place of abode and the bodily abode of the soul'.

---

[679] The Shrine of Our Lady of Walsingham booklet, Jarrold Publishing and Guardians of the Shrine of Walsingham 2002, p.2

[680] Analytical Concordance to the Holy Bible, Robert Young, United Society for Christian Literature, Lutterworth Press London, 1973, p. 496-499

[681] Analytical Greek Lexicon, Samuel Bagster & Sons Ltd, London, 1973, p. 284-5

The home of Zechariah and Elizabeth was a house of joy recognizing Jesus *(Luke 1:40-44)*. This word is used for the **house** in Bethlehem where Mary, Joseph and Jesus were living at the time of the visit of the Wise Men *(Matthew 2:11)*. Simon Peter and Andrew's home in Capernaum was a house of healing and hospitality *(Mark 1:29-31)*. Jairus's **house** was a place of sorrow turned to joy and healing *(Matthew 9:23-26)*. Jesus' coming to that house brought the good news of God's healing love. When Jesus sent out the twelve they visited people in their homes to share the good news. Those houses were places of mission and evangelism *(Matthew 10:11-14)*. Jesus healed the Roman Official's son in Cana of Galilee, assuring him 'your son will live' *(John 4:50)*. When he arrived **home** he discovered the boy recovered at 'the exact time at which Jesus had said to him, "Your son will live." He and all his **household** believed' *(John 4:53)*. That became a house of joy and faith in Jesus.

Jesus' parable about **two houses** teaches us that 'everyone who hears these words of mine and puts them into practice is like a wise man who built his house on the rock' *(Matthew 7:24)*. We need to hear and follow the teachings of Jesus to be wise and safe in the storms of life; unlike the foolish man building on the sand *(Matthew 7:26-27)*. Jesus said to Zacchaeus, 'I must stay at your **house** today' *(Luke 19:5)*. That house became a house of repentance, good choices and receiving forgiveness. Mary and Martha welcomed Jesus into their **home**. Martha worked hard preparing the meal and Mary sat listening to Jesus. *(Luke 10:38-42)*. We all need to do practical tasks and listen to Jesus. When their brother Lazarus died, Martha declared her belief in Jesus *(John 11:27)*. How wonderful that Lazarus was raised from the dead *(John 11:1-44)*. There was a dinner at their **house** in Bethany for Jesus and his disciples *(John 12:1-7)*, when again Martha served. Mary expressed her love for Jesus by anointing his feet. The house of Lazarus, Martha and Mary was a home with hospitality, serving, listening, learning, revelation, healing and a place where Jesus received love, worship and care.

When Paul and Silas were in Prison in Philippi, they told the jailor, 'Believe in the Lord Jesus, and you will be saved – you and your **household**' *(Acts 16:31,33-34)*. That house was a place of hospitality, with growing faith and joy for the new believers.

The Early Church met in homes *(Romans 16:3-5)*, to worship, have teaching and fellowship. Those early **house churches** 'devoted themselves to the apostles' teaching and to fellowship, to the breaking of bread and to prayer' *(Acts 2:42)*. Church leaders should be a good example by the way they live. Paul tells Timothy a deacon 'must manage his children and his **household** well' *(I Timothy 3:12)*.

The word οικος is used to describe the bodily abode of the soul. 'Now we know that if the earthly tent we live in is destroyed, we have a building from God, an eternal **house** in heaven, not built by human hands' *(II Corinthians 5:1)*. Jesus reassures us about our heavenly home, saying: 'In my Father's **house** are many rooms; if it were not so, I would have told you. I am going there to prepare a place for you' *(John 14:2)*.

Peter uses the image of stones in a house to describe the Church. We are being built into a spiritual house: '... you also, like living stones, are being built into a **spiritual house** to be a holy priesthood, offering spiritual sacrifices acceptable to God through Jesus Christ' *(I Peter 2:4-5)*. Our hearts should be a home where Christ dwells. Jesus said: "If anyone loves me, he will obey my teaching. My Father will love him, and we will come to him and make our **home** with him." *(John 14:23)*. Paul prays: 'that Christ may **dwell** in your hearts through faith' *(Ephesians 3:16-17a)*. 'And **we are his house**, if we hold on to our courage and the hope of which we boast' *(Hebrews 3:4-6)*. We need to keep trusting and following Jesus, having the joy of knowing we belong to Him.

We pray in the Prayer of Humble Access that when we receive Holy Communion: [682]*Grant us therefore, gracious Lord, so to eat the flesh of your dear Son Jesus Christ and to drink his blood... that we may evermore **dwell** in him, and he in us. Amen.*

Now we turn to some of the Biblical references about **water**. Jesus turned **water** into wine at the Wedding at Cana *(John 2:1-11)*, showing Jesus' love as he [683]'transforms situations of sadness and embarrassment into experiences of gladness and rejoicing.' Nicodemus was told by Jesus

---

[682] Common Worship Services and Prayers for the Church of England, Church House Publishing, London, 2000 p. 181

[683] The Way of Love: Brother Ramon SSF Marshall Pickering 1994 p.69

that 'no one can enter the kingdom of God without being born of **water** and the spirit' *(John 3:3)*. This reminds us about the baptism of repentance with the waters of Christian baptism; the dying and rising with Christ that they signify; and the living water of the Holy Spirit that is received. The Holy Spirit refreshes and enables us to bring the love of Jesus to others. Jesus said to the Samaritan woman at the well: '... those who drink of the water that I will give them will never be thirsty. The water that I will give will become in them a spring of water gushing up to eternal life' *(John 4:13-14 NRSV)*. Br Ramon[684] recognises Jesus' compassion: 'He looked upon her searchingly, and that saving look brought forgiveness and joy.' At the Feast of Tabernacles, Jesus invites the thirsty to drink living water and receive the Holy Spirit *(John 7:37-39 NRSV)*. The New Testament Greek says [685]'out of his belly shall flow rivers of living water'; this is the Greek word *'koilia'* κοιλία meaning [686]'belly, stomach, **womb**, inner self'. The word 'womb' is significant as Jesus grew surrounded by water in Mary's womb.

When Jesus met with his disciples for the Passover Last Supper *(John 13:1-11)*, Jesus surprised his friends by washing their feet with **water**, which was the job of the lowest servant. We remember this on Maundy Thursday, when we are invited to participate in the foot-washing. This is a sacramental act, when the outward and visible sign of the water poured on our foot is a sign of an inward and spiritual grace of receiving cleansing and forgiveness of our sins. The water from the well at Walsingham can represent cleansing, when we are reminded of our Baptism. [687]Brother Ramon reflects on the foot-washing by encouraging us to 'Yield, surrender yourself to the loving forgiveness and cleansing that Christ offers, and then let his spirit of humble service mark your life.'

On the Cross **water** flowed from Jesus' side as well as his precious blood *(John 19:34)*. Bishop Stephen Cottrell reflects: [688]'Jesus, whom we

[684] Ibid., pp 22f

[685] The Interlinear Greek-English New Testament, Samuel Bagster & Sons Ltd, London, 1958, p.392

[686] Analytical Greek Lexicon, Samuel Bagster & Sons Ltd, London, 1973, p. 234

[687] When they Crucified my Lord: Brother Ramon brf 1999 p.61

[688] I Thirst: Stephen Cottrell, Zondavan, 2003, p. 172 -173, p. 176 177

see thirsting on the cross, is the source of living water. He is the one who will cleanse and revive us, the one who slakes our thirst…. It is from the dead body of the Saviour that the signs of new life flow….The one who thirsts is also the one from whom the living waters flow. ….. Here the waters of refreshment are flowing. This is the place of healing. This is the place where burdens can be laid down…It is also the sign of baptism, cleansing, redeeming and refreshing all those who die with Christ in order to share his risen life.'

How can Mary be addressed by the title Our Lady of Walsingham?

Mary is given this title **Our Lady of Walsingham** because she appeared to Lady Richeldis at her home in Norfolk, England, in 1061. [689]'In 1061 according to tradition' the Virgin Mary appeared in a vision to Lady Richeldis de Faverche at Walsingham asking her 'to build a replica of Mary's **house** in Nazareth, the house where Gabriel appeared to Mary.' *The Pynson Ballad* records that Richeldis was *'a noble widow'*. [690]'The Ballad goes on to tell of the miraculous building of the house, by angels, beside a pair of wells in a location chosen by Mary herself… Records indicate that Walsingham rapidly acquired huge popularity as a place of pilgrimage. As to 'England's Nazareth' many pilgrims including monarchs came.' [691]*The Pynson Ballad* tells:

> *'Many sick been here cured by our Lady's might*
> *Dead again revived of this is no doubt*
> *Lame made whole and blind restored to sight…*
> *And also lepers here recovered have been*
> *By our Lady's grace of their infirmity.'*

[689] The Shrine of Our Lady of Walsingham booklet, Jarrold Publishing and Guardians of the Shrine of Walsingham 2002, p.2

[690] The Shrine of Our Lady of Walsingham booklet, Jarrold Publishing and Guardians of the Shrine of Walsingham 2002, p.2

[691] A transcription of the "Pynson Ballad", Manuscript 1254/6 The Pepys Library Magdalene College Cambridge

Many people received healing at Walsingham, the sick went on Pilgrimage to Walsingham and still the pilgrims come today. Walsingham continues to be a place where pilgrims seeking healing come to the daily Services of Sprinkling with water from the holy well; and to the Healing Services with anointing and laying-on of hands. The daily Shrine Prayers include prayer requests, written by pilgrims, for the sick. At the Service of Sprinkling[692] at the well pilgrims receive a sip of water from a ladle, the sign of the cross on their foreheads and water is poured into their open hands. The prayer for the sick asks: [693]*Father, your Son Jesus Christ brought healing in body and soul to those who turned to him in faith. Hear our prayers for all the sick: restore them to health and strength, comfort them with the presence of your Holy Spirit, and lead them to know and do your will. We ask this through Christ our Lord. Amen.* At Walsingham Mary points us to Jesus. We ask for Mary to pray for us in the *Hail Mary*, but our prayers for healing are addressed to God. Walsingham is a place of healing where people think of Mary as **Health of the Sick**, which I explored in Chapter 16.

Michael Rear writes: [694]'As a measure of how important Walsingham was between the reigns of Henry III and Henry VIII at least forty-five visits of reigning monarchs to Walsingham can be identified, and no other shrine comes close to that. It is suggested that the Holy House at Walsingham was considered to confer a kind of divine blessing upon the 'house' of the dynasty itself.' Walsingham grew in wealth and popularity. Erasmus, the Dutch scholar, visited Walsingham in 1513 and he was impressed by the splendour of the Shrine. He wrote: [695]'When you look in you may say it was the mansion of the saints, so much does it glitter on all sides with jewels, gold and silver'.... Our Lady stands 'on the right side of the altar ... a small image, remarkable neither excelling in material or workmanship.' There were pilgrim routes leading to Walsingham. [696]'All over Europe, on the pilgrim routes, wayside chapels were built to assist

---

[692] The Walsingham Pilgrim Manual 2016, p. 63-65

[693] Ibid., p.49

[694] Walsingham Pilgrims and Pilgrimage: Michael Rear, Gracewing, 2019, p. 117

[695] Ibid, pp 62f

[696] Rear, op. cit., p. 77

pilgrims, the Slipper Chapel being the last of them before pilgrims reached Walsingham.' Pilgrims often left their shoes or slippers there to walk the last mile barefoot as a sign of penitence.

How sad that by 1563 [697]'all the Marian Shrines, including Walsingham, were destroyed; within two generations the Mother of God had faded in the memory of Anglicans.' Henry VIII, who had visited Walsingham on pilgrimage, paid for a candle to burn there for him in March 1538. [698]'However in July of that year the wealth of the Priory was seized by the King's commissioners, the Shrine destroyed, and the image of Our Lady of Walsingham taken to London and burnt at Chelsea.' 1538 was a year of great sorrow at Walsingham.

The restoration of pilgrimage to Walsingham began in 1896 when Charlotte Boyd bought the Slipper Chapel.[699] The Roman Catholic Church and visitors' centre are next to the Slipper Chapel and form a part of the pilgrimage of many Anglicans who walk there along the Holy Mile from the Anglican shrine.

[700]'In 1921 an energetic and charismatic young priest named Alfred Hope Patten was appointed as the Vicar of St Mary's Walsingham.' He arranged for a replica statue of Our Lady of Walsingham, based on the image depicted on the seal of the medieval priory, to be made and placed in the Parish Church of St Mary. A new chapel was dedicated in 1931 and the statue was moved to it. The chapel was extended in 1938 to form the current Anglican shrine. How wonderful that [701] 'the Shrine of Walsingham, which had been destroyed in 1538, was restored in the early twentieth century and is now a place of pilgrimage for Anglicans as well as Catholics.' The Roman Catholic Church and visitors' centre are next to

---

[697] Mary A History of Doctrine and Devotion, Hilda Graef, Christian Classics, Westminster, 1987, The Liturgical Press, p.16

[698] The Shrine of Our Lady of Walsingham booklet, Jarrold Publishing and Guardians of the Shrine of Walsingham 2002, p.2-3

[699] Ibid., p. 4

[700] Ibid.

[701] Graef, op. cit., p.134

the Slipper Chapel. Many Anglicans on pilgrimage walk there along the Holy Mile from the Anglican Shrine.

The picture of the Statue of **Our Lady of Walsingham** on the front cover of this book shows the Blessed Virgin Mary enthroned as Queen wearing a golden Saxon crown and golden slippers carrying the Child Jesus with the Gospel book and a lily flower.

The Holy House in the Anglican Shrine of **Our Lady of Walsingham** is a place for silent prayer. Mass is celebrated there and at healing Services people receive prayer with the ministry of laying-on hands. Just like the homes we reflected on earlier, the Holy House at Walsingham is a place for meeting Jesus, receiving healing and listening to Jesus. Mary, **Our Lady of Walsingham,** always points us to Jesus. There is worship, repentance, receiving forgiveness, listening, learning, revelation and receiving Jesus sacramentally at Holy Communion. It is a **house** of peace, prayer and the presence of the Lord. The Holy House is built inside the Shrine Church at the Anglican Shrine of **Our Lady of Walsingham**. Fr (now Bishop) Philip North described Walsingham as a 'thin place'[702], where we are close to Heaven; described by Jeffrey John[703] as a place where 'the veil between this world and eternity seems to fade away, and we know that we are united with Christ and his saints.' Many pilgrims feel that they have 'come home' when they return to Walsingham for another Pilgrimage.

What does this mean for us?

The Holy House at Walsingham is a place of healing, like Simon Peter's house *(Mark 1:29-*31), and Jairus's home *(Matthew 9:23-26).* It is a place where pilgrims repent of sins, like Zacchaeus's house *(Luke 19:5).* It is a place of listening to Jesus, learning and expressing our love for him, as Mary and Martha's house *(Luke 10:38-42, John 11:1-44, John 12:1-7).* Is

---

[702] 'England's Nazareth' Video about Walsingham

[703] 'Welcome from the Dean' in the Services booklet for Saturday March 5th when the Image of our Lady of Walsingham came to St Alban's Cathedral

your home a place of repentance, healing, listen to Jesus and expressing love for Jesus?

The house of Lazarus, Martha and Mary was a place of hospitality, serving, listening, learning, revelation, healing and where Jesus received love, worship and care. Is your home a place of welcome, hospitality, serving, listening, learning, worship, love and care? Do you recognise Jesus with you in your home and feel joy? *(Luke 1:40-44)* Is your home a place of mission and evangelism where you tell others how Jesus has helped you? *(Matthew 10:11-14)* Is there faith and joy in your home? *(John 4:43-54, Acts 16:31,33-34)* Let us turn to Jesus in trust in ordinary situations of our lives. *(John 2: 1-11)*

The Samaritan woman *(John 4: 13-14 NRSV),* reminds us about [704] Jesus' compassion and our need to receive forgiveness. Do you need to say 'sorry' to God and receive forgiveness? Does Jesus dwell in your heart? *(John 14:23, Ephesians 3:17a)* Commit your life afresh to Jesus asking Jesus to come and live in your heart by faith praying: [705] *O come to my heart Lord Jesus, there is room in my heart for thee.* We sing: [706] *Sweet Sacrament of peace, dear **home** of every heart.* Are you being built up by being an active part of the Church, as a living stone in His spiritual house? *(I Peter 2:4-5)* Ask Jesus to re-fill you with the Holy Spirit and let the love of Jesus flow through you like a river! *(John 7:37-39 NRSV)*

We need to keep trusting and following Jesus and have the joy of knowing we belong to Him and 'we are his house' *(Hebrews 3:4-6).* Do you have reassurance about your heavenly home? *(John 14:2)* Bishop Lyndsay encouraged us to make Mary at home in our homes: [707]'Spend time with Mary in the Holy House, and be sure to spend time with her in your own home. May your experience of her love and encouragement here in Walsingham be echoed there!'

---

[704] The Way of Love: Brother Ramon SSF Marshall Pickering 1994

[705] The New English Hymnal, The Canterbury Press, Norwich, 1987, p. 461, hymn 465 chorus, Emily Elliott 1836-1897

[706] Ibid., hymn 307, v. 2, Francis Stanfield 1835-1914

[707] The Walsingham Pilgrimage Manual 2014, p. 3

Water gives refreshment, quenches our thirst, makes us clean and is beautiful! Waterfalls, rivers, streams and the sea are wonderful! Bishop Lindsay wrote the theme of life-giving stream: [708]'honours Mary as the one from whom 'Living Water' is made available to the world. Jesus is the one who offers refreshment that will not leave those who receive it thirsty anymore, and through the sharing of her humanity she makes the incarnation a reality. It is our particular hope this year that every person who finds their way to 'England's Nazareth' during this year will have their spiritual thirst quenched.' Walsingham is a place where spiritual thirst is quenched at every Pilgrimage because Mary always points us to Jesus; inviting us to come into her **home** and meet with Jesus and to be refreshed with the holy **water** at the well.

I encourage you to go on Pilgrimages to Walsingham and invite other people to come with you. That will be a wonderful time of spiritual refreshment for you.

Streams flow, unlike stagnant ponds, and we need to receive and share; so the love of Jesus flows through us. The River Thames is a shallow stream near the source; this is soon joined by other streams flowing in; so together they become the wide and fast-flowing River Thames further down-stream. Our lives should be streams of God's love flowing out to refresh others, because Jesus said: 'Out of the believer's heart shall flow rivers of living water' *(John 7: 38)*. Let us be filled afresh with the Holy Spirit so that our lives indeed become streams of God's love flowing out though us to refresh others.

The Collect for the Mass of Our Lady of Walsingham is: [709]*Lord God, in the mystery of the Incarnation Mary conceived your Son in her heart before she conceived him in her womb. As we, your pilgrim people, rejoice in her patronage, grant that we may also welcome him into our hearts, and so like her, be made a holy house fit for his eternal dwelling. Amen.*

---

[708] Walsingham A pastoral and liturgical guidebook for leaders 2015 p.1

[709] Masses of the Holy House of Our Lady of Walsingham, The Shrine of OLW, CCL Licence No 48724, p. 45

[710] We can pray The Traditional Prayer to **Our Lady of Walsingham**: *O Mary, recall the solemn moment when Jesus, your divine Son, dying on the cross, confided us to your maternal care. You are our Mother, we desire ever to remain your devout children. Let us therefore feel the effects of your powerful intercession with Jesus Christ. Make your name again glorious in this place once renowned throughout our land by your visits, favours and many miracles. Pray, O holy Mother of God for the conversion of England, restoration of the sick, consolation for the afflicted, repentance of sinners, peace to the departed. O blessed Mary, Mother of God, Our Lady of Walsingham, intercede for us. Amen.* [711] *Our Lady of Walsingham, pray for us.*

When you have the First Visit to the Holy House with *The Litany of Our Lady* with [712] **Our Lady of Walsingham** listed at the end; I hope and pray that when you ask Mary to pray for you, using the 51 titles listed there; that you will now have a greater understanding about the Biblical background and the reasons why Mary is addressed with these titles. Just as Mary always points us to Jesus, so I hope and pray that this book will have drawn you closer to Jesus and that the reflective questions have encouraged you to grow in faith and serve the Lord in the ways He is calling you. My prayer is that you have grown into a closer relationship with Jesus; increased in Biblical knowledge, as well as developing in your appreciation of his Mother Mary.

Elizabeth G. Bryson

---

[710] The Walsingham Pilgrimage Manual 2014, p. 4

[711] The Walsingham Pilgrim Manual 2016, p.14

[712] Ibid, p.12-14

BIBLIOGRAPHY

Bibles

Holy Bible, New International Version, Zondervan, International Bible Society, 1984

The Holy Bible, Authorized Version, Cambridge University Press, SPCK

The New English Bible, The Apocrypha, Oxford University Press Cambridge University Press, 1970

British Hodder's NIV Glo Computer Bible, Glo Premium ISBN 978-0-9826978-8-7, Immersion Digital, 2010

The Interlinear Greek-English New Testament: Reverend Dr Alfred Marshall, Samuel Bagster and Sons Ltd, London, 1958

Bible Commentaries and Atlas

Analytical Concordance to the Holy Bible, Robert Young, United Society for Christian Literature, Lutterworth Press London, 1973

Analytical Greek Lexicon, Samuel Bagster & Sons Ltd, London, 1973

What the Bible Teaches: R.A. Torrey, Nisbet & Co., Ltd, London, early 20th century

Glo Computer Commentary, Glo Premium ISBN 978-0-9826978-8-7, Immersion Digital, 2010

The Ministry of the Word, Handbook for Preachers, BRF, 2000

The Oxford Bible Commentary, edited by John Barton and John Muddiman, Oxford University Press, 2001

Oxford Bible Atlas, Ed Herbert G. May, London, Oxford University Press, 1962

Peake's Commentary on the Bible, edited by Arthur S. Peake, London, T.C. & E.C. Jack Ltd, 1931

The Lion Handbook to the Bible, David and Pat Alexander, Lion Publishing, 1973

Believer's Bible Commentary, Early Church Writings, online version

The History of Christianity: A Lion Handbook: T. Dowley, Lion Publishing, Berkhamstead, 1977

Early Christian Doctrines, Fifth Edition, J.N.D. Kelly, Continuum, 2011

Books

Bicknell, E.J., *A Theological Introduction to The Thirty-Nine Articles*, 3rd Edition revised by H.J. Carpenter, Longmans, 1959

Boss, Sarah Jane Ed, *MARY the Complete Resource*, Oxford University Press 2007

Bur, Jacques, *How to understand the Virgin Mary*, SCM Press Ltd, Translation 1994 John Bowden and Margaret Lydamore

Canice, Fr O.F.M.Cap, *A Study of the Mother of God*, M.H.Gill and Sons Ltd, Dublin, 1950

Combier-Donovan, Catherine, *Mary throne of Wisdom: Twelfth Century Statue Twenty first Century Icon* Georgetown Center for Liturgy, 2009

Cottrell, Stephen, *I Thirst*, Zondervan, 2003

Daniel, Evan, *The Prayer Book Its History, Language and Contents*, Gardner. Darton & Co, London, 1892

Davie, M., *A Guide to the Church of England*, Mowbray, London, 2008

Eliot T.S. Selected Poems, Faber and Faber, London, 1972

Graef, Hilda, *Mary: A History of Doctrine and Devotion* Christian Classics, Westminster, 1987, The Liturgical Press Collegeville, Minnesota

Morris, Gilbert, *The Angel of Bastogne*, Digital Edition based on the Printed Edition, B&H Publishing Group, Nashville, Tennessee, 2005

Graham, Billy, *Angels God's secret agents*, Hodder, 1988

Gumbel, Nicky, *Searching Issues*, Kingsway, Eastbourne, 2004

Hahn, Scott, *Hail, Holy Queen,* Darton, Longman and Todd Ltd, London 2010

Hammond, Cally, *Joyful Christianity, Finding Jesus in the world*, SPCK, 2009

Hammond, Cally, *Passionate Christianity, A journey to the Cross*, SPCK, 2007

Hammond, Cally, *Glorious Christianity, Walking by faith in the life to come,* SPCK, 2012

John Paul II, Pope, *The Rosary—Joy. Light. Sorrow. Glory*, 6th Edition, 2005, Agora Printing, Averbode, 2003

Mateo, Fr, *Refuting the attack on Mary,* Catholic Answers, San Diego, 1999

McBrian, Richard P., *Catholicism,* HarperCollins, 1994

McGrath, Alister E., *Christian Theology*, Fifth Edition, Wiley-Blackwell, 2011

Moore, James R., *Religion in Victorian Britain, Volume 111 Sources*, Manchester University Press, 1998

Morris, Gilbert, *The Angel of Bastogne*, Digital Edition based on the Printed Edition, B&H Publishing Group, Nashville, Tennessee, 2005

Parsons, Gerald, *Religion in Victorian Britain, Volume 11 Controversies*, Manchester University Press,1997

Pitre, Brant, *Jesus and the Jewish Roots of the Eucharist*, Image, New York, 2016

Price, Hope, *Angels True stories of how they touch our lives*, Pan Books, 1994

Ramon, Brother, *The Way of Love*, BRF, 1994

Ramon, Brother, *When they Crucified my Lord*, BRF, 1999

Rear, Michael, *Walsingham Pilgrims and Pilgrimage*, Gracewing, 2019

Sri, Edward, The New Rosary in Scripture, Charis Servant Books, Cincinnati, Ohio, 2003

Springer, Rebecca, *Within the Gates*, Christ for the Nations, Dallas, Texas, 1984

Thurian, Max, *Mary Mother of the Lord Figure of the Church*, The Faith Press, Tufton Street London, 1963

Vollert, Cyril, S.J., *A Theology of Mary*, Herder and Herder New York, 1965

Waddell, *Joy the meaning of the sacraments*, Canterbury Press, Norwich, 2012

Williams, Jane, *Angels*, A Lion Book an imprint of Lion Hudson plc, 2006

Time to heal: A Contribution towards the Ministry of Healing, Report to the House of Bishops, Church House Publishing, 2000

Booklets, periodicals and leaflets

Anthony, Fr Peter, *Do you know what the Ark is? Walsingham Review*, December 2010

Anthony, Fr Peter, *Notes of a Pilgrimage to Loreto, Subiaco & Rome, Walsingham Review*, Candlemas, 2020

Barker, Margaret, *The Images of Mary in the Litany of Loreto*, Usus Antiquior, Vol 1, No. 2, July 2010

Bryson, Fr Neil, *Rosary leaflet for the Parish of All Saints Boyne Hill*, 6th October 2012

Gumbel, Nicky, *Why Jesus?* Kingsway Publications Ltd, 2013

Marshall, Fr Rodney, *AVE The Magazine of The Society of Mary*, Sermon given in Sheffield in October 2016, Annunciationtide, 2017

Wedgewood Lady, Pamela Tudor-Craig, *The Virgin Mary as Seat of Wisdom*, The 1986 Assumptiontide Lecture

A *Pastoral and Liturgical Guidebook for leaders*, Walsingham, 2013

A Pastoral and liturgical guidebook for leaders, Walsingham, 2015

Aylesford Priory Information from 1242 to the present day, leaflet

Bray Church Advent Carol Service, leaflet, 27th November 2016

Church Times, No. 8084, 23rd February 2018

Called to be Saints, Lent 2002, Churches Together in Britain and Ireland, Church House Publishing, 2001

Glastonbury Pilgrimage, Booklet, 2013

House of Gold, Welcome, Nathaniel Literature Distributors, Canada, 1983, 1984

Masses of the Holy House of Our Lady of Walsingham, The Shrine of OLW, CCL Licence No 48724

Praying at Home, A resource for those praying at home as a result of the Coronavirus pandemic, produced by The Church Union and The Society, 2020

Pilgrim Course for the Christian Journey, The Beatitudes Church House Publishing 2015

The "Pynson Ballad", Manuscript 1254/6, The Pepys Library, Magdalene College, Cambridge, transcription

The Shrine of Our Lady of Walsingham, booklet, Jarrold Publishing and Guardians of the Shrine, 2002

The Order of Sung Mass, St Michael & All Angels Maidstone

The Walsingham Pilgrimage Manual, Annual Edition 2014, Twenty-fourth edition

The Walsingham Pilgrim Manual, 2016, Twenty-sixth Edition

Walsingham Bible Week leaflet 2017, Monday 23rd October 2017

Welcome from the Dean, Service booklet, Saturday March 5th 2011, St Alban's Cathedral

Dictionaries

An Expository Dictionary of Biblical Words: W.E. Vine, Thomas Nelson Publishers, 1985

Dictionary of Mary 'Behold your Mother', Catholic Book Publishing Co. New Jersey 1997

Pocket Oxford Dictionary, F.G.Fowler & H.W.Fowler, Oxford, Clarendon Press, 1962

The Concise Oxford Dictionary, Oxford University Press, 1985

The Shorter Oxford English Dictionary on Historical Principals, Clarendon Press, Oxford, 1973

Hymn Books and Apps

Carols for Choirs 2, edited and arranged by David Willcocks and John Rutter, Oxford University Press, 1966

Celebration Hymns for Everyone, McCrimmons, Great Wakering, Essex, England, 1994

Common Praise, Canterbury Press 2001

Common Prayer. Hymns A & M, WM Collins & Sons, Glasgow, pre 1953

Hymns Ancient & Modern Revised, William Clowes & Sons, pre 1964

In Praise of Mary, Hymns from the first millennium of the Eastern and Western Churches, St Paul Publications, May 1981

The English Hymnal with tunes, Oxford University Press, London W 1, 1967

The English Hymnal Service Book, London, Oxford University Press, A.R. Mowbray & Co., Ltd. 1969

The New English Hymnal, The Canterbury Press, Norwich, 1987

The Walsingham Pilgrim Manual, 2016, Twenty-sixth Edition

Universalis App, Universalis publishing, 1996-2019

Liturgy and Prayer Books

Exciting Holiness Collects and Readings for the Festivals and Lesser Festivals, Canterbury Press, 2012

The Common Worship Lectionary, NRSV Anglicized Edition, Oxford University Press, 1999

Common Worship Services and Prayers for the Church of England, Church House Publishing, 2000

Common Worship Ordination Services Study Edition, Church House Publishing, London, 2007

Order for the Order for the Eucharist and for Morning and Evening Prayer in the Church of England 2017, Tufton Books

Common Worship, Services and Prayers for the Church of England, Christian Initiation, Church House Publishing, 2006

The Book of Common Prayer, Collins Sons & Co., Ltd, Glasgow

Common Worship Festivals, Church House Publishing, 2008

Walsingham Pilgrim Manual, 2016, Twenty-sixth Edition

Talks

Mary in the New Testament, Jeffrey John, Talk at St Alban's Cathedral, March 5th 2011

Videos and DVDs

England's Nazareth, about Walsingham

The Song of Bernadette, about Lourdes

The Alpha Course, Nicky Gumbel

Printed in the United States
by Baker & Taylor Publisher Services